The Design of Virgil's *Bucolics*

The Design of Virgil's *Bucolics*

Second Edition

John Van Sickle

Bristol Classical Press

Second edition 2004
published by
Bristol Classical Press
an imprint of
Gerald Duckworth & Co. Ltd.
90-93 Cowcross Street, London EC1M 6BF
Tel: 020 7490 7300
Fax: 020 7490 0080
inquiries@duckworth-publishers.co.uk
www.ducknet.co.uk

First published in 1978 by Edizioni dell'Ateneo e Bizzarri

© 1978, 2004 by John Van Sickle

All rights reserved. No part of this publication
may be reproduced, stored in a retrieval system, or
transmitted, in any form or by any means, electronic,
mechanical, photocopying, recording or otherwise,
without the prior permission of the publisher.

A catalogue record for this book is available
from the British Library

ISBN 1 85399 676 9

Printed and bound in Great Britain by
Antony Rowe Ltd

CONTENTS

PART THREE: DESIGN

INTRODUCTION

And where should an austere philologist
Relax but in the very world of shade
From which the matter of his field was made....
A culture is no better than its woods.

W. H. Auden, "Woods" from *Bucolics*
in *The Shield of Achilles* (1955)

On my first encounter with the eclogues (via numerological "chapels" unveiled for a Harvard classroom by G. E. Duckworth in the spring of 1956), they remained a closed book. It began to open a little in 1962 with hints inviting quests that would lead to a concerted argument – *The Design of Virgil's* Bucolics (1978) – now republished here. *Design* scans the *Bucolics'* various reception down through time for interpretative cues. Hence it stresses not only their instant stage success – a hint of dramatic and mythopoeic power – but equally their impact – early and long-range – on book poetics. The argument penetrates dramatic and thematic surfaces to discern the self-reflective vein that now is styled poetological or metapoetic: it infers that Virgil created reciprocal myths – political and literary: Golden Age and Arcadian – masking innovation in each as return to an originary state. With scrupulous attention to modern scholarship, *Design* credited insights and queried faults to foster dialogue and responsible reading.

In reaction to a seminar on Latin style in the early 1960s, I was scouting verse for mannered word arrangement when I discovered that Virgil's fourth eclogue shared certain stylistic mannerisms with Catullus' sixty-fourth poem – "Argonautica" or "Wedding of Peleus & Thetis." A reader less narrowly focused would have remarked contrastive themes as well, since Catullus used his mannered version of heroic verse to express nostalgia for the heroic age and despair at a corrupt present. Themes and patterns began to make sense only when I found in a recent eclogue book an echo of Virgil's fourth likewise composed in mannered, archaizing style and expressing nostalgia for an edenic past. The new book's eclogue sequence skipped from three to five and put the hint of Virgil's fourth in an appendix, because (the poet told me) such a positive vision of history and ambition to write epic were inconceivable in our time.

My resultant questions about linkage between history, style, and confident poetics reached a provisory coalition in my doctoral thesis – *The Unnamed Child: A Reading of Virgil's Messianic Eclogue* (1966).[1] The title stemmed from my initiation to close reading with R. A. Brower. Yet my findings looked beyond new-critical horizons towards cultural studies or nascent new-historicism – meriting a title more like "*Vates* – Virgil as Poet-prophet. Reclaiming Roman Epic from Lucretius & Catullus in the Messianic Eclogue." I realized that Virgil here anticipated the *Aeneid*, projecting ideological myth and epic ambition in a vatic voice. The fourth eclogue would have been a prime exhibit in my senior thesis (1958) on the concept of *uates* ("poet-prophet, bard"),[2] had I only taken a hint from Horace's prophetic epode (16) that matched with eclogue four and struck the self-promoting note, *uate me* –

----

[1]   Dissertation Abstract, *Harvard Studies in Classical Philology* 71 (1966) 350-351, advised by Wendell V. Clausen; published with foreword and afterword that reported and criticized subsequent researches – among them both his and mine – as John Van Sickle, *A Reading of Virgil's Messianic Eclogue* (New York: Garland, 1992), thanks to Gregory Nagy.

[2]   Advised by Zeph Stewart, although he had proposed that I work on

"with me as bard."

Not staying (ill-advisedly no doubt) to shepherd into print a dissertation that pointed through the single eclogue towards the wider contexts of politics, genre, and book poetics, I pressed the inquiries entailed. One led to the eclogue book and its famously elusive relations with Greek bucolic, a dual track foreshadowed by "The Unity of the Eclogues: Arcadian Forest, Theocritean Trees" (1967):[3] how Virgil elaborated Arcadian myth through increments that culminate in *B.* 10.

Exploratory essays on Theocritus led to a turning point for the entire project. First came signs of correspondence between "The Fourth Pastoral Poems of Virgil & Theocritus" (1970).[4] Then fruitful dialogue during a year's fellowship at the Johns Hopkins Humanities Center informed "Is Theocritus a Version of Pastoral?" (1969),[5] and "Poetica Teocritea" (1970).[6] Their lessons shaped my reaction when asked, while at the Hopkins, by Henry Rowell to review a new Theocritean study.[7] Its notion of a simple pastoral genre proved, when I retraced interpretive history, a secondary imposition that caused much mischief: witness Servius' lame note that three eclogues depart from pure rusticity, whether in hope to please or incapacity to invent ten variants of rustic themes,[8] not to mention latter-day fixation on a simple generic type.[9] The ill-

Catullus 66 and Callimachus' "Lock of Berenice."

   [3]   *Transactions of the American Philological Association* 98 (1967) 491-508, J. A. Hanson, ed.

   [4]   *Atti Arcadia* 3.V.1 (Roma 1970) 82-97, thanks to Scevola Mariotti.

   [5]   *Modern Language Notes* 84 (1969) 942-946, with Richard Macksey.

   [6]   *Quaderni Urbinati di Cultura Classica* 9 (1970) 82-97: Scevola Mariotti sent me to the editor, Bruno Gentili.

   [7]   Th. Rosenmeyer, *The Green Cabinet: Theocritus & the European Pastoral Lyric* in *American Journal of Philology* 93 (1972) 348-354.

   [8]   Thilo-Hagen III 1.3.20-24.

   [9]   Van Sickle, *Messianic Eclogue*, 8; "Shall we ever get rid of that

conceived focus on simplicity ruled out the ancient classifica-
tion of bucolic as a mode of *epos*. Yet the concept of *epos*
[poetry in dactylic hexameters] as a system comprising diverse
modes proved able to co-ordinate previously heterogeneous
objects of my research. The several eclogues now appeared as
complementary exercises foreshadowing the successive modes
of *epos* – *Bucolics, Georgics, Aeneid* – in Virgil's full career,
made intelligible as a graduated reply to Theocritus, Hesiod,
and Homer – themselves seen as differentiated modes within a
single tradition. As concept, *epos* provided a generic frame
that gave new point to similarities and differences between
specific texts.

Inquiry into book poetics and conversations at the Hopkins
made me still more conscious, too, of self-reflective poetics
that unfolded through oppositions: "Dialectical Methodology
in the Virgilian Tradition" (1970).[10] I also arranged to publish
the eclogue book that had set off my whole project: *The
Arminarm Eclogues* (1971).[11] Yet the design of Virgil's book
still lacked essential components, most egregiously a program
where any considered structure would have one – at the start.

The way out of this particular aporia came when I recog-

---

simplicity, a curse on nearly all general studies and poetological ap-
proaches?" asks Ernst A. Schmidt, "Ancient Bucolic Poetry and Latin
Pastoral Writing (Reviewing P. J. Alpers, *What is Pastoral?*)," *International
Journal of the Classical Tradition* 5 (1998) 234; cf. the welcome move to
historicize Alpers et al. by Joy Connolly, "Picture Arcadia: The Politics of
Representation in Vergil's *Eclogues*," *Vergilius* 47 (2001) 106.

[10]   *MLN* 85 (1970) 884-928, with thanks to Paul de Man, Richard
Macksey, Elias Rivers, and Charles Singleton, cf. below, pp. 32-33.

[11]   W. Antony, *The Arminarm Eclogues with the Hexercises (For the
Heclogues) Pieces*, including *The Works of Imbry Miles* [echo of eclogue 4]
(La Quercia 1971), with Giulia Battaglia. The authorial name is a *nom de
guerre* [scilicet *de plume*] that would give way to another, David Mus, in
subsequent poems and critical writings. With his given name, David Kuhn,

nized in eclogue one a programmatic pattern from Theocritus: "Epic & Bucolic (Theocritus, *Id.* vii / Virgil, *Ecl.* i)" (1975).[12] Presented first as a shop talk at the American Academy in Rome (invited by Frank Brown), the paper focused on the anecdote attributed to one herdsman about a "cause" for the situation of the poem. The story – recounting *Tityrus'* travel to Rome and empowering encounter with a god – served as a causal narrative (etiology), I came to see, for Virgil's bucolic venture. He recast to suit his own new situation a narrative of poetic authorization that Theocritus (*Idyll* 7) had adapted from Homer and Hesiod to define his own bucolic mode of *epos*.[13]

With eclogue one anchored as an energetic program refounding old bucolic through new Roman myth, I queried a recent interpretative fashion that denied the first eclogue programmatic import, finding only in the sixth a program for the entire book and proclaiming it Callimachean: "Virgil's Sixth Eclogue & the Poetics of Middle Style" (1977).[14] The rage for Callimachus fomented error, too, about the figure of *Gallus* – assigned a role lofty and uplifting in eclogue six, but in ten lowly and tragic. Again theoretical discrimination seemed imperative to sift out elusive hints: "ET GALLVS CANTAVIT: a Review Article" (1976-1977).[15]

---

he wrote a Sorbonne doctoral thesis that would inspire the approach to poetics in *Design: La poétique de François Villon* (Paris, 1967).

[12]   *QUCC* 19 (1975) 45-72; an insight carried further in "Theocritus & the Development of the Conception of the Bucolic Genre," *Ramus* 5 (1976) 18-44, A. J. Boyle, ed.; cf. also "Revising the Eclogue Tradition," *Rivista di Cultura Classica e Medioevale* 1977 (Rome) 791-797, Nino Scivoletto, ed.

[13]   Though concerned with "representative anecdotes," modern pastoralists ignore anecdotes of travel that define pastoral modes (e.g., Spenser, *SC* 1 or Wordsworth's *Prelude*), cf., e.g., Schmidt, "Alpers Review," 241.

[14]   *Liverpool Class. Monthly* 2 (1977) 107-108: the good John Pinsent.

[15]   *Classical Journal* 72 (1976-1977) 327-333.

A parallel investigation benefited from other conversations in Rome. Talks with Piero Pucci on deferral and Derrida as well as contacts with topography and topographers helped me learn how a poet could marshal themes of Roman place and myth in one moment for a vatic voice, only to develop a reciprocal project by returning to recuse the first in a counter anecdote, backing off from one ambition to (re)authorize another: "Propertius (*uates*): Augustan Ideology, Topography, & Poetics in Elegy, IV, 1" (1974).[16]

At last the makings of a system could be glimpsed: premised growth and incremental progress to public myth, then its redirection in a gradual move toward the reciprocal – new literary myth achieved in a climactic and paratragic close:

i. Disruptive & transumptive program: Latin epic expropriated ("sing no songs": "impious soldier" as new regime's agent) –

Meliboeus (vatic lapse, citizen-farmer's exile, goatherd singer silenced, grotto lost; cf. goatherd silenced, *Id.* 3) –

vs –

Tityrus (cowherd-shepherd aged but endowed with pipe [*auena* vs *calamo*], sc. of *Daphnis-Pan, Id.* 1) –

Resumptive & incrementative (vatic) program: bucolic reauthorized by oracle ("god" at Rome as new regime's agent).

ii-iii-iiii. Programmed increment of song (renewed epic):

ii. Erotic passion as cause – *Corydon* (goatherd-shepherd singer), pipe from dead master *Damoetas* (sc., tradition from Theocr. to Virgil): pipe invented by *Pan* – but then

iii. Emulative passion as cause – *Damoetas* challenged by *Menalcas*, Latin Muses "love dialectical song" (*amant alterna* [sc. *carmina*] *Camenae*): both validated by *Palaemon* (synthesizing voice) –

iiii. Full vatic increment – "Cumaean song, fates" – mythemes of return & novelty (new hero & olden times restored) –

---

[16] *Dialoghi di Archaeologia* 8 (1974) 116-145: *ROMA* vs *AMOR*.

new epic project ("tell ... deeds") would defeat *Pan* even, even in Arcadia.

  v. Vatic songs of new bucolic hero-god (from shade to grotto, cf. *Meliboeus' B.* 1):

      Mopsus (sc., bard at Grynean grove in etiological epic by Euphorion – sequel to dying *Daphnis*, *Id.* 1)

    vs

      Menalcas "greater" (trumps even *Mopsus'* sequel to *Id.* 1 by fuller hint of new god at Rome, cf. *B.* 1) co-opts Pan.

  vi. Recursive & recusative (re)program of first half-book for reciprocal project (anti-vatic, "song led down"):[17]

  vatic voice minus Rome & moved by love (~~ROMA~~ *AMOR*) –

  Tityrus (recast as narrator, reduced to shepherd by *Apollo*) –

  Pierides –

    Silenus (cosmic rise & fall) sings apostrophes –[18]

    Pasiphaë (bucolic error towards tragic scope) –

    appeal to "Nymphs of Netting" (sc. "enclosing")[19] –

    [*A Muse*] to **Gallus** (anecdote of upward shift from erotic error [elegy] to etiological epic, cf. *B.* 5) –

  Eurotas mediates song (river from Arcadian source)

  Apollo meditated first (emulating music of spheres).[20]

---

[17] Sc. *deductum carmen*: "Nella nuova poetica...l'enfasi cade non più sull'incremento, ma sullo sfruttamento e l'affinamento di un materiale già ammassato": John Van Sickle, *Poesia e Potere*. *Il Mito Virgilio* (Roma: Laterza, 1986) 122.

[18] Virgil represents *Silenus* producing song in terms that recall Homer's account of *Hephaestus* producing *Achilles'* shield (*Il.* 18): B. W. Breed, "Silenus and the *Imago Vocis* in *Eclogue* 6," *HSCP* 100 (2000) 327-339 – a further hint that in *B.* 6, revising the incremental thrust of *B.* 4 and *B.* 5, Virgil pulls back and works out a different mode of epos – pitched to the middle range and styled *agrestis musa* (*B.* 6.8) – by appropriating a Homeric paradigm of craft: cf. above note 14 and below, pp. 146-158.

[19] Below, p. 156, n. 23.

[20] Below, p. 235; Godo Lieberg, "L'Harmonie des sphères chez Virgile? Remarques sur l'épilogue de la sixième églogue," *Bull. Assoc. Budé*

vii-viii-viiii. Recursive & recusative critique through dialectics
builds reciprocal myth of return to song in Arcadia:
Meliboeus (reintroduced as distracted goatherd-narrator)
reports discernment (*certamen*, sc. "means of sifting") still
dialectical but now recursive (*alternos* [sc. *uersus*] *Musae
meminisse uolebant*):[21]

	[vatic powers of song played down or out]	[Arcadian craft sorted out: adopted by eclogue poet]
vii	*Thyrsis* would-be *uates* (defeated)	*Corydon* poetics of limitation (adopted by *Meliboeus)*
viii	*Alphesiboeus*: song as vatic spell (cf. *Moeris*)	*Damon*: Maenalian verses, *Pan* inventor (tragic love)
ix	*Moeris uates, Menalcas* disempowered	*Lycidas* rejects title *uates* that herders give *Moeris*

x. Reciprocal myth complete (sc. *carmen iam deductum*) – return
to Arcadia as originary place & time of best song –
goatherd-narrator (cf. *Meliboeus*) – *Arethusa* (not yet fled
from Arcadia for Sicily, cf. *Idyll* 1), *Maenalus, Lycaeus,
Silvanus, Menalcas, Apollo, Pan* –
Gallus as bucolic hero (reduced from etiological to
bucolic epic, supplants dying *Daphnis, Id.* 1) –
Virgil supplants Theocritus as inventor of bucolic epic mode.[22]

The synthesis in *Design* spurred collateral study and critical dialogue:

"The Bookroll & Some Conventions of the Poetic Book"

(1978).

[21]   Opposed to incrementative *amant alterna Camenae*, *B.* iii.59, cf. J.
B.Van Sickle, "Pastoral Contests," *Classical Review* 54 (2004) 94-95.

[22]   The index was the most important part of a book for Eduard
Fraenkel, someone had told me (Gordon Williams?). An ideal index would
cross-link main motifs and their supports. Securing the requisite concentration, in 1978 a January blizzard delayed return to school.

(1980):[23] book structure and scroll format.

"Reading Virgil's Eclogue Book" (1980):[24] spelling out persistent errors in eclogue criticism (*uestigia non iam irrita*).

Also *Design* offered perspectives on a papyrus scrap from Cornelius Gallus with motifs for a book opening or close.[25]

Further occasions stemmed from the bimillennium of Virgil's death, including lectures as a Fulbright Professor at the University of Rome *La Sapienza*, where I gathered further evidence that theater performance of the *Bucolics* helped father Caesarist ideology and the vatic fame of Virgil:

> "*Commentaria in Maronem Commenticia*: a Case History of Bucolics Misread" (1981):[26] *B.* 8 addressed to patron of *B.* 1.
>
> "Order in Callimachus & Virgil (*Aitia* III-IV / Liber Bucolicon)" (1983).[27]
>
> "Dawn & Dusk as Motifs of Opening & Closure in Heroic & Bucolic Epos (Homer, Apollonius, Theocritus, Virgil)" (1984).[28]

Poesia e potere. Il mito Virgilio (1986).[29]

The charts of structure in *Design* and the Fulbright lectures reached new theoretical synthesis in the Virgil encyclopedia:

---

[23] *Arethusa* 3 (1980) 5-42, with thanks to John Peradotto.

[24] *Aufst. u. Nied. d. röm. Welt* II.31.1 (Berlin 1980) 576-603.

[25] "Gallus & Callimachus: Parallel Texts," *LCM* 5 (1980) 109; "Poetics of Opening & Closure in Meleager, Catullus & Gallus," *Classical World* 75 (1981) 65-75; "Style & Imitation in the New Gallus," *QUCC* 38 (1981) 115-124; "Neget quis carmina Gallo?" *QUCC* 38 (1981) 125-127.

[26] *Arethusa* 14 (1981) 17-34, with thanks to Jenny Clay. Also notes critical of misprision: "Bucolic Variatio & Single-Minded Reading," *LCM* 6 (1981) 189-191; "Theocritus Vergilianus?" *Rivista di Filologia* 110 (1982) 245-246, Scevola Mariotti ed.

[27] *Actes* VII Congrés F.I.E.C., I (Budapest 1983) 289-292.

[28] *Atti del Convegno di Studi Virgiliani,* I (Milano 1984) 124-147, presented as part of a delegation led by M. C. J. Putnam.

[29] Roma: Laterza 1986: "Poetry and power: the Virgil myth."

"Le Bucoliche. 11. La Struttura" (1984).[30]

Theory also informed an Oxford lecture revisiting the initial causal myth. Fundamental to the argument in *Design*, the myth was now convicted of ideological manipulation:

"How Do We Read Ancient Texts? Codes & Critics in Virgil, Eclogue One" (1984):[31] against crudely literalist historicism.

Ensuing work traced book poetics before and long after Virgil:

"The Hellenistic Background" (1989).[32]

"Riscoprendo una sequenza poetica del cinquecento: *Ioannis Casae Carminum liber"* (1989).[33]

Giovanni della Casa's Poem Book: Ioannis Casae Carminum Liber *Florence 1564* (1999).[34]

Interpretative optimism greeted a new decade, but reductive

---

[30] *Enciclopedia Virgiliana* I (1984) 549-552, by F. della Corte, who also printed my detailed supplement: "Strutture interne di singole egloghe nel libro bucolico di Virgilio," *Maia* 35 (1983) 205-212. Structures – recursive (sc., resonant), cyclical, chiasmic, numerological – constitute an area ripe for theoretical and comparative redevelopment; cf., e.g., Bruce Heiden, "Cyclic Design and Thematic Resonance in *Iliad* Books 3 and 6," *Gaia* 7 (2003): 162, n. 6, with bibliography on "cyclic design in Greek poetry"; and Paul Claes, *Concatenatio Catulliana: A New Reading of the Carmina* (Amsterdam: Gieben, 2002), with findings that should be fruitful to weigh, adapt, and criticize in any further studies of book poetics and intratextual cross-reference in the *Bucolics*.

[31] *Materiali e discussioni per l'analisi dei testi classici* 13 (1984) 107-128, thanks to Angus Bowie and Gian Biagio Conte. Another correction ensued: "'Shepheard Slave': Civil Status & Bucolic Conceit in Virgil, Eclogue 2," *QUCC* 56 (1987) 127-129.

[32] In "Recent Structural Studies on the Augustan Poets," *Augustan Age* 9 (1989) 42-48.

[33] *Res Publica Litterarum* 12 (1989) 223-227, Sesto Preti, ed.

[34] Medieval & Renaissance Texts & Studies (Tempe, Arizona, 1999),

and dismissive pieces – neglect, even erasure, of Virgil's theater reception and book poetics – provoked:

"Response to a *Georgics* Reader Bemused by the *Bucolics*" (1990):[35] hope for more systematic readings.

"A Review Article: The End of the Eclogues" (1995):[36] dismay at lack of system with respect to either scholarship or the book.

"Staging Vergil's Future and Past" (1997):[37] praise for etymological learning, reproach for neglect of the system of causal myths in the eclogue book; corrective to misreading of climactic intertext – *B*. x >< *Id*. 1.

"Eclogues in Receivership, *Bucolics* to Reread" (1998):[38] criticizing a throwback to abstractive mysticism, reductive receptionism, and crude intertextualism.

Despair of "epic in our time" restrained the eclogue book that sparked these studies. Lessons learned about epic continuity and renewal – deflation and reflation through drastic shifts in dominant themes – shaped my approach to a poet who dared in 1990 to publish an epic. With *Omeros* Derek Walcott created new versions of the epic modes – bucolic, georgic,

with strenuous advice from P. O. Kristeller.

[35] *Vergilius* 36 (1990) 56-64, by Ward Briggs. This and subsequent studies along with some dialogue provoked may be consulted at http://academic.brooklyn.cuny.edu/classics/jvsickle/bbground.htm.

[36] *Vergilius* 41 (1995) 1-25, a "searching" (one reader called it) report of W. Clausen, *Virgil's Eclogues* (Oxford 1994); like dismay from Ernst A. Schmidt, "Review of W. Clausen *Eclogues*," *Gnomon* 46 (1997): 720-722.

[37] *Classical Journal* 93 (1997) 211-216, reviewing *True Names* by J. J. O'Hara (Michigan, 1996), and *Extremus Labor: Vergils 10. Ekloge und die Poetik der Bucolica,* by Lorenz Rumpf, Hypomnemata 112 (1996).

[38] Shared between *Vergilius* 44 (1998) 113-115 & *Bryn Mawr Classical Review* [http://ccat.sas.upenn.edu/ bmcr/1998/1998-11-39.html]: reviewing R. Leclercq, *Le divin loisir: Essai sur les Bucoliques de Virgile*. Coll. Latomus 229 (Brussels, 1996); Ch. Martindale, "Green Politics: The

civic-heroic – and posited metaphoric links with Homeric myth that he then pretended to deny, thereby gaining recursive and recusative momentum for a moving close:

"The Design of Derek Walcott's *Omeros*" (1999).[39]

Meanwhile, new work on Theocritus was showing ever more fully his programmatic intertexts with Homer, inviting return to the first eclogue with fuller credit for a neglected narrative of cause and implied program: the story of *Meliboeus'* displacement – rife with intertextual crossings and poetological hints – proved if anything prior and more far-reaching than the tale of *Tityrus'* replacement via travel to Rome and back:

"Virgil *vs* Cicero, Lucretius, Theocritus, Callimachus, Plato, & Homer: Two Programmatic Plots in the First Bucolic" (2000).[40]

In the course of research for the previous piece, I came across a note on the poetics of *B.* 1 that defied belief and provoked a response:

"Virgil, *Bucolics* 1.1-2 & Interpretive Tradition:
A Latin (Roman) Program for a Greek Genre" (2004).[41]

Invited back to Genoa, where my work had found support from Franco della Corte, I determined to test a long held sense that a certain piece, although enjoying currency in Italian and even English, badly misconstrued the capstone of Virgil's design:

Eclogues," *The Cambridge Companion to Virgil* (Cambridge, 1997) 107-124; A. Cameron, *Callimachus and His Critics* (Princeton, 1995) 454-475.

[39] *Classical World* 93.1 (1999) 7-27. Cf. John Van Sickle, "Virgilian Reeds in Derek Walcott's *Omeros,"* *Essays Presented to Michael C. J. Putnam* (Providence: Brown University, 2003) 409-434.

[40] *Vergilius* 46 (2000) 21-58: constructively edited by Joseph Farrell.

[41] *Classical Philology* 99.4 – the editors of *HSCP* did not see fit to accept this detailed critique of a note they had found fit to print.

"Quali codici d'amore nella decima egloga? Il poeta elegiaco contestualizzato nel *Bucolicon liber* di Virgilio" (2003).[42]

Elsewhere, in a panel advertised as *The Virgilian Century*, one paper augured understanding how "all elements in a culture participate equally in making the national myth,"[43] which took me back to *Design* with its sequels and theoretical ground:

> L'écriture, étant la forme spectaculairement engagée de la parole, contient à la fois, par une ambiguïté précieuse, l'être et le paraître du pouvoir, ce qu'il est et ce qu'il voudrait qu'on le croie.[44]

The phrase brought deconstructive force to bear on Virgil at his most vatic (*B*. iiii.7-14): *iam nova progenies* ("now new line"), *ferrea primum | desinet ac...surget gens aurea* ("iron race first desist, then golden rise"), *...si qua manent sceleris uestigia nostri | irrita perpetua soluent formidine terras* ("if any traces of our crime remain, canceled they will free the lands from endless dread").[45] Realities of revolutionary change were masked in mythemes showing power as power would wish. Who might be meant by "iron race" or "traces of our crime" or "new line" and "golden race," what actual change be mystified by "first desist" and "surge" or "canceled" to "dissolve" whose dread of whom? What of murdered senators, proprietors proscribed, of Cicero – the class of *Meliboeus*? Was this a kind of photo-op or spin binding poetry to power?

---

[42] *Giornate Filologiche "F. della Corte"* III (Genova, 2003) 31-62, with thanks to Ferruccio Bertini and Silvana Rocca.

[43] Michèle Lowrie, "Literature is a Latin Word," *Vergilius* 47 (2001) 37.

[44] "Writing, as the form of the word that is visibly engaged, contains now and again, with precious doubleness, what power is and what it would have one believe it is": Roland Barthes, *Le Degré Zéro de l'Écriture* (Paris: Éditions du Seuil, 1953) 39: acquired in 1967.

[45] *Irrita* the most important word in the poem, according to my con-

Another paper by its title – "A Study of *Eclogue* 9" – raised suspicion of neglect for the book as context.[46] The *Menalcas* figure in *B*. 9 remains elusive unless construed recursively as a structuring element that unified the book's initial Roman suite but now recurs to help prepare and effect the final shift to Arcadian myth. Likewise the figure of *Moeris* as a defeated *uates* must be understood in context with the concerted rise but then revision of vatic voicing through the book.

A third essay would surmount nostrums of simple pastoral by surveying representation in poetry and painting from theoretical heights.[47] But Greenberg, Alpers et al. do not in practice guarantee properly close looks – careful of textual ramifications let alone real landscape. Error – "Mincius, a river that flows from the Po" – alerts. Recurrent generalizations – "each poem" or "almost always" or "the only eclogue" – fail the test of close reading. Incertitude mounts, perhaps not unlike that which the essay rightly finds in the shifts of shade and shadow in Virgil's works from first to last.[48] What the essay confesses for its treatment of other texts – an "inexcusably hasty glance" – comes back to haunt its tour of the *Bucolics*, which merit (and reward) more worthy use of such originary, intellective passion. *The Vergilian Century* – still preoccupied with scholiastic eclogues and pastoralismic theory – does scant honor to the poet's *liber* ("bark" and "book").[49]

temporary eclogue poet, cf. above note 11.

[46]   Christine Perkell, "Vergil Reading His Twentieth-Century Readers: A Study of *Eclogue* 9," *Vergilius* 47 (2001) 64-88; but for the import of book position, recognized even by an ancient reader: below, pp. 19, n.9; 31.

[47]   Connolly, "Representation," 105-106, cf. above note 10.

[48]   Connolly, "Representation," 110-111, cf. already below, pp. 230-232, on shade and flight opening *B*. 1 and closing *Aeneid* 12.

[49]   Cf. *B*. v.13; x.53, 67: below, p. 248; "Quali codici," 56.

Failure, too, by recent studies to absorb Virgil's early reception as described in *Design* and *Poesia e Potere* has prompted theoretical reflection and supplementary research.[50] The theoretical platform starts with questions posed by Michael Reeve: does our reading "explain things in the [text] that had seemed puzzling? Does it reveal things that no one had noticed? In short, where does it lead?"[51] Answers, indeed the very questions, suppose attentive study of prior reception, fulfilling, too, an ideal of scholarly community, described by Reeve as "less intellectual than moral," that rewards priority with "credit given where credit is due,"[52] in keeping with the honor accorded "first," to say nothing of scholarly desire to avoid the embarrassment of claiming to discover the wheel or of neglecting evidence that may impair or reinforce one's case. Also, facing Reeve's "fundamental question why [still today receive such works]," reception studies must reopen texts to contemporary conversation. Questioning views that have long constrained discussion, e.g., "simple pastoral" or "chronology of separate eclogues," would revitalize reading.

In practice, the present query began with Richard Thomas,

---

[50]   A combination of theory with practice welcomed not in venues controlled by the receptionists it queries but by the Classical Association of Great Britain (Centenary session, April 2003, Coventry) and the Arcadia conference (April 2003, Oslo). For the latter, however, I chose instead to recall, as fundamental background for such a session, how Virgil created the Arcadian literary myth through emulative response to Theocritus: *Id.* 1 >< *B.* x [http://academic.brooklyn.cuny.edu/classics/jvsickle/bbarcad.html].

[51]   Michael Reeve, "Reception/History of Scholarship: Introduction," *Texts, Ideas, and the Classics* (Oxford, 2001) 249. Of course "explain," "reveal," and "lead" as metaphors for the hermeneutic process must be interrogated: cf. other papers in the same volume: Susanna Morton Braund, "(Genre) Introduction," 139; Alessandro Barchiesi, "The Crossing," 148; and Marcus Wilson, "Seneca's *Epistles* Reclassified," 185.

[52]   Reeve, "Reception," 245; Richard F. Thomas, *Virgil and the Augustan Reception* (Cambridge, 2001) xx, citing Heinze: "honour where

who delineated and deconstructed what he called an "Augustan reading" of Virgil. Thomas emphasized actual focus on texts, seeking with J. M. Ziolkowski "a middle ground between the deconstructive aims of some theory and the reconstructive project of all philology."[53] He aimed to free Virgil of tralaticious incrustations, making the text seem less familiar,[54] and to freshen conversation through rereading. The goal was welcome, achievement considerable, which increased disappointment at his shortfall in the primary case.

Thomas's eclectic blend of theory with philology succeeded for the *Georgics* and *Aeneid* only to slight Virgil's first work; for such categories of reception theory as "implied reader" and "reader response" assume the library and study; and the effort to "establish an 'original' climate of reading" neglects the requirement that interpretation be "historically plausible in terms of the culture that produced the text."[55] In short, Thomas slighted ancient testimony for Virgil's initial success in the public media of his day.

Actual reception. The Suetonian-Donatan life of Virgil reports: *Bucolica eo successu edidit ut in scena quoque per cantores crebro pronuntiarentur* (§ 26: "Virgil gave the *Bucolics* out with such success that also on the stage by performers they were frequently recited"). The report has passed its most recent muster with no less redoubtable a Virgilian than Nicholas Horsfall, who cites it in his Virgil *Companion* along with other evidence for the poet's "fame in his own

honour is due."

[53]   J. M. Ziolkowski in Thomas, *Reception*, xvi.

[54]   For "defamiliarization" (*Entfremdung*) see Thomas, *Reception*, xvi: he cites a reader's complaint at his *Georgics* commentary – "This is not the poem that I have been reading and rereading" – as "quite heartening, since that was really my aim": likewise mine for the *Bucolics*.

[55]   Thomas, *Reception*, xvii, occluding documented reception via suc-

lifetime and immediately after his death."[56] The report, while ignored by Thomas, does get casual though uncredited notice from Charles Martindale in *his* Virgil *Companion*, inferring a bit more and much less than the text implies: "in antiquity some of the poems (which indeed are indebted to mime and show some interest in characterisation) were performed on stage as miniature dramas."[57] Ignoring the initial success and frequent performances, Martindale also neglects Horsfall's evidence from graffiti that the *Bucolics* figure in Virgil's popular notoriety disproportionately to their length.[58]

Cultural matrix. Wishing to reconstruct Virgil's cultural matrix by means of philologico-historical methods, we first have to deconstruct the dubitative account by Thomas:

> What, first of all, do we know of the period in which Virgil wrote, roughly speaking, the period in which the voices of Caesar and Cicero have fallen silent, before the time of Velleius, and in a world where Livy's contemporary history is available only in epitome?[59]

Against this counsel of despair, one may relate the report, *eo successu edidit* ("gave out with such success"), to well documented cultural practices at Rome, where the elites had long shared texts among themselves, both orally and in writing, in private and public contexts, as Horsfall himself and Mario

---

cess in recitation that led to stage performance.

[56]   Nicholas Horsfall, *A Companion to the Study of Virgil* (Leiden: Brill, 2000) 249. Cf. Nicholas Horsfall, "Aspects of Virgilian Influence in Roman Life," *Atti del Convegno di Studi Virgiliani*, II (Milano: Mondadori, 1984) 51-52: presence of the *Bucolics* in popular media is greater than for the *Aeneid*, while the *Georgics* were largely ignored.

[57]   Martindale, "Green Politics," 119.

[58]   Cf. above, note 56.

[59]   Thomas, *Reception*, 27.

Citroni, among many, have observed;[60] Virgil's friend Asinius Pollio made a point of reciting his own works before invited audiences, setting a fashion that later even Augustus would feel constrained to humor.[61] Success in recitations, then, might catch the interest of those able and eager to promote frequent repetitions, also in the theater: *in scaena quoque crebro*.

In welcome reinforcement for my own views concerning the theater's political roles,[62] Richard Beacham in 1992 reminded readers that in the late Republic "politicians looked to the theater as a platform both for impressive display and for mass communication and manipulation of popular feeling."[63] Also Peter Wiseman in 1995 wrote that "in republican Rome, the theater was the arena for the 'making and remaking' of the community's myths."[64] Beacham noted that Pompey completed Rome's first permanent theater in 55 BCE providing a new venue for crowd manipulation and propagandistic display, which Julius Caesar promptly exploited to celebrate his final

---

[60]   Nicholas Horsfall, "Poet and Patron Reconsidered," *Ancient Society* (Macquarie, 1983) 1-3; Mario Citroni, *Poesia e Lettori in Roma Antica. Forme Della Communicazione Letteraria* (Roma-Bari: Laterza, 1995) 3-56.

[61]   Seneca, *Controv.* 4, praef. 2, *Pollio Asinius...primus...omnium Romanorum advocatis hominibus scripta sua recitavit*; Suetonius, *Aug.* 89, *recitantes et benigne et patienter audiit*; cf. Llewelyn Morgan, "Creativity Out of Chaos: Poetry Between the Death of Caesar and the Death of Virgil," *Literature in the Roman World* (Oxford, 2001) 80, "in the first instance this was Pollio's work, but the practice was picked up by others and became a central institution of Roman aristocratic life in the imperial period."

[62]   Below, pp. 9-10; Van Sickle, *Poesia e Potere*, 17-25; Van Sickle, *Messianic Eclogue*, 15-36.

[63]   Richard C. Beacham, *The Roman Theatre and Its Audience* (Cambridge, Ma., 1992) 156.

[64]   T. P. Wiseman, *Remus A Roman Myth* (Cambridge, 1995) 132. Cf. Cicero, *pro Sestio* 118-124, *ad Atticum* 2.19 and 14.3, *de orat.* 2.240-243, *Phil.* 2.65, 67; Macrobius, *Saturnalia* 2.7.1-9.

defeat of Pompey.[65] Beacham, then, in 1999 would devote an entire chapter to the "Statecraft and Stagecraft of Augustus," documenting how the young Caesar deliberately and persistently used public spectacles in the theater and games to play on public opinion, how he capitalized on his status as *divi filius*, "son of the deified one."[66] The latter theme of course figured especially in Octavian's coinage, to ingratiate and define himself with the public, as Paul Zanker had shown.[67] Moreover, in the years between 46 and 29 BCE propaganda had to deal with an audience that included some of the several hundred thousand persons who had suffered loss of their lands to veterans of the civil wars, as Keith Hopkins has pointed out.[68] Consequently, in Zanker's words,

> The uncertainties of the present and the capriciousness of politics in Rome, along with the absence of any concrete or realistic expectations of what the future might bring, provided fertile soil for seers and soothsayers, irrational longing for a saviour, and predictions of a new and blessed age.[69]

Also, Andrew Wallace-Hadrill has treated what he described as "the whole matter of new mythology and cultural innovation in the Augustan age."[70] The audiences were volatile, primed to spot allegory and gossip, the opinion makers alert and wary, as we know from Cicero, who anxiously monitored the theater's mercurial moods.[71] He himself reportedly told

[65]   Beacham, *Roman Theater*, 160-162.

[66]   Richard C. Beacham, *Spectacle Entertainments of Early Imperial Rome* (New Haven, 1999) 92-108.

[67]   Paul Zanker, *The Power of Images in the Age of Augustus*, translated by Alan Shapiro (Ann Arbor: U of Michigan P, 1988) 35-39.

[68]   Keith Hopkins, *Conquerors and Slaves* (Cambridge, 1978) 67.

[69]   Zanker, *Image Power*, 44.

[70]   Andrew Wallace-Hadrill, "Rome's Cultural Revolution," *JRS* 79 (1989) 156-164, cited by Van Sickle, *Messianic Eclogue*, 148, n. 19.

[71]   Beacham, *Spectacle*, 92-108.

young Caesar of dreaming that a miraculous youth was sent down from heaven on a golden rope and honored by the gift of a whip from Capitoline Jove (Suetonius, *Div. Aug.* 94.9).

Features that fit the matrix & favor response. Such reminders of Virgil's cultural matrix should prompt receptionists to try a fresh look at his first work, in search of features apt to strike that susceptible public, whether we suppose it assembled in some great atrium, library hall, or the vast, unruly theater, not in any case just a solitary reader curled up with a scroll. As potential allegory, however, Thomas cites only three passages as possibly referring to Octavian:[72] "*Ecl.* 1.6-10, Tityrus, unnamed *deus* the salvation of Tityrus, with *Ecl* 1.42-5, Tityrus, unnamed *iuvenis* allows Tityrus to herd"; also, but with a question mark,[73] "?*Ecl.* 8.5-13, Virgil, unnamed *tu* to be subject of future song." Thomas then infers "a single and dominant function to all of these passages: each one creates a close identity between Octavian and Jupiter...."[74] This ought to have led him to coins, reported by Zanker, that

---

[72] Thomas, *Reception*, 41.

[73] But in the context of the book's whole design, less dubious: Van Sickle, "Commentaria," note 26 above.

[74] Idem 42. Thomas sees *B.* 8.11 as the only time in the *Bucolics* that Virgil addresses Octavian. He cites *Iupiter in caelis, Caesar regit omnia terris* (Anth. Lat. 813R, attributed to Virgil) as well as Aratus 1, & Theocr. 17.1 and *B.* 3.60, "at the beginning of amoebeans which end possibly with a riddle on Aratus' poem. A secondary reference, close in rhythm, to Homer, *Iliad* 9.97 (ἐν σοὶ μὲν λήξω, σέο δ' ἄρξομαι) seems to complicate by bringing in Agamemnon, but the words that follow make it clear that even here Zeus is very much in the air..."; cf. praising the Muses "both first and last," Hesiod, *Theog.* 34: σφᾶς δ'αὐτὰς πρῶτόν τε καὶ ὕστατον αἰὲν ἀείδειν.

identify young Caesar with the Dioscuri and Jupiter himself.[75] Further research would have found in other *Bucolics* stage potential – dramatic, rhetorical, and ideological.[76]

One basis for a fresh look at the *Bucolics* comes from Beacham's account of the art of pantomime, seen as probably an Augustan development from mime. He quotes Lucian:[77] "To sum it up, [the pantomime] will not be ignorant of anything that is told by Homer and Hesiod and the best poets, and above all by tragedy"; and Beacham elaborates:

> This individual silent performer was backed by musicians ... accompanied by either a single actor or a chorus that sang the part and provided the narrative continuity, during which the pantomime impersonated all the characters, male and female, in a series of interlinked solo scenes consecutively arranged.

Beacham goes on to report:

> Quintilian notes that there could be two *pantomimi* "contending with alternate gestures" and says that Augustus called one of them *saltator* (dancer) and the other *interpellator* (interrupter) (*Inst.* 6.3.65). The task of the performers was to give an impression of the whole ensemble and the relationship of one character to another while preserving the sense of the plot and creating graceful and expressive movements and gestures.

In such a context, the first eclogue seems brilliantly calculated to prompt the actor and captivate the turbulent crowd. Credit must go to N. W. DeWitt who in 1923 saw the theatrical excitement and propagandistic effect of the clash of pronouns and contrastive themes in the opening words of the persona called *Meliboeus*: the famous "you, *Tityrus*" at rest making music as opposed to "we ..., we are fleeing our fatherland,"

---

[75]   Zanker, *Image Power*, 38, 54-56.

[76]   Thomas believes, at least in theory, "that Virgil's oeuvre is ideologically complete and susceptible to interpretation": *Augustan Reception,* xvii.

[77]   Beacham, *Spectacle*, 143, citing Lucian (*De Salt.* 37-71).

which dramatizes the ideological divide between beneficiaries and victims of the revolution, only to be overshadowed by the ensuing triple run of three third person demonstratives – "that one ... that one's ... that one"– directing an actor's gestures towards the young Caesar in the front row as a present benefactor and savior, which was a preferred theme of Octavian's propaganda, as Zanker underlines.[78]

The savior theme recurs with increased emphasis towards the poem's center: *nec tam praesentis alibi cognoscere divos* (*B.* 1.41: "nor elsewhere than at Rome could I know such saving gods"). Then at the very center, Virgil makes his *Tityrus* aver that in Rome for the first time he met the one who delivered the oracle that determined his happy fate:

> *Tit*: hic mihi responsum primus dedit ille petenti:
> 'pascite ut ante boues, pueri. summittite tauros' (*B.* 1.44-45)
> (here [sc. at Rome] that one first gave me the oracle as I petitioned:
> 'graze cattle as before, boys; bring up bulls.')

The image of the saving, present divine force invites comparison with the Dioscuri on the coinage.[79] However, the message of return to business as usual, doing things as before, does not address the petitions of a *Tityrus*, represented as an old slave motivated by the cause of getting free to go to Rome (*Quae causa...? Libertas*, 1.26-27). The theme of return to things as they were, *ut ante*, seems rather calculated to assuage if not mystify those members of the crowd represented in the figure of *Meliboeus*, portrayed as a citizen land-owner dispossessed by barbaric soldiery. The supplementary message, "bring up bulls," suggests not merely restoration of the past but new development, albeit along traditional lines. (What

---

[78]   Norman W. DeWitt, *Virgil's Biographia Letteraria* (Toronto, 1923) 129-130: cited in critique of those who ignore the ideological clash by Van Sickle, *Poesia e Potere*, 20-22, "Dal mimo al mito."

[79]   Cf. above note 75.

could be more traditional in bucolic yet innovative than more bulls?) Thus the oracle, promulgating a program of restoration augmented by growth in a traditional manner, formulates and projects what will become the Augustan political and cultural program, even as it implies Virgil's program in poetics: return to bucolic tradition but with growth.[80]

From the ideological clash, centered on Caesar and capped with a mystifying image of a peaceful countryside at day's close, as Alfonso Traina has shown,[81] Virgil's dramaturgy shifts to the hot son and restless passion of *Corydon* for the master's darling, *Alexis*. The lively monologue provoked allegory to the poet's erotic vicissitudes and captivated scribblers of graffiti, generating also an inscription over a portal in Via Monserrato at Rome – "TRAHIT SVA QVEMQVE VOLVPTAS" (*B.* 2.65, "Each man's pleasure drags him on"). Sudden apostrophes cue emphatic gestures and shifts of tone, while epigrammatic points mimic the often sententious style of mime.

Next the dramaturgy switches back to dialogue and stirs intense by-play in comic language about sex, work, and song, giving an actor plenty of scope for stagy switching back and forth between voices and attitudes, before rising to a majestic center that projects fertility in every tree and field at the height of spring. The formal exchange opens by invoking Jove and Apollo, two deities associated with the young Caesar in propaganda and cuing further gestures with demonstratives:

Dam: ab Ioue principium musae, Iouis omnia plena:
　　　ille colit terras, illi mea carmina curae.

Men: Et me Phoebus amat. Phoebo sua semper apud me
　　　munera sunt – lauri et suave rubens hyacinthus.

　　　　　　　　　　　　　　　　(*B.* 3.60-63)

---

[80]　Van Sickle, "Codes and Critics," note 31 above.

[81]　Alfonso Traina, "La Chiusa Della Prima Ecloga Virgiliana," *Lingua e Stile* 3.1 (1968): 45-57; Van Sickle, "Dawn & Dusk," 132.

(*Dam*: From Jove our muse begins; of Jove all things are full:
that one keeps lands safe, him my songs concern.

Men: And me Phoebus loves. His gifts on hand I have
for Phoebus ever – bays and hyacinth blushing sweet.)

This Jupiter seems at once more comprehensive and more
immediately present than the Zeus in Theocritus' seventh Idyll
to whose throne report of one singer reached (*Id.* 7.93) or than
the Zeus evoked by Aratus (*Ph.* 1-5). The ensuing rapid-fire
exchanges dictate their own form of dramatic intensity, larded
with tidbits of names that could be gesticulated to the crowd.
Closure comes again with a touch of proverbial lore, again
sententious as in mime (love whether bitter or sweet deserves
reward, meadows have drunk their fill).

In abrupt contrast, then, the dramaturge calls for greater
things and consular scope, putting love and satisfaction behind
in the reach for Rome: strong clues to actor and audience of
the departure about to unfold in eclogue four, which alone
among the eclogues Zanker and Beacham cite for its currency
of prophetic motifs, to mention only *ultima Cumaei uenit iam
carminis aetas* (4, "now Cumaean song's last age has come");
iam noua progenies caelo dimittitur alto (7, "now a new line is
being sent down from heaven on high"). The latter shares the
conceit of Cicero's reported dream about the youth let down
by a golden rope and honored by Jupiter. The anecdote smacks
of political etiology even as philosophically it counters
Lucretius. He denied a Stoic allegory on Homer concerning
the descent of human life from heaven on a golden rope.[82]

Also, with renewed emphasis and cues for gesture, eclogue
four features the gods important for Octavian's propaganda:
tuus iam regnat Apollo (10, "already now your Apollo reigns")
and *magnum Iouis incrementum* (49, "Jove's great scion"), the
latter a ponderously spondaic, Roman adaptation of poetic

---

[82]   Below, p. 133, n. 73.

praise from the seventh idyll: "a sprig from Zeus fashioned all for truth" (*Id.* 7.44).

If the fourth eclogue, therefore, founds Virgil's reputation as a *uates*, the role would only be enhanced by the fifth, where the twin epitaphs for the dead Daphnis would prompt ways to remind the crowd of the dead and deified Julius – *extinctum ... crudele funere* but then *candidus insuetum miratur limen Olympi* (*B.* 5.20, 56: "snuffed out by a cruel death" but "shining he marvels at the unfamiliar threshold of Olympus") – an impression of vatic scope reinforced by an echo of the first eclogue, again with its gestural demonstrative: *'deus, deus ille'* Menalca (64: "a god, a god that one, Menalcas"). The literate mime recalled by Lucian might be expected to find in the contentious *Mopsus* an echo of the bard who competed with Homeric *Calchas* in the etiological epic by Euphorion about Apollo's Grynean Grove.[83]

After the vatic climax of eclogues four and five, resonant with Caesarist themes, a stagy retreat from public matter opens the sixth. Virgil brings back and reduces the figure of *Tityrus* with a different directive from a god – no longer expansive from the stand-in for Octavian but now restrictive from Octavian's favorite Apollo (the notorious downward shift of key that has prompted such aberrant scholarly receptions and provides such lively performative cues).[84]

Apollo frames – first down-grading the returned *Tityrus*, then expecting homage from an upgraded *Gallus*, and finally revealed as the originator of the entire outburst of song. Again apostrophes cue gestures, now emphatic in their own right though not directed to the front rows of the audience. The passion of Pasiphaë with its climactic apostrophe to the Nymphs of Netting echoes and redoubles the already paratragic dimensions of *Corydon*'s singing. Indeed the whole eclogue brings

---

[83]   Cf. note 77 above; also below, pp. 138-139, n. 84.

[84]   Below, pp. 148-149; cf. above, note 14, also http://academic.brook-

to mind Lucian's dictum that the pantomime not be ignorant of
Homer, Hesiod, the best poets, and above all tragedy.[85] The
spectacle of *Gallus* accompanied by the Muses triggered the
scholiastic fancy that the putative mistress of Cornelius Gallus
– the mimic actress Cytheris – performed this piece to the
amazement of Cicero.[86]

By marked contrast, eclogue seven opens with a static set-
ting deliberately and recollectively composed – *Daphnis* pro-
jected prior to *B.* 5, set in shade that never fails, *Meliboeus*
prior to exile and relieved of toil, exotic Arcadians on Min-
cius' woven bank: *Corydon* playing self-restrictive counter-
point to *Thyrsis*, the swelling poet, would-be *uates* scheduled
for defeat – where motifs of earlier vatic confidence return
with diminished emphasis: the adjective "golden" qualifies not
a returning race but a prospective image of Priapus (7.36) and
Jove figures only as a soaking rain (60).

The counterpoint between a retreating vatic strain and its
reciprocal builds further drama in eclogues eight and nine.
Two apostrophes evoke the vatic motifs of the first half-book
and help convey a sense of recursive structure in the whole. In
eight, the narrative prefaces contrastive songs of tragic
intensity with an apostrophe to an figure unnamed but linked
with the book's structure – its opening and prospective close –
and called worthy of tragic boot and laurel crown:

> a te principium, tibi desinam: accipe iussis
> carmina coepta tuis, atque hanc sine tempora circum
> intra uictricis hederam tibi serpere lauros.

(B. 8.11-13)

> (from you my start, for you will I desist: receive these songs
> begun by your commands and let this ivy creep
> among victorious bays around your brow.)

---

[85]   Cf. note 77, "best poets," sc. Callimachus, Calvus, Euphorion?

[86]   Servius, Thilo-Hagen III.1.66.16.

Again, the ideological language provides a gestural cue to the actor and audience. Among the perquisites granted the young Caesar was the right to wear a wreath of laurel at all times,[87] one that reinforced his emblematic association with Apollo; and the laurels also feature in his coinage.[88] Then, too, within the framework of the book, the young Caesar figured at the start as the savior evoked by *Tityrus'* anecdote of travel to and from Rome;[89] and bringing this structure to a close will free the poet to push on to higher modes of praise.

In the ninth eclogue, then, Virgil imagines a fragment of scarcely remembered song in which the old *uates* named *Moeris* had once in happier days evoked the *Caesaris astrum* ("Caesar's star"), which was one of the earliest and most prominent motifs in young Caesar's propaganda.[90] Here no demonstratives direct attention to the front rows; but the retreat from vatic poetics leaves Virgil free in eclogue ten to transfer his field of operations from Italy to Arcadia, bringing back the structuring figure of *Menalcas* as an Arcadian, joined at last with Pan in the place of bucolic origins.

In eclogue ten, the figure of *Gallus* dying for unrequited love affords the actor and gossipy public a climactic mix of local gossip and tragic posturing. The tragic range of *Gallus* echoes and outdoes that of Theocritean *Daphnis* in the first idyll. Virgil achieves his new version of bucolic tragedy recursively by recalling the tragic *Damon* and demonic enchantress of eclogue eight, the paratragic Pasiphaë in six, and in two the histrionic *Corydon*:[91] all erotic dramas that tickle popular fancy and feed graffiti, while the historico-mythopoeic flights mystify political consciousness and promote identification

---

87   Zanker, *Image Power*, 41.

88   Zanker, *Image Power*, 42.

89   Below, pp. 179-182; cf. "Commentaria," n. 26.

90   Zanker, *Image Power*, 35-37.

91   A tragic mode grows in the second half-book: cf. Lucian's dictum,

between the future princeps and his poet-prophet.

Some such development must lie behind two pieces of evidence for Virgil's public status in his own day. The Suetonian-Donatan life reports (39-40):

> si quando Romae, quo rarissime commeabat, viseretur in publico, sectantis demonstrantisque se subterfugeret in proximum tectum.
> (If ever he was seen in public at Rome, where he most rarely traveled, he would take refuge from the pursuing and cheering crowds under the nearest roof.)

Tacitus, in the *Dialogue on orators*, makes the poet Maternus recall that Virgil lacked neither favor with Augustus nor notice by the public:

> testis iste populus, qui auditis in teatro Vergili versibus surrexit universus et forte praesentem spectantemque Vergilium veneratus est sic quasi Augustum
> (A witness is that public of yours, which in the theater having heard some verses of Virgil's, who happened to be present among the spectators, rose all together and paid him homage almost as if he were Augustus himself).[92]

A view, then, of "Poetry and Power" by Richard Tarrant must be emended: "Virgil can be said to have fashioned a literary myth to support the political myth of the principate."[93] Our evidence would transfer this from the *Aeneid* to the *Bucolics*, where we have seen how Virgil fashioned his myths. They must have prompted the young Caesar to promote theatrical presentations, inspiring popular response and interpreting power, casting the poet as its prophetic voice, thus gaining him quasi-mythic status as the regime consolidated control. The

---

note 77 above, and the "Sophoclean buskin" of *B.* 810.

[92]   *Dial.* 13: before the origins of eloquence (12) came a Golden Age (*aureum saeculum*) rife with poet-prophets (*poetis et vatibus*), no lawyers but Orpheus and Linus, Apollo: cf. *B.* 4: 8-9, *gens aurea*; 56-57, *Orpheus, Linus, Apollo*, cf. Van Sickle, *Messianic Eclogue*, 150.

[93]   R. J. Tarrant, "Poetry and Power: Virgil's Poetry in Contemporary

whole dynamic of the unfolding and varying spectacle eludes theoretical radar fixed on reading, despite scholarly duty to make evidence (philological, historical) interrogate familiar habits handed down.

Receptionists have neglected not only the vatic persona of Virgil but also the other myth created through the book: Arcadia as the originary locus of bucolic song. Not to repeat arguments offered in *Design* and elaborated at Genoa, suffice it to recall the time and place parameters of the tenth eclogue and their metapoetic implications. Virgil greets the nymph *Arethusa* in Arcadia, which implies a notional date before her flight to Sicily, where she was addressed by Theocritean *Daphnis* in the first idyll. By thus claiming priority for himself with respect to Theocritus, Virgil reaches beyond the story in the second eclogue of *Corydon*'s pipe as a legacy from dead *Damoetas*. It acknowledged initial debt to Theocritus, whom now Virgil bids to supplant: a marked poetic ambition neglected by interpreters like Richard Jenkyns,[94] or Martindale in his *Companion*, and now Thomas, who in consequence purvey inevitably reductive versions of Virgil's achievement in the *Liber Bucolicon*.

Theory – reductive and simplistic, bent on closure – has long infected pastoralistic studies. To be sure, Virgil made his *Meliboeus* praise his *Tityrus*' enclave –

> Fortunate senex, ergo tua rura manebunt
> et tibi magna satis, quamuis lapis omnia nudus
> limosoque palus obducat pascua iunco:
> non insueta grauis temptabunt pabula fetas
> nec mala uicini pecoris contagia laedent
>
>   (*B.* 1.46-50)
>
> (Lucky old man, therefore your countryside will stay
> and great enough for you: however much bare rock

Context," *The Cambridge Companion to Virgil* (Cambridge, 1997) 169-178.

[94]   Richard Jenkyns, "Virgil and Arcadia," *JRS* 79 (1989) 26-39, taken

and marsh with muddy rush hem in your pasture all:
no unfamiliar feed will threaten pregnant ewes
nor neighbor flock's contagion do them harm)
– tending to distance and mystify the causal link with Roman power. Servius stumbled on the issue,[95] Schmidt complained, "Shall we ever get rid of that simplicity, a curse?"[96]

Schmidt argued, too, that Anglo-Americans ignore Germanic scholarship, including his: and he augured dialogue with Alpers crossing borders.[97] That would be a start, yet both have often been and still seem closed to another dialogue long sought and urged. Busy isolating one eclogue or another for the sake of abstractive theory, they, like the receptionists, neglect in Virgil's text the fabric of design with its impact on book poetry. They ignore concerted mythopoeia that identifies the poet via causal anecdotes both as Roman bard and as (re)-founder of epic tradition in its originary mode, supplanting Sicilian bucolic with Arcadian pastoral song.

Nevertheless dialogue with texts in hand would still be welcome, even at this late date, when one hears talk already of "pastoral post-Alpers,"[98] if only age, menacing circumstance, and minds ingrained with habit will allow.

Springs (East Hampton)[99]

---

to task by Van Sickle, *Messianic Eclogue*, 153, n. 42.

[95]   Cf. above note 8.

[96]   Cf. above note 9.

[97]   I have found it necessary to query two younger German scholars who attempted theoretic flights that proved short on careful reading of texts (cf. notes 21 & 37). Here, too, dialogue would be welcome.

[98]   So M. Skoie closing the Oslo conference on Arcadia (cf. note 50), which raised many hopes for dialogue, among them, e.g., on *B.* 3 with A. Fenton, *B.* 6 & *Iliad* 18 with B. Breed, and metapoetics with T. Saunders.

[99]   Deborah Blake ably shepherded this project, which I dedicate to Gail Levin for her scholarly example, patience, and unswerving support.

PARENTIBVS
MAGISTRIS
ET
AVCTORI

PREFACE

No one doubts that Virgil finished his own *Bucolics* and
gave them the order handed down by a unanimous tradition;
but the book he made has passed most commonly for a some-
what heterogeneous gathering of ten poems—the *eclogae*,
'selections'—where a norm of genre, the simple pastoral, is
violated now and again by complexity. The eclogues, it is
tacitly assumed, were composed with greater care than the
book.

Taking an opposite tack, I have explored the idea of
some modern readers that Virgil may have created in his book
a highly artful and unified whole. Since I assume that, if a
whole really differs from what we always thought, then our
view of its parts must also change, I have approached the
several eclogues not as miscellaneous, however skillful, poems
but as the differentiated segments (only in this sense 'selec-
tions') of a single composition, as the products of a thorough-
going and programmatic design.

In seeking to identify the terms in which such a design
might have been conceived, I have let myself be guided by
the history of the work. The *Bucolics*, in the course of some
two thousand years, have shown that they are able to speak
at the most diverse levels to many different interests. Thus
it would have been arbitrary to presume that their unity
existed at only one level and could be expressed in only one
set of terms.

In the first place, the *Bucolics* appealed to a broad listening public. They scored, so we hear, an immediate and clamorous success in their own time; and it is easy for us to imagine the original recitations, perhaps even with separate pieces circulated privately among the poet's friends. We hear, too, how success led to repeated performances on the stage and to the author's celebrity: Virgil pursued by admirers in the streets of Rome and applauded thunderously in a theater. Hence we know that the poetry both entertained sophisticated hearers and caught the people's ear and heart. We can infer that part of the reason will have been the dramatic eloquence, expressing mingled fear and hope of something new out of the long torment of civil war, the sense of a turning point after seven centuries in the history of Rome. A whiff of gossip, too, will not have lessened the entertainment.

We are, if anything, even more aware that the *Bucolics* command reflective readership. Here, too, our first evidence comes from Virgil's time. It suggests that his book, once published in its final form, immediately prompted a mode of reading appropriate to itself as a whole entity: I mean the emulation of contemporary poets, who responded by writing books of ten that likewise were informed by self-reflective and programmatic designs. We infer that the plan and the theoretical import of Virgil's book were perceived as something new and a challenge in poetics.

Another kind of readership also began early, provoked, so we are told, by the poet. Asconius Pedianus tells of hearing Virgil say that, in the riddles of the third eclogue, he 'set up a cross for scholars, for he wished to make trial, which one of them would be found most learned', *se grammaticis crucem fixisse, uolens experiri quis eorum studiosior inueniretur.* That is how Servius tells it (on E.iii 105). Yet Asconius' birth followed Virgil's death by a decade. Servius, at a remove of three centuries (and with his characteristic imprecision) will have been thinking of Asconius' book,

'*Against Virgil's Detractors*'. Our inference, however, can be precise: scholars very soon set to arguing about the *Bucolics*' value and sense. They leapt to Virgil's bait.

Given the tenor of the poet's remark, may we perhaps infer, too, that he knew what he was starting and had mixed feelings about it? After all, torture for getting the truth out of slaves (*crucem, experiri*) was still in use, the metaphor still current—its tone colloquial, with parallels in comic diction. Does it betray a trace of sarcasm? Virgil's work drew on an already ripe tradition of scholars and scholar-poets, to mention only such contemporaries as the imported Greeks Parthenius of Nicea and Asclepiades of Myrleia and the Italian M. Terentius Varro. Virgil knew the breed. They were exacting, tireless, had preserved, classified, ransacked and purveyed a cultural heritage. Yet, like some of their modern heirs, they could squabble in the birdcage of the Muses, show themselves relentlessly ingenious in the trivial but in the main things insular and obtuse. They could be counted on to minister to and to administer a text like his, but in their fashion: ever trying.

These multiple and diverse responses, from the applause, with its later echoes in masque and show, to poetic readership, with its rich and still varying sequel in the eclogue tradition, to scholarship, still racking its brains, all dictate that the unity of the *Bucolics* be pursued on different levels and that study adopt by turns the modes of interpretation appropriate to each level. No doubt the closest thing to a precedent for such system would be in della Cerda (1608). His commentary follows a graduated progression from the simple representation of a gist to more complex and analytic modes. The ideal might be something on the order of "well-tempered criticism" (the phrase is owed to Northrop Frye: both fully voiced like the clavier and well-disposed). The aim would be comprehensive and irenic rather than exclusionary and polemical: a program grounded in awareness of the complexity of the poetry, in respect for the diversity of values and points of view through two millenia, and in hope to learn from each.

Although the present book does build on previous essays that explored various and complementary interpretative approaches, it traces its immediate development to an invitation to write a review of scholarship for a German series called 'Ascent and Decline of the Roman World'. A first version was finished punctually in 1972. Two years delay in publishing made revision and expansion necessary. The lapse of three more years, in which new work by others appeared and my own thinking continued to evolve, recommended something still further. Hence this book. I should like to think of it not as an end of study but as an occasion for taking stock and a prolegomenon to further reading.

Whenever my work approached the level of poetics, the question of Theocritus would arise. Comparing him with Virgil promised one of the surest means of surprising the poet at work. Points of similarity assured a continuum in tradition. Specific departures gave the measure of development, departures that exemplified the *poetica urbanitas*, 'nicety in craft', that Servius remarked (2.22. Th.-H.). But Servius, like so many since, merely thought of Virgil as making complex what had been simple in Theocritus. The dichotomy was crude, 'simple Theocritus / complex Virgil': it always lent itself to the abuses of evaluative critics, who deprecated sometimes the one, sometimes the other, poet, according to the vagaries of taste; now it has been widely discredited. For example, my own effort to reconstruct the literary concerns of both poets, including their criteria for genre, suggested that neither one imagined himself as writing "simple pastoral lyric," a genre foisted on the poets by later critics. Both poets looked to the tradition of *epos*, in which Theocritus' work claimed a place as a complex though limited enclave, and to which Virgil more expansively returned. The need for an adequate study of Theocritus became evident. It remains to be written.

Thus, suggestions about Virgil's emulation of Theocritus still have to be offered provisionally. Here I have touched only a few of the principal cases, some of those most prominent in the outline of Virgil's design.

Aid for my preliminary studies and this book came from several sources, which I gratefully acknowledge: the Commission for Cultural Exchange between America and Italy (*già Commissione Americana per gli Scambi Culturali con l'Italia*), Fulbright fellowship in Rome; University of Pennsylvania, summer research grant; the Humanities Center of the Johns Hopkins University, post-doctoral fellowship; Trustees for Harvard University, The Center for Hellenic Studies, Junior Fellowship; and the City University of New York, Faculty Research Award. The Staff of the Library of the American Academy in Rome has been unfailingly courteous in its help.

Many students and colleagues have contributed to the development of these ideas. Some of the earlier essays drew especial benefit from criticism and encouragement by William S. Anderson, Thomas Cole, Paul de Man, Sears Jayne, Michael Putnam, and Charles Segal. Scevola Mariotti gave invaluable encouragement near the start and has remained an acute and generous critic. To Bruno Gentili, my debt is particularly great. He published two of my preliminary articles in *Quaderni Urbinati di Cultura Classica*. He invited me to present my basic analysis of the eclogue book in a seminar at Urbino, where he has welcomed me also as a visiting scholar and now collaborator for his journal. He made possible this publication. None of these readers, however, must be held accountable for what I have finally added, omitted, or retained.

My study of bucolic poetry began in a peculiarly appropriate setting—riparian and rife with umbratile passions. If the work has grown, much depends on the privilege and good fortune of being able to turn to Rome. Yet this would hardly have been possible in such measure without the warm and unstinting hospitality of the late Annie Battaglia and her family, who have given me so much more than a place to work. I owe the most, of course, to her daughter, Giulia, whose patience and sure judgment, vision and timely impatience have sustained and helped to bring these pursuits to this point.

La Quercia / New York

PART ONE: ORDER

Chapter 1
SOME SENSES OF ORDER

In the past, when scholars spoke about the order of Virgil's eclogues, they meant one of two things: either the temporal sequence in which separate pieces had been written,[1] or their final arrangement by the poet in the book.[2] In the course of nearly two millenia of discussion, neither line of speculation led to any firm and generally accepted conclusions. The various attempts to establish chronology cancel each other out, as any review of scholarship will show, even when the reviewer professes optimism that he at least has the good explanation at last.[3] No single reckoning holds the field, partly, no doubt, because of the lack of uniform criteria and consistent methodology. The sole instance of general agreement on chronology provides a case in point.

A. Chronology

Almost all scholars believe that Virgil wrote the second eclogue first and then the third, on grounds that these two pieces show the greatest simplicity and fidelity to Theocritus; and it is also believed that the fifth eclogue came next,

---

[1] "De eclogis multi dubitant, quae licet decem sint, incertum tamen est, quo ordine scripta sint." Servius 3.4. Th.-H.

[2] "Sed non eodem ordine edidit, quo scripsit." Probus (?) 328.10 Th.-H.

[3] Schmidt 1974.passim; Büchner 1955.1251-55; and, without review of scholarship, the unintentional *reductio ad absurdum* of the approach in Coleman 1977.14-21.

as being likewise simple and Theocritean, but especially because it closes with an express reference to the first and second eclogues. [4] Yet a closer look at the text in the light of some recent studies suggests that the general belief may be quite superficially based. The second and third eclogues emerge as works of considerable complexity in internal design, and they make significant departures from their Theocritean predecessors: in short, they are no more "simple" or "simply Theocritean" than, say, the tenth, ninth, eighth, seventh or first eclogues, where complexity and complex transformation of Theocritus are known. [5] As for the fifth eclogue, far from being simple or Theocritean, its lament for the dead Daphnis forms a sequel, not a simple return, to the first idyll, since the lament is a development of post-Theocritean bucolic. Moreover, the image of Daphnis amplified to the proportions of a culture hero and god overshadows any other bucolic figure in Theocritus or Virgil. [6] To be sure, the closing verses of the fifth eclogue do recall the openings of the second and third, but this need not be interpreted in the habitual way as merely a sign of chronology and autobiographical allegory. The sign, instead, might be one, for example, of thematic relations within the eclogue book, [7] or even of continuity in dramatic character, as one scholar has recently argued. [8] But we can return to this in due course.

[4] Soubiran 1972.72; and e.g. Posch 1969.10; Skutsch 1969.168; Otis 1964.131.

[5] Schmidt 1972.61; idem rev. Posch; Otis 1971.248; Posch 1969. 30; Williams 1968.294; VS 1967.498-99. Skutsch 1970.95-100 would have at least E.ii 44-55 late, non-Theocritean.

[6] Frischer 1975.13, 50-51; Berg 1974.122-23; idem 1965.11, 14; Otis 1964.144; cf. Putnam 1969.166-171: signs that the singing not to be simply generic.

[7] VS 1970b.907-910; Becker 1955.320.

[8] Flintoff 1976.21.

B. *Variatio*

The discussion of arrangement within the book also had precedents in ancient times. The commentary attributed to Probus says that first Virgil must have written his complaint at losing land (E. viiii) and then later his thanks to the Emperor for its recovery (E.i); but in order not to vex the Emperor the poet must have given the complaint its less prominent place in the book—in the middle, where things can be overlooked, and not first or last, *ne uel sic insigniter legeretur.*[9] In addition to such criteria, variation itself was supposed to dictate both the length and arrangement of such a book. This at least is implicit in the remarks of Servius, commenting on Virgil's departures from the norms of Theocritus: (3.20 Th.-H.; cf. 29.12)

sane sciendum, VII eclogas esse meras rusticas, quas Theocritus X habet. hic in tribus a bucolico carmine sed cum excusatione discessit, ut in genethliaco Salonini et in Sileni theologia, uel ut ex insertis altioribus rebus placeret, uel quia tot uarietates implere non poterat.

Some principle of variation, then, lies behind most of the modern attempts to explain the arrangement, although scholars differ about what alternates with what, whether theme or some aspect of form.[10] To cite only one example,

---

[9] "Gratias ergo agens Augusto, quod recepisset agros, Bucolica scripsit. Sed non eodem ordine edidit, quo scripsit. Est enim ecloga, qua ereptos sibi agros queritur (E.viiii), ... et ea posita est in paenultimo. At prius fuit queri damnum, deinde testari beneficium. Ergo praeponi illa ecloga debuerat et sic haec substitui, qua gratias agit. Sed Vergilii consilium hoc fuit: ne offenderet imperatorem, cuius saeculo librum legendum praebebat, maluit instare testimonio. Nam ipsa ecloga, quae de damno refert, nec in ultimo posita est, ne uel sic insigniter legeretur. Plerumque enim, quae in medio ponuntur, inter prima (et ultima) delitescunt." Probus (?) 328.9-19 Th.-H.

[10] Soubiran 1972.43; Büchner 1955.1255-58.

a recent variant on this approach divides the eclogues into those where the "Eclogue Poet" speaks (E.ii, iiii, vi, viii, x) and those in which the "characters speak for themselves" (E.i, iii, v, vii, viiii): [11] in short the familiar hypothesis of alternation between varieties of representational form (*diegematikon* and *dramatikon*). It always breaks down because E.vii, too, is narrative; and this version adds the further inconsistency of attributing E.vi to the impersonal "Eclogue Poet," although the narrative personae in both the sixth and seventh have highly significant, recurrent bucolic names, a point to which we will return. In any case, a pattern of *uariatio* at this level would leave us, as Jean Soubiran has remarked, "sur le plan de l'esthétique extérieure, à la surface des choses. " [12]

C. *Design*

By contrast with the inconclusive speculation about chronology and alternation, one hypothesis can be said to have broken through the impasse, since it has opened the way to a series of discoveries that gradually but radically has altered our conception of Virgil's book and art. Already in 1884 W. Krause observed that Virgil made a point of separating pieces with similar subjects, thus E.i and viiii (dispossession), E.ii and viii (love), E.iii and vii (amoebaean exchange), E.iiii and vi (revelation of future and past), although the criteria for what is "similar" shift, as Karl Büchner has objected. [13] But in 1944 Paul Maury argued that each of these thematic or formal correspondences also had a numerical value in the sum of the lines in the related pieces; [14] and in 1969 Otto Skutsch, after

[11] Leach 1975.263-274, who makes this account the basis for comparisons with "structures" in painting.
[12] Soubiran 1972.43.
[13] Krause ap. Büchner 1955.1256.
[14] Maury 1944.71-177.

an earlier rejection, accepted Maury's discovery in principle, although prudently still refusing to supplement the text, as Maury proposed, to procure perfect symmetry within the book and coincidence with certain Pythagorean numbers. [15] The numerical scheme, after the censorship of Skutsch, stood as follows: [16]

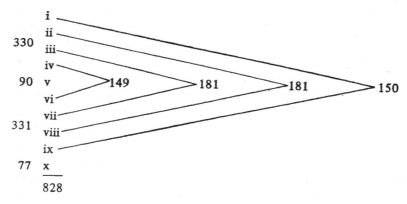

Defending Maury's discovery, Skutsch wrote that "the numerical pattern cannot possibly be the result of chance, because it accompanies and confirms the pattern observed in the content and to some extent in the form of the poems concerned." [17]

Meanwhile, independently of these developments, other discoveries were in progress, arising from a different source. Although Skutsch generally was reluctant to attribute sense to the numbers he defended (no doubt because Maury had attributed too much), even he admitted to an exception: [18]

There is one eclogue only where the structure may be a little more than a senseless pattern. *Eclogue* iv, the Messianic eclogue

[15] Skutsch 1969.161.
[16] Idem 155.
[17] Idem 159.
[18] Idem 158. Skutsch's warning was directed against a jejeune study also criticized by VS 1967.506, n. 31.

announcing the birth of the wondrous child and the coming of
the Golden Age, is structured in groups of seven lines. ...the
number 7, as we know from the *Aeneid,* has a way of turning
up in solemn and especially in prophetic contexts—a warning,
perhaps, against unduly playing down the seriousness and signi-
ficance of the Messianic eclogue.

Thus it is not surprising that the fourth eclogue directed my
own contemporary but independent study to the importance
of number in Virgil's art. [19] From this followed an article
looking from E.iiii to the eclogue book but supposing,
unlike Skutsch, that numerical patterning and sense must
be correlated, in particular that the numbers and theme
of Arcadian poetics in the fourth eclogue had a further
development: [20] the image of Arcadian poetry undergoes
amplification in two successive pieces that are placed at
regular intervals and have numbers of verses that are
sequential multiples of seven—E.iiii, 63 lines, distant hope
of poetic victory in Arcadia (iiii 58-59); E.vii, 70 lines,
report of two Arcadians competing on Italian ground;
E.x, 77 lines, report of full cast of Arcadian characters in
Arcadia itself.

From this first observation, others followed. It was
clear that the second eclogue had ten lines less than the
first (E.i, 83; E.ii, 73), an evident symmetry with the end
of the book (E.viiii, 67; E.x, 77); but there also seemed
to be some possibility of a relation to the fourth eclogue
(83, 73, 63). But what of the third? Inquiry into its inter-
nal structure showed that it had 48 lines of amoebaean
exchange, a length inherited from Greek bucolic; [21] but the
surrounding frame, a number of verses that Virgil was free
to calculate for his own devices, proved to be 63 lines in

[19] VS 1966.349-352.
[20] VS 1967.492-494.
[21] VS 1973/1974.198-99; cf. Skutsch 1971.26-28.

length. Thus we had a group at the start of the book—83, 73, 63+48, 63—and Skutsch's question, what could it mean? That it meant something in relation to E.iiii seemed likely, especially when further inquiry suggested that the internal structure of the first and second pieces, too, is based on a module of 63: E.i, $5+5+63(+)5+5$, and E.ii, $5+63(+)5$. Suddenly the first four eclogues stood apart as a group in which the fourth seemed to determine structure. Clearly a fuller investigation of theme would be required.

Finally, close analysis of the structure of the book as a whole showed that it divided into two equal halves (accepting Skutsch's exclusion of E.viii 78) not at the boundary between the fifth and sixth pieces but precisely at the point towards the end of the fifth that harks back to the second and third, that well known "sign of chronology" that initiates a process of pointed reflection on the first half-book (E.v 85-90 = B. 415-20, out of 828 lines). [22]

Bringing together these observations generated by the fourth eclogue with those of Maury-Skutsch, we can summarize the general design of the book as follows:

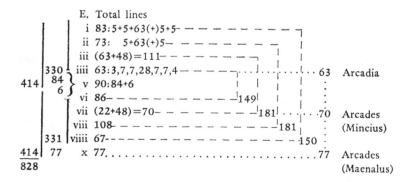

[22] VS 1970b.907-910.

Reading down from the top, we first observe the group of the first four eclogues; then, glancing down and back, we may begin gradually to piece out the system of responsion in the second half-book; and finally we may pursue the progression of Arcadian motifs through north Italian Mincius to a place near Maenalus. Also, once we have posited a link between the first and the fourth pieces, we have the makings of a framework for the book as a whole: E. i, iiii, vii, x. This, too, will require interpretation.

D. *The Actual Writing*

The order that these divers studies, in spite of occasional missteps, have succeeded in delineating is more complex than anything scholars had imagined, although we cannot exclude the possibility that poets mastered some of its essentials— Horace perhaps, [23] Propertius, [24] Calpurnius, [25] or Spenser. [26] Evidently we are dealing no longer with simple sequence or variation but with an intrinsic order in a highly integrated system—a comprehensive design in the poetic text. This will require a new and higher order of discipline from interpreters. It has already placed one of their most unexamined assumptions in doubt: *non eodem ordine edidit quo*

[23] C. A. Van Rooy, "'Imitatio' of Vergil, Eclogues, in Horace, Satires, Book 1" *AClass* 16 (1973) 69-88; cf. n. 5.37 below.

[24] Cf. nn. 1.32, 39 below, and more generally on Propertian emulation of Virgil, VS 1974.116 ff.

[25] Leach 1973.53 suggests that Calpurnius, with marked structure, "may have aimed to remedy what seemed to him defective in Vergil's uncertain symmetry (Sic!)." For evidence that Calpurnius was an accurate interpreter of Virgil, Damon 1961.298; for Leach's own perception, see n. 11.

[26] Alpers 1972.367, "If Spenser's great achievement is to bring a variety of eclogue types together in the same sequence, Milton, with his usual heroic relation to poetic tradition, brings them together into a single poem."; see A. Fowler, *Triumphal Forms* (Cambridge 1970) on number in Spenser.

scripsit. [27] It was always assumed that Virgil completed separate poems and put them together in an order different from that of composition. But this model of operation no longer seemed adequate once it became clear how comprehensive the design was. Hence new, complex models of operation had to be posited to allow for rewriting at least, [28] or even for the creation of entire poems or blocks of poems to fill out a design which was presumed to have taken shape gradually in the course of the work. [29] Yet the old attachment to chronology still persisted, with the hope of distinguishing earlier and later parts. [30] Now, however, even this vestige of our old habits seems destined to be given up. Virgil is simply too accomplished a stylist not to have covered his tracks. The *Bucolics* are a uniformly finished work. No stages of rewriting can be discerned. [31]

But, if this is so, it will be necessary to devise yet another model of operation, one that presupposes no separately completed poems at all but rather some initial sketches, nuclei, such as exercises in response to prior texts (e.g. the simple Theocritean translation, E.viiii 23-25) or in response to events (e.g. expropriation, E.viiii 27-29), but then gradual elaboration by sharpening the poles of contrasts, articulating parts, differentiating forms and themes, each element taking shape in response to others, conditioned by and conditioning the design of the whole. In the end, the several eclogues would not be separate poems but pieces realized and completed only in and with the whole. Thus

[27] Cf. n. 1.9 above.

[28] Clausen 1964.193.

[29] Otis 1964.131.

[30] E.g. Skutsch 1970.95-99; assumptions by Otis 1964.131 ff.; Duckworth 1969.49-53, who seeks to use dactyl-spondee structure to determine priority, yet admits that it might be an index to matter rather than time, p. 60, n. 12.

[31] Skutsch 1969.168, more prudently than in 1970 just cited; Büchner 1955.1255.

an eclogue would have a peculiar status, between autonomy (its own inner coherence) and subordination to the design. The situation may be compared with that in Propertius: [32]

Once we accept that a poem was written to complete a programme, it follows that it cannot be interpreted in isolation as a separate entity (in accordance with certain tenets of modern literary criticism), but that the whole question of its context or function in the wider plan needs to be taken into account. And this may be the key to poems whose intention is not immediately clear.

Some of the apparently irreducible difficulties in interpreting some eclogues might in fact be overcome if we conceived of eclogues as pieces, parts or movements (as in music), rather than isolated lyric poems.

Such an operative model also entails a new approach to the interpretation of dates. Under the old model, it was readily assumed that an entire piece would have been completed not merely after any date mentioned by any verse but actually during and within the year. [33] Thus the fourth eclogue had to have been rushed to completion in the fall of 40 B.C., though no one that I know of went so far as to time the ninth after the comet, in the autumn of B.C. 44. Such crude identifications between actual composition and what might better be called historical allusions or dramatic dates will have to be given up if a piece like the fourth eclogue as we know it cannot be supposed to have been completed apart from any of the others. Dates in the eclogues can no longer be assumed to indicate the years of separate poems. Chronologically they will serve only as terminus post quem for the final completion of the book, as late, then, as 35-34 B.C. [34] although they retain all their

---

[32] Barsby 1974.137.

[33] E.g. Coleman 1977.15; Berg 1974.122-23; Berkowitz 1972.22; Hardie 1970.1123b; Otis 1964.131; et multi.

[34] Bowersock 1971.74-76 supports Servius, who took E.viii 6-13

ideological importance for study of the *Bucolics* in their time; and mention of a datable event in a certain manner also reveals the poet's stylistic concerns.

E. *Interpretation of the Design*

Without our old addiction to chronology, we remain with what no one doubts we have, the product of Virgil's *ultima manus*, complicated now by the strange design. Faced with a new fact of this magnitude, some critics have been tempted to deny its existence. [35] Those who tried, instead, to come to terms tended naturally to perceive the design in ways pioneered by Maury. [36] Even his sharpest critics, unconsciously, were conditioned by his approach.

1. *The Concentric(-Static) Thesis*: Paul Maury was a man of singular sensitivity and vision, so much so that one reads him with mingled admiration and dismay and in reporting runs the risk of travesty. He perceived the corresponding pairs of eclogues as rings in a spiritual itinerary, the mind moving through one and nine, two and eight, three and seven, four and six, in an ascending spiral that culminated in the fifth eclogue, the high point and the center, with Daphnis as Caesar become a god. This movement of the mind in a gyre has provoked a series of scholarly affirmations and grimaces that we need not reproduce here; [37] the evolution of one of Maury's most telling critics

as alluding to Octavian's Illyrian campaign of 35-34 B.C. A closer look shows that the identification on historical grounds is tenuous; but it is bolstered by a correct reading of the passage in the design of the eclogue book, see nn. 6.71-72 below.

[35] Coleman 1977.19; E. de Saint-Denis, "Encore l'architecture des 'Bucoliques' virgiliennes," *RevPhil* 50 (1976) 7-21; Leach 1975. 274; Putnam 1969.6; Williams 1968.328; Skutsch 1956.195; cf. n. 37. Instead there is a reasoned discussion of "poetry books" in B. Otis, rev. Williams 1968: *AJP* 92 (1971) 325-26.

[36] Eg. Skutsch 1969 (cited n. 41); Otis 1964 (cited n. 50).

[37] Soubiran 1972.43-45, Posch 1969.61, n. 3, give bibliography.

will suffice to illustrate the fate of Maury's basic views before their incorporation in the design presented above. In 1956, as we noted earlier, Otto Skutsch rejected Maury out of hand, heaping particular scorn on the proposed pairing of E.iiii and E.vi, since these contained mutually contradictory poetic programs: *maiora canamus* (iiii 1) and *deductum dicere carmen* (vi 5).[38] In 1969, however, after the experience of working out an intricate numerical structure in another Augustan poetry book,[39] Skutsch came to the conclusions quoted above: the numbers could not be denied, but they had to be more sparingly construed:[40]

Now it is no good saying "I don't believe in numbers" and burying your head in the sand. These are facts, and they have to be faced. They were, of course, first stated by P. Maury, and they would have been accepted sooner and more widely if he had not gone too far in his pursuit of the significance of number. Nor indeed is there anything wrong with patterns formed by numbers arrived at by adding together the verses of several poems. We find the same thing in the *Monobiblos* of Propertius, the structure of which was explained five years ago.

True to these strictures on Maury, Skutsch pruned away the mystical vision, the spiraling spiritual itinerary, and the unconscionable supplements to the text. What survived was a perception of the design as static, but still essentially as in Maury concentric, with rings of eclogues around E.v conferring special sense:[41]

Standing thus right in the centre of the group from i-ix, numerically as well as structurally, *Eclogue* v is bound to have a special significance. And if we recall that in the internal structure of *Eclogue* i it was the reference to Octavian, unnamed, which occupied, or rather usurped, the central position,

[38] Skutsch 1956.196.
[39] O. Skutsch, "The Structure of the Propertian Monobiblos," *CP* 58 (1963) 238-39.
[40] Skutsch 1969.159.
[41] Idem. 167.

it would require some hardihood to deny that the idea of the death and deification of Julius enters, indirectly but inevitably.

Although the mind no longer circles and soars, E.v still is perceived as in the center and centrality as the key to significance; only now Skutsch supports this perception by analogy with the first eclogue, which he also perceives as concentric and static. The sense, then, that he infers from these centering designs is narrowly ideological—"Octavian" or "idea of the death and deification of Julius."

2. *The Linear-Dynamic Thesis*: it is notorious that one and the same text will produce quite different senses when approached with different preconceptions. So the first ec-logue, in which Skutsch perceives concentric-static order, has been read by Brooks Otis, among others, as an example of dynamic and linear construction: [42]

...tension of the poem as it grows to a climax that permits a new and more exalted confrontation of Tityrus and Meliboeus...

Similarly, in the second eclogue, Otis perceives not the con-centric pattern with myth of poetic authority at the center but the dynamism of the unhappy lover in speech that builds to one feverish peak, collapses in remorse and self-reproach, but builds again to "the climactic significance of the second lament." [43] Or again, in the cases of E.iii and E.iiii, Otis and others have minimized containing and purely symmetrical or concentric patterns and have emphasized climactic move-ments through repeated and cumulative *amplificatio*—the

[42] Otis 1971.247; cf. Otis 1964.13; and Wormell 1969.17, Kling-ner 1967.23-26 (object of review by Otis 1971), and Pöschl 1964.13, 150-151.

[43] Otis 1971.247; cf. Otis 1964.13; and Wormell 1969.17, Kling-ner 1967.23-26 (object of review by Otis 1971), and Pöschl 1964.13, 150-151.

auxesis of themes and stylistic means. [44] Of course the fifth eclogue easily lends itself to like perceptions, as we shall see, both in its setting, with the pointed move away from familiar bucolic shade to a more select locus, and in its songs, where the first is advertised as something freshly added and the second, raising the dead Daphnis to heaven, is announced in terms that strongly suggest an advance beyond the first (cf. E.v 51-52).

In turn, these perceptions of the first and other eclogues ought to suggest some linear and dynamic readings of the book as a whole, if Skutsch was right to draw an analogy between the design of a single piece and that of the book. In fact a number of efforts have been made along these lines, taking the eclogues in given order and seeking to discern continuities and developments in character or theme that extend through successive pieces, even shaping the entire work. [45] We shall investigate such studies in a moment, but first it may be useful to look at an influential work that pointed in their direction only to fall back into the concentric thesis of Maury.

In 1964 Otis wrote: [46]

It is clear (whatever else may not be clear) that *Eclogues* 1-5 are relatively forward-looking, peaceful, conciliatory, and patriotic in a Julio-Augustan sense. *Eclogues* 6-10, on the contrary, are neoteric, ambiguous or polemic, concerned with the past and emotively dominated by *amor indignus*, love which is essentially destructive and irrational and is implicitly inconsistent with (if not hostile to) a strong Roman-patriotic orientation. The con-

---

[44] E.iii: Otis 1971.248; Segal 1967.281-89. E.iiii: Otis 1971.250 faults Klingner's failure to analyse "climax building" and his attempt to "minimize progressive schemes of development in the poem"; cf. analyses of such schemes by VS 1969a, Williams 1968. 276-280, VS 1966.251, Otis 1964.139.

[45] E.g. Soubiran 1972; VS 1967; Galinsky 1965 (1968), although accepting E.ii as first in time, p. 162; J. Ruelens, "Les saisons dans les 'Bucoliques' de Virgile, *AntClass* 12 (1943) 79-92.

[46] Otis 1964.131.

clusion is suggested that *Eclogues* 6-10 were in large part written to form a contrast with *Eclogues* 1-5 and that the general design of the complete *Eclogue Book* emerged *before* Virgil had completed the whole series of ten poems.

Here we had the makings of a bold linear and dynamic reading of the book—contrast between the first and the second halves,[47] movement from affirmation to negation. On such terms it seemed possible to detect in the whole design a principle of dialectical construction like that which Viktor Pöschl at the same time was finding in the first and seventh eclogues—unity of opposites as a means of grasping a complex reality entire, contrast as a means of advance.[48] Also, the play of contrast and reversal in a whole structure seemed to lend itself to semiological analysis: the effort to assert a positive ideological moment in the first half book entailing deferral (temporary mystification) of negative themes, but these then surfacing, even in disguised forms, in the second half of the structure (e.g. the moment of effective Roman force: positive in the first half book—god reassuring slaves, 'Carry on as before, boys!' [E.i 45]—but in the second half negative, and thus assigned to a more nondescript speaker—'These are mine. Old cultivators, get off!' [E.viiii 4] *sic minus insigniter*, as the scholiast said).[49] But even without dialectical or semiological models, the large reversal seemed to deserve study as a clue to Virgil's, indeed the forming Augustan, mind. But Otis merely reverted to speculation about the chronological sequence of separate poems and closed with a variant of the concentric-static thesis:[50]

The centre of his (sc. Virgil's) real devotion, the goal of his true

[47] Cf. Becker 1955.317; Büchner 1955.1251.
[48] Cf. nn. 53, 54, 55 below.
[49] See n. 9; for the concept of deferral of the negative, VS 1974. 121-22, and Benevelli 1973.263.
[50] Otis 1964.142.

poetic instinct, is not *Amor* and its service (sc. the theme of E.vi-x) but the new *Romanitas*... star of the deified Caesar...

So strong was the grip of Maury's concentric perception. And yet even the ancient critics recognized that first and last are the most emphatic positions, and Virgil himself placed the passionate and neoteric not the obliquely Julian version of Daphnis last.

3. *Contrast of Theses*: without the support of a full-scale interpretation of the design in linear-dynamic terms, the suggestion of a large ideological contrast between half-books made an easy target for rebuttal from a more strictly centristic and static point of view. Hence Skutsch, in his own palinode in 1969, ironized: [51]

Well now, a priori: if I were a poet and wanted to represent five positive aspects of one thing or another and five negative aspects, would I really put all the negative aspects in the second half of my book and let the reader sink into gloom and despair? The answer obviously is No. But let us look at the evidence: it seems to me that violence is done to several poems to force them into the positive-negative mould....

No, there is no symbolic structure in the book as a whole. Just as the structures of the individual poems are pretty patterns devoid of meaning except in one instance, [52] so the structure of the whole book reveals, with one notable exception, nothing of the essential significance of individual poems.

Denial, not merely of negation in the second half-book but of any non-centristic dimension of meaning in the whole, could hardly be more absolute. Like any antithesis worth its salt, this one bids to demolish and supplant the thesis. And yet this very relish for the attack betrayed itself. It seemed less likely to persuade Virgilian initiates than to

[51] Skutsch 1969.161-62.

[52] Elsewhere Skutsch allows two instances of significant structure: E.i (p. 167) and E.iiii (p. 158).

remind them of the rhetoric of argumentation and the symmetry of opposing extremes, to which Pöschl had just called attention in the eclogues themselves, as we have noted. As a rule, each extreme is so conditioned by the necessity for contrast with the other that neither can comprise the whole truth. Needless to say, these conditions of dialectical construction appear not merely within single works but in separate works sequential in time. Hence the very forcefulness of thesis and antithesis in Otis and Skutsch seemed to necessitate a glance beyond them both in search of some kind of interpretative synthesis. The hope was for an approach that would incorporate contributions of both the concentric-static and linear-dynamic perceptions of design, above the perhaps inevitably dogmatic polarities of exploratory work. The requisites could be found in Pöschl: perception of "Symmetrie" and the centrality of the god (E.i); [53] but also of "Kontrast," which could have either static or dynamic effects; [54] and perception, too, of "Steigerung," which was linear and dynamic. [55] But it remained to press analogies between single pieces and the whole. A step in this direction had meanwhile been taken by the study, mentioned above, of the fourth eclogue and Arcadian imagery in the book, with hints, too, of syntheses of centering and linear patterns. [56] What seemed called for, then, was an advance beyond the dichotomies of academic dispute toward an integrated discourse that could deal with the poetry as both "still and still moving." [57]

[53] Pöschl 1964.68-71.

[54] Idem. 73.

[55] Idem 13, 150-51. Flintoff 1976.23 compares Virgilian contrast and building to Hegelian dialectic: apt, and a reminder that dialectical method is not the exclusive property of any one age or genre. Cf. Johnson 1977.2, 16, 20, 22.

[56] VS 1967.493-94, 498-500.

[57] Benevelli 1973.263 attributes to Barthes a critical practice that is "il superamento della dicotomia di sincronia e diacronia, sostituen-

4. *Toward Synthesis—The Approach through Ideology*:
the text justifies Otis in the sense that certain traditional
negative themes, which were subdued in the first half-book,
do return to the fore in the second half: for example, what
we might have expected from bucolic poetry, a refusal of
heroic and historical *epos* (E.vi 1-12), together with themes
of deforming and destructive passion in human life (E.vi
45-60, 74-81); or, again, the humiliation of losing a contest
(E.vii 69); and suicide from unrequited love (E.viii 14-61);
and a disheartened, forgetful old age that fragments song,
singers defeated, unlucky, forced to abandon the pastoral
foreground (E.viiii 2-6, 51-55); then, finally, unrequited
passion again, causing defeat, death, alienation from Arcadia
(E.x 10, 69). As another attentive reader has put it, be-
tween the two half-books we feel "une opposition de mode
majeur/mode mineur." [58] Still the antithesis, too, finds
strong support in the text: such positive themes as resolve
for new poetic enterprise (E.vi 8), with an *epos* of cosmic
generation (E.vi 27-40), instances of constructive passion
(E.vi 26, 61-73, 82-83); and ideal poetic 'play' and victory
(E.vii 17, 69-70); or powerful and concretely effective
song (E.viii 1-5, 64-108); or youthful enthusiasm for sing-
ing (Lycidas, E.viiii); [59] or the image of Arcadian poetry
consoling passion with skillful, eternal entertainment (E.x
31-34), and poet's constructive passion for poet (E.x 73-
74). In short, every one of these last five eclogues has its
share of both positive and negative themes. Skutsch is right
to deny the thesis of simple negation; yet a feeling lingers
that at some level some shift of tone or mode occurs. The
book that opens with 'thanks to the Emperor' does end

do alle metafore di linee e di forme la metafora del diagramma
musicale." Cf. the exemplary critique of reductive and dichotomizing
interpretations ("myths") by Johnson 1977.1-22.
[58] Soubiran 1972.45-46.
[59] VS 1967.500, cf. nn. 22, 23; Leach 1975.209.

with poetic honors to a friend and evocation of the theme of love's distress.

The impasse begins to resolve itself once we distinguish between the kinds of themes at issue. Skutsch points in this direction when he reproves Otis for misconstruing *amor indignus* as 'unworthy love' and for suggesting that Virgil condemned erotic passion on moral grounds (e.g. Otis' judgment that such love is "implicitly inconsistent with, if not hostile to, a strong Roman-patriotic orientation"). [60] This moral standard, of course, came from the first half-book, which Otis saw in moral and ideological terms— "relatively forward-looking, peaceful, conciliatory, and patriotic in a Julio-Augustan sense." [61] And yet the second half-book opens by conspicuously putting off a public theme and closes with the display of sympathy for fatal, private love. Ideology hardly seems the first concern of such poetry, in spite of the lesson inferred by Otis. Indeed the real lesson would appear to be of another order: that we as readers not continue merely to compare and contrast predominant themes in general, whether "negative" or "positive," without distinguishing their level or kind. Instead we should begin specifically to isolate themes that are ideological in fact (not just "implicitly" as Otis says): [62] in other words, ideas of socio-political order and change. These flourish in the first half-book, to judge by Otis ("patriotic... Julio-Augustan") and Skutsch ("Octavian... center... idea of the death and deification of Julius"), who seem not to disagree substantially on their positive thrust. Granting, then, that a positive ideology predominates in the first half-book, we can inquire whether it is reversed by the socio-political assumptions of the second half.

Approaching, now, the last five eclogues from just this

[60] Skutsch 1969.162 against Otis 1964.131.
[61] Otis loc. cit.
[62] Ibid.

standpoint, in the sixth we observe a narrative persona that introduces and frames the entire piece. Here, then, if anywhere, we should expect to find the underlying ideas of the work; and in fact an ideological premise does emerge. The narrator takes for granted a stable order in society as the background for his work. He speaks confidently of the authority and success of a powerful friend, and he anticipates an outpouring of literary energy and ambition by others (E.vi 6-7, 9-12). Hence for his own poetry socio-political change, either anxiety or ambition, need not be an issue. He can claim freedom in the poetic foreground (the narrative present) to go about his business as defined by artistic or personal imperatives rather than political considerations or beliefs.

Likewise in the seventh eclogue we find a narrative persona presuming a secure social order in the background. The narrator mentions coming from a 'home' that is characterized as a place of property and ordinary occupations that are dictated only by the changing of the seasons. He tells of arriving in a poetic locus that was occupied by herdsmen at 'play' and is represented as an idyllic north Italian setting, with no hint of political strife and social change (E.vii 1-20, Mincius, 13).

The eighth eclogue, too, is a narrative that presupposes a secure order in the background, although a dynamic one. Like the background of the sixth, it offers scope for poetic ambition, perhaps demanding poetic attention, however, more insistently and thus threatening to distract the narrator from pastoral concerns (E.viii 6-13).

The ninth eclogue changes from mixed narrative to purely dramatic representation; but it, too, articulates a division between background and foreground. Its background, like the others, contains an established order that is not about to change; but here the background does finally compel abandonment of the pastoral locus. The pastoral speakers are represented as journeying toward the background, which appears differently to each. One perceives it as the seat of a harsh new master, who has driven his old master out and requires him to make this trip (E.viiii 4, "These are mine; old cultivators, get off!": the negative version of change, expressed *sic minus insigniter* as noted above); [63] but the other thinks of the background in terms of paragons of urbane art, whom he admires but does not pretend to reach (E.viiii 30-36).

Finally, in the tenth eclogue, back to mixed narrative-dramatic form, a narrator tells of satisfactorily completing work in the bucolic foreground and speaks of withdrawing to a 'home' (E.x 77, cf. vii 15) that is imagined as some-where in a secure background, where animals and men can safely retire, well filled, after grazing, weaving, and singing in the bucolic locus (E.x 70-77). The image is one of peaceful, unchanging life. It presupposes a stable order in society and the world at large, without threat (or hope) of change.

Altogether, then, the last five eclogues share a common idea of stability in the background as the socio-political context of operation. Ideologically this cannot be said to reverse the "peaceful" image of the first half-book, though it may somewhat subdue the positive tones. If anything, then, the second half continues the ideology of the first half, but as a background or general frame, within which the poetry can busy itself with a number of matters, among which human passion, both constructive and degenerative, and human mortality certainly figure.

---

[63] Cf. nn. 9, 51.

Chapter 2

IDEOLOGICAL ORDER IN THE ECLOGUE BOOK

The general framework of socio-political order that emerges beyond the contrasting theses of Skutsch and Otis looks by and large uniform. Its very stability appears above all suited to a concentric-static order; thus ideology would seem to confirm that perception of the design in the eclogue book. But before settling down to this conclusion, we must remember that it depends on accounts of the ideas in the first half-book by critics whose opinions on the second half have had to be sifted out and reordered.[1] Once we bring to bear on the first half of the eclogue book the same criteria for ideology, we cannot speak so simply of a uniform and peaceful background as the general ideological frame. Right at the start the most prominent place (*sic insigniter*) contains not only 'thanks to the Emperor' but eloquent protest at his policy's effect. This initial clash of ideologies used to be so famous that it could stand alone as type and summary of the pastoral as genre: (Sidney, *Defence of Poesie*, 1595)

...is the poore pipe disdained which sometimes out of *Meliboeus* mouth, can shewe the miserie of people, under hard Lords, and ravening souldiers? And again, by *Titerus*, what blessednesse is derived, to them that lie lowest, from the goodnesse of them that sit highest?

A. *Contrast of Ideological Images (E.i)*

It would be difficult to conceive of a more total contrast

[1] Cf. nn. 1.58, 60-63.

than the one between the images of socio-political change associated with these two personae. Sidney's "miserie of people" and "ravening souldiers" reflect the fact that Virgil has represented 'Meliboeus' as belonging to the class of citizens, the *ciues miseros* (E.i 71-72), who have been dispossessed by revolutionary force—*impius . . . miles, barbarus* (E.i 70-71). These are emphatic terms in a comprehensive and expressive, forcefully negative image of what is lost and who unjustly gains from violent change. Virgil shapes the image through the persona of the citizen-farmer imagined as reduced to herding only goats. He pictures them straggling into the bucolic foreground (E.i 11-18) from a complex background where an entire social, political, economic and artistic order has been displaced: we hear of loss of beloved farmland (E.i 3), exile from the fatherland (i 4), violence on every hand (11-12), citizens abandoning ancestral homes; a brute soldier the new owner of their carefully tended fields, preempting the fruits of georgic labor (67-73), disrupting pastoral care and song (74-78). The viewpoint is that of the republican and conservative oligarchy, and of those who were simply blessed with land, who suffered from the proscriptions and expropriations in the years when the heir of Julius Caesar and his allies were consolidating their position in Italy and Rome: [2]

The proletariat of Italy, long exploited and thwarted, seized what they regarded as their just portion. A social revolution was now carried out, in two stages, the first to provide money for the war, the second to reward the Caesarian legions after victory.

Both great and humble, both militant noble and hapless yeoman, lost property; but Virgil cloaks the interests and activity of the great conservative landowners in the generic term, *ciues*, with the pathetic *miseros*, and masks the re-

[2] Syme 1939.194.

publican cause, its vigorous military resistence, indeed the entire Roman commonwealth, in the image of the defenseless victim. Further, by way of moving contrast, he paints the new forces from the conservative point of view. *Impius* imputes to them exclusively the guilt for fratricide in civil war with disregard for established bonds and laws, both human and divine; *barbarus* echoes the conservative slurs against the Gauls, Germans, and Spaniards who formed a new proletariate in Caesar's ranks; [3] it depicts the new owner as a usurper from beyond the civilized pale. From the viewpoint of conservative ideology, the republican cause seems pacific and composed of all citizens, while the new forces encroach from outside. Here is none of that stability of the background of the second half-book. The persona, far from being drawn to a stable background, is imagined driven into a bucolic foreground that affords no enjoyment or satisfaction, only an occasion to articulate loss of previous order with doubt whether it will ever be regained.

At the same time, however, Virgil also imagines this foreground in another kind of relation to a very different background, as Sidney puts it so well: "blessednesse... to them that lie lowest, from... them that sit highest." Virgil pictures the other persona as a shepherd-cowherd (E.i 8-9) in a tranquil, prosperous and stable foreground, occupied with love and religion and poetic play (5, 8, 10). Only the advent of 'Meliboeus' interrupts this idyl and elicits an account of the background of 'Tityrus': in old age, he says, he set out for Rome to seek social change for himself—his freedom from slavery (27, 40). But in the city, instead of the expected master or even some official

---

[3] Arnaldi 1938.13. Leach 1975.132 notes that Servius saw this as implicit criticism of Octavian, who as a soldier offended against *pietas*.

who might manumit,[4] he found a god who made an oracular and authoritative pronouncement: (E.i 45)

'pascite ut ante boues, pueri; summittite tauros.'

'Graze cattle as before, boys; bring up bulls.'

Addressed as to a whole class of inferiors, in the context evidently rural slaves,[5] *ut ante* clearly imposes a return to *seruitium*. The only change contemplated by the authority of Rome is increased productivity from the herds. Yet nothing in the eclogue suggests disappointment at this failure to obtain the longed-for change in status. 'Tityrus' is shown devoted to the god, offering regular sacrifice with a piety that is exemplary (if not actually overdone),[6] and grateful for freedom at least to compose what he wants with his humble, 'countrified', reed (10).

Whatever we choose to make of the discrepancy between freedom from slavery (sought) and freedom to play (gained), the ideological import of the whole is unmistakeable. Here the beneficiary of the new order is drawn as a pacific model of piety, no *impius miles*, and the motive force for change becomes not barbarian rapacity but an old slave's desire to move up a rung within the existing order. How authentic the motivation, and how contrived

---

[4] A censor according to Leach 1975.120.

[5] Williams 1968.311; misconstrued by Berg 1974.115-16.

[6] Leach 1975.126: only the *Lar familiaris* and *Jupiter Capitolinus* received monthly sacrifice, the former a private offering of a handful of meal, the latter public offering of a sheep or lamb (cf. E.i. 8, 43); *deus* is imagined being adopted as *Genius* by Tityrus, thus monthly lamb extravagant. Clausen 1972.202-03 cites monthly sacrifice in Hellenistic ruler worship as Virgil's model, absolutely excluding any allusion to the *Lar*. Without ignoring the Greek background, we must ask how the language would have been intelligible to an ordinary Roman (cf. n. 2.15). J. H. D'Arms in conversation also notes how closely the term *deus* is linked to the personal perception and experience of Tityrus (E.i 7), i.e. to the fiction.

the rest, can be gathered by comparison with a contemporary account of real slaves and their master in the vicissitudes of civil strife. In the *Civil War*, Julius Caesar mentions that L. Domitius Ahenobarbus levied workers from his estates to man ships in defence of Marseilles: (*B.C.*I 34, 3; 56, 3; 57, 4)

...quas (sc. nauis) Igilii et in Cosano a priuatis coactas seruis libertis colonis suis compleuerat.

...certas sibi deposcit nauis Domitius atque has colonis pastoribusque, quos secum adduxerit, complet.

...pastoresque Domiti spe libertatis excitati sub oculis domini suam probare operam studebant.

These shepherd slaves left the land not for Rome but for the sea, and they fought beneath their master's gaze, pricked on by the hope of freedom. This, too, was Tityrus' motive (*spes libertatis*, E.i 32), but he, between the state of *seruus* and *libertus*, is shown as doing nothing more than make petition (i 44); and Virgil depicts him as a veteran of only commerce and sex (i 31-35): no doubt a shade more realistic than some Greek bucolic precedents, yet certainly more idyllic far than those shepherd slaves from Cosa. Moreover, Virgil has here again disguised the class of "hard Lords". The militant, anti-Caesarian nobles like Domitius disappeared behind the affecting image of Meliboeus. Now, instead of the *dominus* with whom a real slave might expect to deal, Virgil imagines the 'god'. Here, of course, he both flatters and dissimulates the role of the commander of the revolutionary troops, the ultimate authority for expropriation. Caesar's heir might take pleasure in the allusion to the divine status that a malleable Senate conferred on his late adoptive Father in 42 B.C. He himself had been hailed as 'divine youth' and *spes libertatis* not long since by Cicero,[7] who provoked an angry judgment from Caesar's assassain, Brutus:[8]

Let Cicero, who is able, live servile and dependent, if he is not ashamed. No conditions of slavery, however favorable, will ever dissuade me from the fight against regal pretense, exceptional military offices, domination, and force exercised beyond the law.

Cicero was among the first casualties of proscription in 43. Brutus committed suicide in defeat in 42. In Virgil's imagination, the young Caesar appears as a 'god' responding to the aspiration of a slave with the conservative message, 'as before'.[9] Republican language and ideas have been expropriated, values inverted, for the sake of new order.

In the context of political history, attributing such an idea to such a figure (a watchword less suited to an heir of Caesar than of Pompey) may be Virgil's truest or most interested, most prescient or most wishful, touch. In the context of the work, however, it raises a problem, for it sacrifices dramatic consistency for the sake of ideology—a thematic consideration. At the level of the dramatic fiction, Tityrus' desire (and its fulfilment—*seruitio me exire*, 40) cannot be reconciled with the injunction to carry on 'as before'. But we need not assume that the crafting of rustic character and inner psychology must be

---

[7] *Philip.* 5.43.

[8] Cicero, *Ad Marc. Brut.*25.6; "At Rome all men paid homage to *libertas*, holding it to be something roughly equivalent to the spirit and practice of Republican government..., most commonly invoked in defence of the existing order..., could not be monopolized by the oligarchy—or by any party in power...Caesar's heir...*Libertatis p. R. Vindex...*" Syme 1939.155. Hence liberty as change of state is conceiveable only from the viewpoint of a slave.

[9] But Leach 1975.127 asserts, "There is no reason why a slave in the course of a journey for manumission should encounter one of the chief men of the Roman world"(!).

the only, let alone the primary, concern in this or any eclogue. We should expect, in the words of a recent critic, [10]

not... flexible, many sided personalities as... in narrative fiction, but rather individuals of set disposition whose idiosyncrasies designate them as symbolic types. What really happens in the *Eclogues* is not the development of character but the exploration of themes.

The exploring, it must be emphasized, gets done through the personae not by them. Each is constructed as a discrete entity, associated with a distinctive class, mode of work, and historical experience, hence useful as the representation of a specific ideological position. 'Meliboeus' is not endowed by his maker with knowledge of Rome and the 'god'; "he" does not know, in the dramatic fiction, what we observe in reading, that Virgil has distorted the reality of the revolutionary party by splitting it into two components and picturing its head and its members as totally different kinds of force at the opposite extremes of an imaginative hierarchy (*impius barbarus / deus*). [11] Nor is 'Tityrus' imagined as knowing about the uproar in the surrounding fields. To the contrary, all he is supposed to see around him across the valley to the hills is peaceful farmland (i 82). Nor, of course, is either persona imagined as knowing about the concentric disposition of the piece, the placement of the epiphany of the 'god'. Thus we are talking about something other than the level

[10] Leach 1975.144-45. Yet she all too often treats the character as personal rather than thematic (e.g. n. 9), as does Flintoff 1976.16 et passim. Cf. the strictures of Perutelli 1976.775, 779 quoted in n. 6.39.

[11] I cannot agree with Fredricksmeyer 1966.208-09 that 'Meliboeus' connects *deus* and *miles*. Generally we risk overpersonalization of dramatic fictions when we lapse into the convenient critical shorthand of writing, "Meliboeus says..." or "Tityrus knows...": e.g. Leach 1975.141, "although Tityrus has not seen and probably not heard of Octavian..."; cf. nn. 9, 10.

of the dramatic fiction when we note that the theme of the god's utterance does respond not to the imagined request of slaves but to the socio-political crisis articulated through the persona of 'Meliboeus'. To the outcry of the old order—'we are leaving lands'—answers the message—'carry on as before'. In theme, at least, the eclogue gets beyond the stark contrast of ideologies (complacency/distress), even though in the dramatic fiction there is "no true communication between the speakers." [12] At the same time, the expressive force of protest quite outweighs this hint of ideological reconciliation. [13] The piece as a whole, although in theory, as it were, projecting the outline of a new ideological frame, "peaceful" and "patriotic in a Julio-Augustan sense," in practice derives its main force from nostalgia for the order that is replaced. So too in the last half-book the ideological framework contains the variegated, more expressive songs.

B. *Growth of Contrasting Images (E.i)*

If in retrospect the first eclogue presents a general contrast of ideologies, in the course of actual reading the ideological images grow step-by-step through a series of particular oppositions that amplify each image in turn. This process is linear and dynamic, [14] taking impetus from the moving contrast in the initial dramatic fiction: (E.i 1-10)

M: Tityre, tu patulae recubans sub tegmine fagi   1
   siluestrem tenui musam meditaris auena;   2
   nos patriae finis et dulcia linquimus arua.   3
   nos patriam fugimus; tu, Tityre, lentus in umbra   4
   formosam resonare doces Amaryllida siluas.   5

T: O Meliboee, deus nobis haec otia fecit   6
   (namque erit ille mihi semper deus); illius aram   7

---

[12] Leach 1975.138, cf. 117.
[13] Putnam 1969.67, 73; cf. Soubiran 1972.48, n. 35.
[14] Cf. nn. 1.42, 43, 44, 54, 55.

saepe tener nostris ab ouilibus imbuet agnus;   8
ille meas errare boues (ut cernis) et ipsum   9
ludere quae uellem calamo permisit agresti.   10

M: Tityrus, you lying back beneath cover of outspread
                              beech   1
     work to make a woodland muse with slender oat;   2
     we leave fatherland's borders and sweet plowlands.   3
     We flee fatherland; you, Tityrus, pliant in shade   4
     teach woods to sound back "comely Amaryllis."   5

T: O Meliboeus, a god made this ease for us   6
     (for to me he always will be "god"). His altar   7
     often tender lamb from our pens will stain.   8
     He let my cattle wander (as you see) and self   9
     play whatever I would with country reed.   10

The first vignette we see contains a rustic figure resting in the cover of a single tree and engaged in modest artistic work, all in the bucolic foreground (1-2). But in contrast with this very restricted start on a positive image, we get the far-reaching and emphatically negative terms of 'Meliboeus' reporting loss of familiar territory and regular agricultural occupation (e.g. 'fatherland' and 'plowlands', 3), all this imagined as elsewhere; then, in still stronger terms, exile from the ancestral state (4). As a contrast, then, to this strong antithesis, the speech returns to the rather weak initial thesis and adds to the positive image ever so slightly, amplifying the generic terms of art into a specific subject and activity — 'Amaryllis' and 'teach' (5). The terms for place also grow to include 'shade', *umbra*, less abstract than 'cover', *tegmen*, and finally·'woods', more ample than a single 'beech' (4-5, cf. 1).

In response, then, to the very strong negation of order at the center of the first speech, the second speech commences with a strong affirmation of order (6), which expands the positive image still further by adding a causal myth (*aition*), which comprises a figure of authority, a key generic quality, and definite act of authorization in time (*deus, haec otia, fecit,* 'god', 'this ease', 'made, set aside'). With these details, we have a virtually complete outline of positive ideology; and in fact the rest of the speech (and of the work) only keeps returning to dwell upon it, articulate it, and fill it in.

This process of ideological amplification begins at once. The speech proceeds by returning to the most ambitious and ideologically loaded term of the outline — *deus*, 'god' — and qualifying its use before going on to dwell on its positive implications (7). The series of demonstratives that refer back to the mention of 'god' — *ille* (7), *illius* (7), and *ille* (9), 'he', 'his', and 'he' — underlines its force and adds still further details to the image of the bucolic foreground which the 'god made'. The positive image grows to comprise 'sheep pens', 'tender lamb', regular piety (8), and then also 'cattle', the imagined space of pasturage in which they might 'wander', and the artistic freedom to 'play' (9-10).

From this point on, the positive and negative images grow by turns through a sequence of discrete augmentations, each of which has some imagined psychological motive in the unfolding drama. These successive dramatic inventions need not detain us here, since our concern for the moment must be with ideology. But, if one wanted to speak of a subjective style in Virgil, it is clear (whatever else may not be) that the first exemplar is the figure of the emotive refugee with its explosive language of contrast and its complex evocation of a lost patrimony: even plowlands become 'sweet' when they are left behind.

In response to Tityrus' revelation of the 'god' (6-10), the figure of Meliboeus is imagined as making a strong defensive rejoinder which adds greatly to the earlier image

(3-4) of the changes and losses occurring elsewhere: (E.i 11-12)

M: haud equidem inuideo, miror magis: undique totis
usque adeo turbatur agris. en ipse capellas...

M: I'm not at all envying, rather amazed: on every side, entire
territories, there's turmoil to such extent. Look, self, goats...

Suddenly Tityrus' peaceful foreground seems isolated, like an inexplicable island amidst the general chaos of the surrounding background. The dramatic thrust of this revelation serves in the ensuing lines to add further pathetic details to the negative image not only of Meliboeus' background but even of his arrival in the pastoral foreground, which he experiences as inhospitable and rocky (13-18); then inevitably the heightened contrast leads to Meliboeus' query about the divine cause of Tityrus' exceptional peace (18; cf. Meliboeus' continuing search for a cause, 26).

In reply, Tityrus is constrained to give an account of himself (19-45). First we see a gradual build-up of the picture of Tityrus as a conventional bucolic figure — inveterate lover, trader in animals and cheese with town, slave who was moved to travel to Rome in the cause of his own freedom (19-40). But then, at the center of the eclogue, we hear that in Rome Tityrus met not his master and manumission but the 'god', and that the 'god' made his decisive intervention there (44-45). The center thus gives Tityrus' initially isolated bucolic foreground an unexpected background of its own, not merely urban but pointedly ideological; the sketchy initial version of the causal myth (6-10) fills out with implications for Roman history and politics: (E.i 40-45)

T: Quid facerem? neque seruitio me exire licebat   40
    nec tam praesentis alibi cognoscere diuos.   41
    hic illum uidi iuuenem, Meliboee, quotannis   42
    bis senos cui nostra dies altaria fumant.   43

> hic mihi responsum primus dedit ille petenti: 44
> 'pascite ut ante boues, pueri; summittite tauros.'   45

T: What was I to do? Nowhere else was it allowed me to get out of slavery or get to know such favoring gods. Here that young man I saw, Meliboeus, for whom each year two times six days our altars send up smoke.
Here first he gave response as I petitioned:
"Graze cattle as before, boys! Bring up bulls!"

Contemporary listeners in the theater would not have doubted whom to applaud at these words. [15] The Roman public had long been used to political allegory on the stage. [16] The Caesarian party had arranged the performance of Pacuvius to arose feeling against the assassains of Julius. [17]

In the development of the eclogue, Tityrus' foreground and background together now form a positive image that counters Meliboeus' image of general disorder in the fields. Between a positive bucolic foreground and its urban background, also positive, we have an extensive, negative georgic middle ground.

The revelation of Tityrus' prestigious and powerful

---

[15] N. Dewitt, *Virgil's Biographia Litteraria* (Oxford 1923) 129. The topical nature of the language, immediately intelligible to its original audiences in terms of ideological myth, is forgotten by Leach 1975.127-28 (again with the fictional status of the personae) when she writes that Tityrus as country slave confuses Veiouis with Jove!

[16] B. Bilinski, *Contrastanti Ideali di Cultura sulla Scena di Pacuvio* (Wroclaw 1962) 5, n. 5.

[17] Suetonius, *Div. Jul.* 84, ap. I. Mariotti, *Introduzione a Pacuvio* (Urbino 1960) 73-74. Clausen 1972.202-03 cites the improvement in Octavian's position after 36 B.C. as a political climate necessary for the conception of E.i. No doubt it would enhance the reception, and clearly the scholiastic dates for composition were too rigid (cf. nn. 1.33, 34); but we should not go to the opposite extreme of insisting too much on 35 B.C. When did Horace write S.1.5, 6, 10, and the allusions to Virgil, Maecenas, the *Bucolics*?

background prompts, in the dramatic fiction, a famous outcry that serves to amplify still further the image of Tityrus' foreground: *fortunate senex* . . . poor, merely pastoral, not georgic, yet enough (*magna satis*, 46-50); *fortunate senex* . . . an ideal bucolic locus (51-58). In turn the drama leads to still further elaboration of Tityrus' background (59-63) and then to Meliboeus' final vision of his exile to the ends of empire (64-66) with doubt about return to his beloved georgic (67-73) and pastoral (74-78) order. Emotionally the eclogue reaches its high point here, with the image of articulated order lost. But in a final, specific contrast the last word goes to Tityrus: (E.i 79-83)

T:	Hic tamen hanc mecum poteras requiescere noctem	79
	fronde super uiridi: sunt nobis mitia poma,	80
	castaneae molles et pressi copia lactis;	81
	et iam summa procul uillarum culmina fumant	82
	maioresque cadunt altis de montibus umbrae.	83

T:	Here, still, this night you could rest with me	79
	upon green branches. We have mellowed apples,	80
	meaty chestnuts, and plenty of cheese in molds;	81
	already now also far off villas' tops are smoking	82
	and shadows falling longer from high hills.	83

The image looks "peaceful" and "conciliatory" after the agitated peroration of 'Meliboeus'. It touches the idea of a conjunction of the contrasting figures (*mecum*, 79), if only momentary (*hanc... noctem*); and adds newly substantial detail to the image of the foreground: hospitality, rest, 'apples', the texture of meaty chestnuts, supply of cheese on hand. But beyond this, positive ideology acquires a component lacking in the outline heretofore—a peaceful version of a middle ground that can stand in direct contrast with Meliboeus' evocation of the middle ground disturbed. The image of smoke rising from roof-peaks far and wide and of shadows falling suggests an entire countryside populated with numerous farms and estates where work ends peacefully, as always, with the sun's setting and workers return to hearth and evening meal. The only interruption for rural work is the diurnal cycle, free from the threat or hope of revolution. The idea is conservative and represented as a sight visible from the foreground. The loss of Meliboeus' middle ground is only a report. [18]

The full outline of "Julio-Augustan" ideology has grown gradually from that first sketch of locus and causal myth through the amplified etiology at the center, followed at once by intensified elaboration of the foreground, to the end, which projects into the gap between Tityrus' bucolic foreground and his Roman background a sketchy but positive image of the middle ground. On reflection, we may still feel that the work draws its life and force from the initial articulation of exile and strong negative attitude towards change; yet the positive idea prevails at least in the structure, holding the center and the end; and the god's response does close, at least in theory, the crisis opened with Meliboeus. How then, we may ask, did the poet himself conceive of the relation between this initial and tentative outline of positive ideology and the confident ideological assumption of the second half-book? Analogy with the process of ideological construction as we have seen it in the first eclogue would suggest a gradual bridging of the gap between beginning and end by means of successive and cumulative augmentations in a step-by-step

[18] A. Traina, "La chiusa della prima egloga virgiliana (vv. 82-83)," *Lingua e Stile* 3 (1966) 48, distinguishes the two contrasting and mutually exclusive images of surrounding space. Leach 1975.130, 132, 134, 137 muddles Virgil's careful discrimination of foreground (bucolic), middle ground (georgic), and background (historical, mythic). Thus she is in no position to mark the further differences between the Tityran and the Meliboean versions of each of the three topics, registers, or thematic levels, e.g. the contrast in the middle register between 'unseen, destroyed' and 'seen, peaceful'. For her, both personae are "farmers."

reinforcement of the outline of positive ideology. [19] In order to test this linear and dynamic hypothesis of development in the book, we are forced to continue for yet another moment to use the approach inherited from recent critics and to inquire into the ideological premises of the intervening eclogues and their relation to the language and ideology of 'Tityrus'. [20]

C. *Continuation of Growth* (*E.ii+iii+iiii*)

Ideology is not, in fact, the first thing that comes to mind in connection with the second eclogue. Here we find no hint of the contrast of political ideas which moved and divided the first eclogue. Instead, the second piece presupposes a stable social order which is undisturbed by political change. Property is safe. The ideological premise, in other words, resembles that image of a peaceful and well-ordered society which grew up around Tityrus. In the brief introduction, an all-seeing narrator tells of a world where masters have their possessions and slaves are in their places; the upper class background controls even the sexual goods for which the servile bucolic foreground pines: (E.ii. 1-5)

N:	Formosum pastor Corydon ardebat Alexin,	1
	delicias domini, nec quid speraret habebat;	2
	tantum inter densas, umbrosa cacumina, fagos	3
	adsidue ueniebat; ibi haec incondita solus	4
	montibus et siluis studio iactabat inani:	5

N:	Grazer Corydon kept burning for comely Alexis —	1
	owner's darling — and hadn't a thing to hope.	2
	Just among thick-standing beeches, shady peaks,	3

---

[19] Cf. nn. 1.54, 55: Contrast and Growth (*incrementum*).

[20] Ideology may be inescapable in "civilized" poetry, but we might envy the terms of another approach to the ending of E.i., beginning of E.ii: Soubiran 1972.48, "La Buc.I est une ouverture, au sens musical du terme, une promesse...".

he constantly kept coming, alone kept hurling   4
with useless zeal these unsettled things at hills and
                                                 woods: 5

One point of generic resemblance between this pas-
sage and the first eclogue is the use of the distinction
between a prestigious background and a humble bucolic
foreground. Also, the locus itself is characterized by some
of the same natural furnishings — 'hills' (ii 5, i 83),
'woods' (ii 5, i 5), and especially 'beech' (ii 3), which
was the leading image of nature in Tityrus' foreground
(i 1). But, though all of this confirms the generic unity
of the first two eclogues, it shows nothing about the
specific nature of the relation which Virgil established
between them. For this, we have to look not only at
the general resemblance but also especially at the par-
ticular differences. For example, the image of 'beech'
changes from the single 'cover of out-spread beech' (i 1)
to 'thick-standing beeches, shady peaks', [21] which looks
like a deliberate augmentation of the terms of the bucolic
locus. Or again, we see continuity in the quality of a
beloved person — *formosum* (ii 1, i 5)—yet change, in
that Alexis here is an inaccessible boy where Amaryllis
was not only a 'comely' but also a willing female. The
shift in sex and availability looks like a deliberate varia-
tion within the generic category of Love, [22] so that this

---

[21] E.i 1, *patulae sub tegmine fagi* / E.ii 3, *densas umbrosa
cacumina fagos*, where we also have an echo of the generic topic,
umbra (E.i 4). In the book, 'beech' becomes an important indicator
of change and development, from the initial bucolic context (E.i 1)
and its expansion (E.ii 3) to an image of a long established context
(*ueteres fagos*, iii 12), and then the material on which more than
simply bucolic matters are inscribed (E.iii 37, E.v 13), then finally
a symptom of exhaustion of the bucolic form (E.viiii 9, *ueteres iam
fracta cacumina fagos*): see Williams 1968.316-318, and VS 1967.
505, n. 30.

[22] On other forms of *uariatio*, see n. 1.10, 11.

bucolic lover moves with restless song rather than re-
clining in musical ease.[23]

The background, too, shows a general continuity with
Tityrus' background in that both contain figures of author-
ity and the means of satisfying some desire (which does
not, however, get satisfied). But within this generic ca-
tegory the change takes the form of a *diminuendo*, from
the emphatic and controversial term 'god' (i 6, 7, cf. 42)
to *dominus* (ii 2), 'owner, master', which is the sort of
authority a rural slave in search of freedom might con-
ventionally be expected to seek in town (cf. i 26, 40).
What is more, not only the authority but also the object
of interest gets reduced to more conventionally bucolic
terms, for Tityrus' desired *Libertas* had inevitable political
overtones in spite of the pastoral guise,[24] while here Alexis
is purely personal and erotic. As a bucolic lover, Corydon
has no hope of change of any sort and moves only within
the foreground; while Tityrus at least moved, hoping,
from foreground to background. At the same time, how-
ever, this ideologically closed system also precludes the
risk of radical displacement like that of Meliboeus.[25] In-
stead, there would be the risk of death through unrequited
love (ii 7).

We have, then, evidence not only for general con-
tinuity but also for particular differences of a kind which
suggest that the second eclogue may well be conceived
as a sequel and development of the first, continuing and

[23] Soubiran 1972.48: "La promesse est tenue. Sur un paysage
plus grandiose que celui de *B.I*,[35] mais dominé encore par de beaux
hêtres...le soleil s'est levé à nouveau."; then, n. 35, "V.5 *montibus
et siluis* suggère un vaste paysage qui écrase l'homme seul (4, *solus*)
Corydon."

[24] Cf. n. 2.8.

[25] The alternative was exile (E.i 4, 64-65); here it is death from
love (E.ii 6-7), not a matter of ideological difference (but cf. E.viiii
16)

elaborating the ideological outline of Tityrus, playing down
the controversial aspect but conserving the secure authority
of Tityrus' background, working up with variation the
erotic pastoral foreground. But it is striking that this
consolidated version of the Tityran outline lacks an image
of the middle ground, apart from 'hills' and 'woods', which
though echoing the first piece give no hint of the tranquil,
agricultural, peopled countryside that was Tityrus' last
telling detail. This lack, however, is more than compensated
in the course of the eclogue, which proceeds by drawing
a contrast between erotic disorientation in the bucolic
foreground and a steady rhythm of work and timely repose
in an agricultural — georgic — middle ground where
harvesters eat herb salad in the shade while the bucolic
lover paces in noon-day sun and where finally plowmen
lead their oxen home in the cool of day's end while the
lover still burns. [26] By the close, through these contrasts,
the positive image of the middle ground has become much
fuller than it was in the Tityran outline, though not yet
as full as in the outline of Meliboeus; while the positive
image of the foreground has also grown still fuller, since
it has come to comprise the lover's boasts of property in
kine, his beauty (19-24), artistic tradition, poetic instru-
ment (35-39), pet animals, and a flurry of blooms, hues
and scents all artfully combined (45-55). The piece actually
closes with a further, retrospective contrast between the
restless bucolic-erotic foreground and the demands of the
orderly georgic middle ground, where 'vines' remain to be
pruned and *usus* (ii 71), 'utility, necessity', requires the
weaving of containers or furnishings for the farm home.

---

[26] E.ii 10-11, 66-67. Here Leach 1975.151 notes the contrast
between georgic "disciplined images" and bucolic "fancies," although
wrongly attributing E.ii 69-73 to the "Eclogue Poet." Putnam
1969.113 compares *incondita* (5) with *semiputata* (70) and contrasts
studio inani (5) with *usus* (71).

At this point, Meliboeus' picture of the social fabric torn by civil war seems distant. That image of the entire countryside distraught (with the bitter allusion to labor lost on 'vines', i 73) has been in part supplanted by a positive version of both the foreground and the middle ground. Our attention has been absorbed by the picture of individual distress that passion, not exile, causes. Here love, not war, breaks off the work on 'vines'. The power of Rome, which appeared in explicit force, here has been relegated and reduced to the status of an unstated but positive political premise for the social hierarchy (master/slave) which is taken for granted at the start of the piece. In effect, the figure of Corydon has the passionate energy of a Meliboeus without the ideological burden. But we will come back to this.

A marked signal of continuity yet change also opens the third eclogue: (E.iii 1-2)

M: Dic mihi, Damoeta! cuium pecus? an Meliboei?   1
D: Non uerum Aegonis; nuper mihi tradidit Aegon.   2

M: Tell me, Damoetas, whose flock? Is it Meliboeus'?   1
D: No, truth, it's Aegon's. Aegon newly passed it to me.   2

The question about Meliboeus suggests general continuity with the first eclogue; yet the answer makes this a different particular situation, expressly characterized as a recent arrangement. Here the name — 'Meliboeus' — has no overtly ironic or negative connotations; it seems just another owner's name, unless we let it take us back to reflect on continuity and change in the foreground, middle ground, and background since the first piece. In any event, these animals are not his. [27]

The situation sketched in the ensuing lines shows a general continuity with the second eclogue, since here,

[27] Meliboeus was a goatherd, E.i 11-18, 74.

too, a master (Aegon) proves to be in the background
and occupied with an erotic object that also interests a
figure in the foreground (3-6). The object, here again
as in the first eclogue, is imagined as female; and the
interest — portrayed in the dramatic fiction as sexual
envy combined with overly zealous, perhaps also envious
concern for Aegon's sheep — gives rise to a dynamic
altercation in the foreground. The quarrel progressively
adds details of property and work to the positive image
of the foreground — above all the possession by each
speaker of two well crafted cups, which implies an articul-
ated technological middle ground and powerful poetic
tradition —, as the contrast, which began with apparently
random insult, transforms itself into poetic rivalry and
finally an agreement to compete in song. [28] At this point
the bucolic cast expands to include a third actor — an
encompassing and unifying figure over and around bucolic
contrast, Palaemon, a 'neighbor', who issues an invitation
to speech: (E.iii 55-57)

P:	dicite, quandoquidem molli consedimus herba	55
	et nunc omnis ager, nunc omnis parturit arbos,	56
	nunc frondent siluae, nunc formosissimus annus.	57

P:	Speak, since we have settled on soft grass,	55
	and now every territory, now every tree gives birth,	56
	now woods leaf out, now is year most comely.	57

This is the most deliberate, generalizing, and comprehen-
sive language that we have seen since the beginning of
the book. Its firm repetitions, alliterations, and exhaustive
terms of productivity in nature amplify the image of peace-
ful order to comprise a tranquil, receptive foreground
where speech is favored by a quickening, abundant middle
ground that has grown to take in every part of nature,
every territory and tree (cf. i 11-12), imagined at the

---

[28] Segal 1967.282-83; VS 1967.499; cf. Putnam 1969.122-23.

pitch of vitality and comeliness in the spring season (cf. i 5, ii 1). The next lines amplify and reinforce this image, abstracting and generalizing still further, and filling in a mythical background as well: (E.iii 60-61)

D: ab Ioue principium Musae, Iouis omnia plena: 60
   ille colit terras, illi mea carmina curae.   61

D: From Jove my Muse's start; with Jove all is filled: 60
   he takes care of lands; he cares about my songs.   61

Here the background and the poetic foreground, as in the first eclogue, are linked and dominated by myth — a figure and causal principle of divine order for all nature and the present art. But this 'Jove' is a greater and more universal, yet more immediate and immanent, image of causality than the 'god' of Tityrus and also of course far less historical and less overtly ideological. By contrast with the first piece, the outline of positive ideology here is colored as if it were traditional and universal, not historical, contingent, and Roman. [29] The problem of change and Rome's causal force is by and large suspended here as in the second piece. The close invokes love as the origin of poetic value (iii 108-111), which, in these two eclogues, has been the case.

By now we have seen two successive pieces follow with general continuity and particular development from what preceded them in the book, and we have watched the language and image of an ordered nature become progressively more comprehensive. Thus it would seem rea-

---

[29] *Principium* and *plena* are predicated simply and absolutely as being always and unchangingly the case (cf. the hint of timelessness in the image of the ideal bucolic locus, *quae semper*, E.i 53). The 'god' of Tityrus was pictured more historically, as having acted decisively at a moment in the past, giving Tityrus' ease a definite *principium* in time — *fecit* (i 6), *permisit* (i 10), *dedit* (i 44): this is the image Tityrus presents; Meliboeus imagines the timeless, changeless *quae semper*.

sonable to expect the cumulative development to go on into the ensuing work. But against this practical inference stand the scholiasts, who have taught us to see the next eclogue as an anomaly — a sport.[30] Hence we have to take particular care in our approach. In any case, we should be alerted by the opening of the piece, which poses the problem of continuity and development still more overtly than even the beginning of the third eclogue: (E.iiii 1-3)

Sicelides Musae, paulo maiora canamus!	1
non omnis arbusta iuuant humilesque myricae;	2
si canimus siluas, siluae sint consule dignae.	3

Sicilian Muses, a bit greater matters let us sing!	1
Trees and groundling tamarisks do not please all;	2
if we sing woods, let woods be consul-worthy!	3

In this narrator-singer, we recognize general continuities with the preceding work: not only the familiar distinction between humble bucolic and things more prestigious, but also the recurrent and productive tension which takes the form of desire to join the lower and the higher (Tityrus and Rome, Corydon and master's darling, questioner and Aegon's woman). Here again, as in the first, second, and third pieces, some pressing interest in distant or higher matters motivates or conditions bucolic speech. But in a striking change, the interested figure here is the poet himself rather than some bucolic *persona*, and he refers to the foreground in the most abstract and summary language we have seen thus far in the book. His phrase, 'Sicilian Muses', harks back to Sicilian details such as 'bees of Hybla' (i 54), 'hills of Sicily' (ii 21), or Daphnis (ii 26, iii 12), and it articulates the generic relation to Theocritus

---

[30] The problem is raised by Servius ad loc. For some recent chapters in the discussion, see Schmidt 1972.154-156, who underlines the need to read E.iiii closely with the others. Cf. Appendix.

that was implicit in all three preceding eclogues.[31] His ensuing mention of 'trees, tamarisks, woods' recalls the terms of earlier evocations of nature,[32] but here the words are practically emptied of natural reference by the baldness of the allusion to the mode that they belong to, equating pastoral nature, in effect, with bucolic art.[33] On the other hand, the language for the background also changes, but in the direction of greater concreteness: *consule* suggests something more official and historical, also more traditionally republican, than *deus* (i 6) with *Romam* (i 19), let alone *domini* (ii 2, iii 16) and *Iouis* (iii 60). Brusquely asserting what has been implied at every boundary between eclogues, the poet claims continuity and growth.

In keeping with this rather abrupt show of his true colors, the narrator-singer goes on to furnish the positive outline with an idea of change far more complex, comprehensive and dynamic than the bare hint of expansiveness detectable in the conservative command of Tityrus' god ('as before . . . bring up bulls', i 45). Again, negative implications of change are dissimulated: (E.iiii 4-7)

Ultima Cumaei uenit iam carminis aetas;	4
magnus ab integro saeclorum nascitur ordo.	5

[31] See nn. 5.61-71 below, for discussion and references to the poetics of the first three eclogues.

[32] *Arbusta* is particularly a word of context in the first three pieces: E.i 39, ii 13, iii 10 (v 64, with echo of i 6-7); *humilis* elsewhere in the book only at ii 29, v 17; *myricae*, Theocritus, Id.i 13, the ideal context for song, hence an appropriate 'Sicilian' generic sign here, and so used again by 'Tityrus'-poeta, E.vi 10, and in the desperate transformations of Tityran bucolic (E.viii 54-55, cf. *Tityrus Orpheus*); *siluae* is generic throughout the book, e.g. E.i 5, ii 5, iii 57, and *passim*.

[33] Berg 1974.148, "It is in fact a convention in Roman literature to allude to a genre through its content"; Putnam 1969.136; Büchner 1955.1195; cf. Schmidt 1972.156. Servius (E.vi 9); *per myricas et nemora bucolica significat* (cf. on E.i 2, 10; E.iii 111; E.x 17). Philargyrius (E.i 8): *agnus tener id est carmen tenue*. Cf. n. 4.2.

iam redit et uirgo, redeunt Saturnia regna,   6
iam noua progenies caelo demittitur alto.   7

Already now Cumaean song's last age has come.   4
Afresh great generations' rank is being born.   5
Now returns Maiden, too; Saturn's realms return.   6
Now a new line is sent down from high heaven.   7

The perfect tense (4) suggests the definite end of an old order, but colors it in the guise of a fulfillment of prophecy. The idea, then, of change is elaborated as a grand new start for the old, a renewal of cosmic process, but then a return of ancient virtues and restoration of an ideal kingdom (5-6). Only after this egregiously reactionary picture (*ut ante* written large) do we get a hint that change may mean innovation; and here the language remains grandiosely mythic but becomes vaguer still: 'a new line' (7), where scholars wonder whether *progenies* implies an individual or a race, and where *noua* is the inevitable, but for a Roman conservative revolutionary, idea, while descent from heaven gives the whole an aura of myth (cf. *deus*, i 6). It all sounds less specific and much grander than Tityrus' god, and of course just the opposite of Meliboeus' harsh terms for new force from outside the established order.

From fulsome generality, the image of change shifts to the extremely particular detail of the well-known birth of the child: (E.iiii 8-10)

tu modo nascenti puero, quo ferrea primum   8
desinet ac toto surget gens aurea mundo,   9
casta faue Lucina: tuus iam regnat Apollo.   10

You to a boy just being born, by whom first race   8
of iron will cease and golden rise whole world throughout,   9
give favor, constant Lucina. Already now your Apollo
                                            reigns.   10

Interest in the identity of this born prodigy need not keep

us from appreciating the advantages of the chosen language
for ideological ends. The image of an infant being born,
whose only effect is future reform, represents change and
dissimulates historical causality in the most innocuous and
natural terms conceiveable. What is a more usual and
welcome form of innovation than a son's birth? What
agent of change more gentle than a babe? [34] In the develop-
ment of the argument, the process of birth (8) is pre-
sented as the cause of the cosmic renovation already
evoked (4-7), an explanation as it were of that portentous
utterance by one concrete detail. Incidentally, by means
of a relative clause, we learn that return of the virtuous
original state entails elimination of the entire existing
society: by the agency of the child the 'iron race' will
give way to the 'golden' (819). How grand yet tidy as an
image of the change from the old order to the new! What
an improvement on the miserable picture of Meliboeus!
Here social change appears as sheer amelioration with no
hint of the troublesome conflict of parties and interests,
values on either side. The ambiguity of change and of
Roman force, which we could apprehend in the first eclogue,
gives way to a triumphalistic ideology, in which the old
is 'iron', the new 'gold', and all historical causality masked
in the miraculous agency of the 'boy'.

   With the ideas of descent from heaven, birth, univer-
sally transforming agency, Virgil has completed the form-
ulation of a causal myth far more ample than that of
Tityrus (*deus fecit*, i 6), although the themes of return
and growth recur. As in the first eclogue so here, elabor-
ation of the myth gives body and impetus to the rest of
the piece. Building on the image of future change, Virgil
first articulates it into three moments: beginning, middle,
and end. Here he adds to the illusion of historical im-
mediacy by associating the beginning with an actual date—
the consulship of C. Asinius Pollio, 40 B.C.—and also
by projecting the imagined influence of Pollio into the

middle stage, when 'traces of our crime and curse, reversed,
will free the lands from fear' [35] (13-14):

te duce si qua manent sceleris uestigia nostri
irrita perpetua soluent formidine terras.

The third stage, then, is imagined as a point of arrival
dominated by the 'boy' as full grown hero, true to the
divine origin implied above (7), and ruler of a peaceful
and Romanized world (15-17). The simple model of devel-
opment as exchange of 'iron' for 'gold' has been sup-
plemented by a complex model: instead of 'birth' the linear
and dynamic process of growth; and instead of the myth
of the metals, dissimulating real social conflict, a mingling
of historical realities (including an allusion to civil war as
'ours', a non-partisan term, in a conception of change as
reaction—voiding, reversing, 'un-ratifying') with heroic-
political myth. With this, the somewhat sketchy outline
of peace and a prosperous but conservative and merely
bucolic future (i 45) has been filled out by a bold, dynamic,
and decidedly "forward-looking" image of Roman history
that also harks back to the start. Though not likely to
be to the taste of the republican-minded consul who lends
his name to the first two stages, an ideology has prevailed
that looks almost monarchical—at least Romulean—in its
image of reversion to ancestral virtue with new heroic,
single rule.

The center of the eclogue (18-45), amplifies the three
part image of the future and reinforces its association with

----

[34] Compare the terms and agents of change in E.i, the implicit
denial of change in E.iii: see n. 2.29 above.

[35] As reported in n. 1.34 above, the dating of the *Bucolics* to a
triennium (inclusive 41-39 B.C.) has been dismissed by Bowersock as
an ingenuous scholiastic fabrication; and the nostrum that E.iiii
itself must have been composed within the year 40 B.C. (let alone
before) must also be given up in spite of the works cited in n. 1.33.

the idea of the gradual growth of the child.[36] First, at the beginning of growth, the poet promises the child (now imagined as actually born, 18) some pastoral miracles (18-25). Next comes a complex middle stage (26-36), suggesting the gradual maturing of the child and advance of the golden age (26-30), but also a gradual, hence still only partial, retreat of the iron age (31-33),[37] but then a recurrence of the old heroic age (34-36) between the end of the iron age and the full growth of the child and the golden age.[38] Only after this transitional stage in the fictional scheme of reversed time, do we move up and back to the moment when the new hero replaces the old violence and the golden age finally can be imagined as commanding everywhere in all lands: perfected image of total order (37-45).[39]

Following this advance into language which spans all mythological time and anthropological development, after and in addition to the earlier language of renewed historical time and extended Roman power (11-17), Virgil goes on to claim a resemblance between his outline of positive ideology and the concept of destiny itself — the 'fates' of the Parcae (46-47). From this it is only a slight step up to the boasts that the 'boy' is 'Jove's great increment'

[36] Virgil, "for the first time ever, used the concept of a Golden Age brought to man in three instalments and in harmony with the growth of a child": Williams 1968.279; cf. Putnam 1969.156.

[37] Williams 1969.279: "Halting of the Golden Age by a residue from the Iron Age is absent from literature before Virgil".

[38] For discussion of this crux of the recent critics, see nn. 5.76 below. Trouble has been caused by failure to see that Virgil imagines the approach of the golden age as gradual, and as the reversal of an earlier decline from golden through heroic to iron.

[39] Williams 1968.279, "When the child becomes a man a full Golden Age will be present"; Putnam 1969.152, "When the boy reaches manhood — has become a *vir* himself, ready to practise the *virtutes* he has seen in others — the world may be all-productive under his guidance".

(49) and that everything participates gladly in his coming new order (52). Here 'everything', *omnia*, coming as it does on top of the images of complete transformation and cheerful conformity in Roman history, human society, and nature, manages to be more far-reaching and absolute than even the language at the center of the third eclogue, which gave a static rather than a dynamic image of universal order and divine authority — *Iouis omnia plena*, 'all filled with Jove' (iii 60) — as opposed to the idea here of an active instrument, scion and agent of divinity, *magnum Iouis incrementum* (iiii 49). The outline of positive ideology thus arrives at the kind of scope, energy, and presumption which usually characterizes the most ambitious, and even totalitarian, ideological language. The heterogeneous views, conflicts, travails represented in the figure of Meliboeus would seem decisively overshadowed if not supplanted by genial totalitarianism of such moment.

If it seems difficult to conceive of a more ambitious and comprehensive utterance, we may well wonder whether Virgil himself ever matched, still less exceeded, this or whether its fullness and absoluteness did not stand as a high water mark, determining the ideological background for everything else he wrote. Not only had he worked out the underlying ideas of the last five eclogues but also the ideological framework of the *Georgics* and the Roman-Augustan 'fate' of the *Aeneid*, which has the precedent of the 'fates' (E.iiii 47), which he imagined here for the first time in his work. [40]

D. *A Total Order* (E.i + ii + iii + iiii)

The progressive growth of a positive ideological image in the course of the first four Bucolics tends to confirm the hypothesis that a linear and dynamic development

---

[40] Cf. VS 1970b.926-928.

links the book's beginning with its second half. In the first eclogue, the positive outline acquires a fairly full foreground, with middle ground and background only sketched; the second and third pieces then amplify the fore- and middle grounds, and the fourth piece vastly expands and transforms the background until the positive ideological image far overshadows the original negative image as presented through the figure of Meliboeus. In view of the totality of the ideological framework thus achieved, not to mention the virtual exhaustion of means of amplifying language, it should not be surprising to find that the fifth eclogue and the others take for granted a stable background of political and social order and return to operate in the middle ground and foreground, with georgic and bucolic materials. For example, the fifth eclogue begins with a bucolic scene carefully constructed to suggest general continuity with the bucolic foreground of the third and second eclogues, but at the same time also showing further particular development, even perfection, of the terms of bucolic art and place (v 1-19). [41] In turn the songs of the fifth eclogue present the bucolic hero Daphnis in greatly amplified form, as we have seen — a god of both herdsmen and farmers, protecting the full middle ground and foreground with their abundant flocks and harvests. [42] The image would be unthinkable in bucolic poetry without the expansive and expressive language of Meliboeus at the start but against it the gradual expansion of the positive outline to comprise a full foreground, middle ground, and dynamic background hence the express echoes of the first and the fourth pieces in the praise of Daphnis as a god. Similarly for the cosmology of the sixth eclogue, which imagines a dynamic development in nature that is

[41] See, for example, the discussion by Putnam 1969.166-170.
[42] See n. 1.6 above.

told by an ample Dionysiac singer who is expressly cut off
from the progressively reordered historical frame (vi 6-12).
Here both the energetic expanse of language and the un-
derlying ideological premise presuppose the development of
the preceding pieces in the book; and we have seen that
this ideological background continues in the eclogues that
ensue.

What we have now observed in the way of a con-
certed and cumulative effort of ideological construction in
the first four eclogues may also help us to interpret one
of those material facts of the book's design which we
noted earlier but did not discuss: namely, that the first
four pieces together form a group that is based on the
number of lines in the fourth Bucolic, the first having
63 + 20 lines, the second 63 + 10, the third 63 framing 48
of contest, and the fourth 63 lines — the shortest of all
in the book. These numbers by themselves would be
perhaps enigmatic, but taken together with the growth of
the ideological image they reinforce the view that Virgil
did calculate his first four eclogues as a special unit within
the book as a whole. In this, the numerical and the ideo-
logical evidence concur; and indeed it seems almost ne-
cessary to speak of number and ideology as two significant
and mutually reinforcing components of Virgil's art. But
if such is the case, it will also be necessary to modify
the assertion quoted above that the structure of the book
reveals nothing of the meaning of individual pieces (apart
from the fifth). [43] At least where the first four eclogues
are concerned, their initial and consecutive placement and
numerical relation confirm and complement their initiating
and unifying ideological function.

But the first four pieces may be a special case; and
it may be that the rest of the book merely fits mechanically

---

[43] See n. 1.51 above.

into the matrix that they dictate. We have seen in fact that they do determine the ideological premise for what ensues; and a closer look at the numerical design shows that the sixth through ninth eclogues do not form among themselves a numerically coherent series like that of the first through fourth but vary in length so as to meet the pattern of correspondences required by the first four pieces. [44] At the same time, however, one of the material facts of structure that remains to be interpreted does suggest a kind of linear development reaching into the second half-book, though within the outline of determined ideology and the requirements of numerical correspondence.

E. *Growth of the Image of Arcadia (E.iiii, vii, x)*

After two thousand years, the most important and most characteristic image in the *Bucolics* must be Arcadia — so familiar in fact that we forget how Virgil actually presented it in his book. Yet we have seen that he mentions Arcadia or Arcadians only in three separate eclogues disposed at regular intervals — iiii, vii, x — in which the numbers of lines are successive multiples of seven: 63, 70, 77. In itself this coincidence of theme and structure would be but a tenuous hint of development were it not for the gradual and progressive amplification of the image of poetic Arcadia in these same three eclogues, a process of growth in significant imagery like that we have now traced in the first four pieces. [45] The fourth makes its

---

[44] If we look at the diagram of the *Bucolics* (page 23 above), we see that the numbers of lines in E.vi, vii, viii, and viiii have no regular relation to each other as a series (86, 70, 108, 67) but that they do fit into the larger design dictated by the first four pieces (149, 181, 181, 150); while the first four themselves do form a group (83, 73, [63+48], 63).

[45] In Sections B and C above.

fleeting reference to potential competition with Pan, for which Arcadia (the god's birthplace) would be the judge.[46] Then the seventh Bucolic presents its recollection of past performance by two skilled singers, who are called Arcadians though they perform in a locus expressly identified as Italian (vii 1-20). Finally, in the tenth Bucolic, Arcady is the locus, with a full Arcadian cast and with the idea of eternal, skilful singing (x 9-43). This gradual augmentation of the Arcadian image in eclogues that are placed in key positions, related by progressive increases in length, first suggested that the general design of the book might be related to thematic elements in individual eclogues and also that the fully realized image of Arcadia might itself be the climax of a dynamic and linear process which takes its impetus from the fourth piece.

F. *A Total Design in the Book (E.i, iiii, vii, x)*

We have now identified two structures in the book as a whole, one starting with the first eclogue and leading up to the fourth, the other growing out of the fourth and reaching to the tenth. Although we called the first ideological and the second Arcadian, both consist in the growth of poetic language and image. Are both, then, parts of one structure, in which the fourth eclogue is the key element, so that we should imagine a significant network framing and unifying the entire book and keyed to four pieces set at regular intervals: E.i-iiii-vii-x? Tentative confirmation of this unitary hypothesis comes from the close of the tenth Bucolic, which establishes

---

[46] E.iiii 58-59; cf. n. 1.20 and Schmidt 1972.175. Yet critics still speak as if 'Arcadia' were a fixed and pervasive idea, even in the Italian-Sicilian georgic-bucolic geography of E.i: so Coleman 1977.89-90, 103, etc.; Dick 1970.292; cf. Becker 1955.322, "Die Gedichte bilden nicht eine Linie, sondern schliessen sich zu einem Raum zusammen; alle sind auf ein und dieselbe Mitte, die "geistige Landschaft Arkadien" (Bruno Snell), bezogen, sie zeigen unter wechselndem Aspekt die gleiche Erscheinung."

a relation of general continuity yet specific differentiation with the first eclogue: (x 77)

ite domum saturae, uenit Hesperus, ite capellae!
Go home, goats, with enough! Vesper's coming. Go!

This both recalls and alters the expressive close of Meliboeus' peroration, which announced departure from the pastoral foreground for an uncertain exile: (i 74)

ite meae, felix quondam pecus, ite capellae!
Go on, my goats, once prospering herd, go on!

The imperatives of departure and the kind of animals are the same in both contexts; and both Meliboeus and the narrator of the tenth Bucolic are characterized as singers (i 77, x 8). But now we hear of a secure home place beyond the foreground instead of civil strife, and the goatherd sees the foreground as the locus of his own satisfying occupation where his goats also thrive. These are slight differences; but along with the other echoes and alterations which the attentive reader will observe they are definite enough to suggest that the book may be conceived as a single and organic work in which something changes for the better between the beginning and the end.

Another confirmation of the hypothesis of a comprehensive structure based on four key eclogues comes from comparison of the dramatic situation in the four, where in each we find some variant of a voice or figure that shows consciousness of much more than the mere bucolic foreground and which is characterized as a goatherd or singer-narrator, or both. Such a voice would appear to be an element of general continuity, from the forceful voice of exile — the goatherd-singer Meliboeus — through the forceful singer-narrator of the fourth eclogue, then the recollective goatherd-narrator of the seventh (Meliboeus), and finally, in the tenth, the closing goatherd-singer-narrator that brings the Arcadian image to its fullest form. We recall that the first Meliboeus enters the bucolic foreground and tells with great expressive force of his homeland lost, with civic life, georgic work, and pastoral song all interrupted elsewhere. Countering this powerful negative image, as we have seen, the powerful and expressive singer of the fourth Bucolic projects his amplified version of the ideology of Tityrus, with its positive image of civic life, georgic work, and pastoral song. In the seventh Bucolic, then, the goatherd narrator called Meliboeus tells of having left a peaceful home to go to a pastoral locus where two Arcadians met. Finally, in the tenth Bucolic, the goatherd-narrator-singer, who echoes and reverses the Meliboeus of the first piece, tells his story of song in Arcadia and speaks of leaving a fully satisfying pastoral foreground for a peaceful home. Since this last singer-narrator, like that of the fourth Bucolic, usually is identified with the poet of the book, it seems reasonable to interpret the type of the goatherd-narrator-singer as a figure of unity and development in the book as a whole, [47] the initiating element or protagonist in poetic imagination, and mediator between the bucolic and larger modes. [48]

In the structural and developmental network which thus emerges, the first eclogue has the role of introducing a strong antithesis and weaker outline of positive thesis. The fourth eclogue then amplifies the positive outline into an all-encompassing vision which answers and supplants the earlier negative; and the fourth also introduces the idea of Arcadian song. The seventh eclogue presumes this new

[47] For the thematic and unifying functions of personae, see nn. 2.10, 11 and VS 1970b.907-910, idem 1967.501-504. Leach 1975. 246-254 reconstructs what she calls the "Eclogue Poet" as a unifying consciousness or figure in the book: in part offering useful suggestions but limited by the failure to treat 'Tityre' (vi 4) and 'Meliboee' (vii 9) consistently; cf. n. 1.11 and discussion there.

[48] Soubiran 1972.48.

full positive background and begins to transform the bucolic foreground by introducing Arcadian singers. The tenth eclogue completes the transformation of the foreground by constructing the full image of Arcadian art. After this there comes the final, deliberate exit from the now Arcadian foreground which still is imagined as part of that general background which the fourth eclogue projected and the seventh presumed, hence the peaceful return 'home'. [49]

[49] Cf. E.vii 15, where 'Meliboeus' left work suspended *domi*; but E.iiii 21 where goats would go spontaneously *domum*.

Chapter 3
SYNTHESIS: FROM IDEOLOGY TOWARD POETICS

Virgil's plan, building up to the fourth eclogue and reaching on into Arcadian myth, makes it difficult to imagine the fifth eclogue as somehow central to a static pattern of eclogue rings. Centering structures figure locally at the extremities of the book (E.i, ii and viiii, x), but the whole design appears now dynamic, even unbalanced; and it seems to impose withdrawal if not actual negation as a characteristic attitude in the second half-book with respect to the fullness of the first. More than ever, too, the role and status of the individual eclogue come into question. If the second and third make a developmental continuum, amplifying between the first and fourth; between the fourth, then, and the seventh do the fifth and sixth also make a transition, winding down from the heady *auxesis* of the fourth toward the calm remembrance of contrast in the seventh? [1] But do the eighth and ninth eclogues then bridge the distance between Arcadians in Italy (E.vii) and

[1] Putnam 1969.194, "... the position of *Eclogue* 5 in the book proves to have been carefully chosen. It sums up the past in idealistic strains which ring harmoniously next to its predecessor. Yet it also prepares the way for the next five poems which, each in its special way, examine particular forces of poetic expression." Putnam does not suppose E.v composed to follow E.iiii, but his careful analysis of the relations of the two pieces provides materials which lend support to this view, e.g. 170, 173, 177, 193. On E.vi as a critique of the ambition of E.iiii, see VS 1977a.107-08; Galinsky 1965 (1968).177; E. W. Leach, "The Unity of Eclogue 6," *Latomus* 27 (1968) 26, n. 3, citing J. Hubaux, *Les thèmes bucoliques dans la poésie latine* (Brussels 1930) 13-14; and VS 1967.501-504.

a Roman in Arcadia (E.x)? Some of the most perennial and acrimonious debates haunt these intervals: type cases of scholarly aporia. Are, then, such eclogues as the sixth and ninth pieces for which only the design of the entire work can reveal the "essential significance?"[2]

These and many other questions open once we begin to deal with the hints of continuity and change, development and differentiation, in the book. But the developing image of Arcadia itself is only ideological by implication, since it grows within the framework and against the background projected in the fourth eclogue.[3] Thus our concern with Arcadian elements finally carries us beyond the ideological approach as well as the centrist dogma, creating a need for other terms in which to interpret the meaning of the growing and changing images in the book, the network of four key eclogues, and the underlying numerical design. From the viewpoint of ideological analysis it may have seemed reasonable to deny that the design had sense; but the denial no longer can be justified when the very review of ideology produces evidence of a comprehensive and considered plan and points beyond itself to other kinds of significance.

In seeking, then, to move beyond ideology, we must take stock of how we have proceeded. Tentatively, at least, we can assume that the method will be the same. The approach must be sequential, taking things as Virgil left them. This does not imply a crudely straight line reading, but only attention to what is presupposed or perhaps even being adumbrated at each point. For example, if we recall only a few of the key passages which we have subjected to ideological analysis, some suggest that Virgil must have expected

[2] Cf. n. 1.32.
[3] See the analysis of the ideology of E.x, Chapter 1.D.4 above; Virgil presents his 'Arcadia' as the original state of bucolic, hence his development of the myth is a return—a conservative if not reactionary idea (cf. *ut ante*, E.i 45).

us to look back and reflect, to estimate change, as a means of reading ahead in greater complexity of sense. Only by observing such signs will it be possible to interpret the book as a comprehensive and cumulative, coherent order, but weigh also the limits to coherence. [4]

Goats, at the close of the tenth Bucolic, seemed to give cause for reflection; but so, too, the opening phrase, 'this end of toil', prompts consideration of the book as a planned ensemble. Then there was the ninth eclogue, with its nostalgia for a more efficacious past; the eighth, harking back to a beginning prompted by a powerful public figure; the seventh, nothing but a story of poetic contrast in the past. The sixth eclogue, too, began by looking back to poetic controversy and then raked up an old story of frustrated desire for song. By contrast, the fourth eclogue, without devious tales within tales, challenged 'Sicilian Muses' to 'a bit more' and made the reader, too, reflect on similarity and difference between the Theocritean matter that precedes and what ensues in the book. [5] But the third and second eclogues also, touching 'Meliboeus' sheep' and 'beech', could give pause to a reflective reader, though they, much like the fourth, seemed more intent on the present and the future than in dwelling, like the last five, on the past.

Among the more and less overt hints of retrospection, the fifth eclogue holds a unique place. To be sure it begins somewhat in the manner of its predecessors by moving

---

[4] Cf. again n. 1.32. Flintoff 1976.16 goes too far in comparing characters in the *Bucolics* to those in a single play (*Hamlet*). Unlike the *Aeneid*, unity in the *Bucolics* and *Georgics* must be something other than narrative-dramatic.

[5] Schmidt 1972.156 recognizes that Virgil here makes a comparison between two modes in his own work, only Schmidt takes *arbusta, myricae* as summarizing all the other eclogues, and not merely the preceding three: but for express echoes of the three in the generic terminology of E.iiii 1-3, see n. 2.32. Leach 1975.249 interprets *Sicelides Musae* as referring only to the previous pieces.

beyond familiar ground, from 'shade' to 'dell', and beyond conventional subjects to a novel song. And its songs of Daphnis dead, then deified, bear out the promise. But suddenly its close evokes preceding work with a kind of express reference to distinct eclogues and their sequence that has no equal in the book: (E.v 85-90)

Me:	Hac te nos fragili donabimus ante cicuta;	85
	haec nos 'formosum Corydon ardebat Alexin',	86
	haec eadem docuit 'cuium pecus? an Meliboei?'	87
Mo:	At tu sume pedum, quod, me cum saepe rogaret,	88
	non tulit Antigenes (et erat tum dignus amari),	89
	formosum paribus nodis atque aere, Menalca.	90
Me:	This frail hemlock we'll make you a gift of before;	85
	this taught us "Corydon kept burning for comely Alexis";	86
	this same one taught "Whose flock? Meliboeus'?"	87
Mo:	But you take a rod that, although he often asked,	88
	Antigenes did not get (and then he was worth love),	89
	comely with equal knots and copper, too, Menalcas.	90

Not a hint of retrospection but the deed itself represented in the dramatic fiction, this signal from the poet was so blatant that no reader could fail to look back. The emphatic statement of identity, 'this same one' (87), following the measured anaphora, but then the nearly verbatim repetitions of the first lines of the second and third eclogues sufficed to make it clear to all that here Virgil meant to think (and us to think) of previous pieces in relation to the fifth. To that extent, at least, the poet's try suceeded, but at best it was a desperate sally, risking loss as much as gain. So much depended on the expectations of the reader. The legions who expected poetry to be autobiography read Virgil's gesture as a sign that he was personally to be identified with 'Menalcas' and that he had written those eclogues earlier, and so on. Once we come to it from other signs of continuity and retrospection, it stands out as the most pointed of them all (almost too pointed); and this very excess demands explanation: why here? The answer to such a question can only be got, if at all, by following the lead of the text.

'Menalcas' did appear in the third and second eclogues, or rather, precisely, a 'Menalcas' was mentioned first in passing as an inferior, presumably a boy, beauty in the background (ii 15). Then we remember the petulant youth, 'Menalcas', with his inculcated sense of property, as the envious protagonist (iii 13). But 'Menalcas' in the fifth eclogue is the elder statesman, sage, protagonist to be sure, but confident, generous, pacific where the younger Mopsus is emulous and aggressive. In short, Virgil's invitation to look back directs us to a continuous pattern of growth— amplification of a dramatic figure in successive pieces. [6] This in itself would be interesting as a further sign of unity in the book, at least linking the three so-called "most bucolic" or "Theocritean" pieces. But the figure of Menalcas raises yet further questions when we remember that we have seen that his song of Daphnis' apotheosis picks up principal themes of the first eclogue and the fourth, such as *otia*, the 'ease' the god established for Tityrus (i 6), and nature's exulant joy at a new heroic-divine presence. [7] Between the figure and the song, 'Menalcas' thus draws on all four preceding eclogues. In the second eclogue itself, of course,

---

[6] Cf. n. 2.47. Flintoff 1976.22-23 gives a useful survey of the traits of 'Menalcas' through the book, but he treats them as the moving biography of a person rather than an index of development in themes.

[7] *Otia*, E.v 61, i 6; *laetitia*, E.v 62, cf. *laetentur ut omnia*, E.iiii 52; *deus, deus ille*, E.v 64, cf. *deus, ille, deus, illius, ille*, E.i 6-9. Putnam 1969.185 notes that the terms for natural spontaneity, *ipsi, ipsae, ipsa*, E.v 62-64, echo and reverse the terms of natural nostalgia for the absent Tityrus, E.i 38-39. Cf. also E.iiii: *ipsae*, 21; *ipsa*, 23; *ipse*, 43; and n. 5.77. It is striking that in the entire bucolic book, *otia* should be mentioned in these two related passages only: see VS 1972.351.

the narrator has no name; only in retrospect are we given the hint, if it is that, that the condescending attitude of the narrator toward Corydon's 'unsettled things' might have reflected Corydon's lack of interest in 'Menalcas'. But these and other moments would properly take their turn in a new sequential and retrospective reading.

PART TWO: POETICS

Chapter 4
BACKGROUND

If, by "poetics," we mean a body of ideas about poetry, the "poetics" of a work must be the ideas of its own nature and status that emerge in the course of reflective reading. [1] The means of gathering such ideas may be divers, varying from passage to passage. In sketching some, we do not pretend to exhaust or preclude.

Most obviously, perhaps, to us one source must be the remarks assigned to fictional personae about their own arts. We make with facility the transfer from fictional discourse about art back to the containing art. 'Tityrus' is imagined declaring his poetic intentions: (E.vi 8)

agrestem tenui meditabor harundine musam.

I'll work to make a country muse with slender reed.

We do not hesitate to construe this as a signal of the leading idea of style, not merely for Tityrus' ensuing song (within the fiction) but for the entire fiction which is the eclogue (comprising, of course, the stylistic utterance itself). [2]

[1] VS 1976.14; Elder 1961.113 poses questions about Virgilian poetics: "How did he feel about his own abilities, how did he feel about past and contemporary poets working in other forms, why did he write these ten poems, what was he trying to do in them, and what literary principles did he strive to adhere to in their composition?"

[2] Servius (E.i 2): *tenui auena, stili genus humilis latenter ostendit, quo ... in bucolicis utitur.* Cf. n. 2.33 and Schmidt 1972.251; Clausen 1964.194.

Perhaps less easily we corroborate such general ideas of poetics by specific inference from the choice of words and placement,[3] to say that the disposition of terms in Tityrus' program exemplifies the named idea of a carefully contrived, selective ('thin' not 'fulsome') style:[4] (vi 8: abvBa)

$$\text{agrestem} \qquad\qquad \text{musam}$$
$$\text{tenui} \qquad \text{harundine}$$
$$\text{meditabor}$$

Such simple modes of inference reinforce each other. They depend, of course, on general knowledge of the language and poetic usage. But a much more specific kind of inference, conditioning and refining the others, becomes necessary in sequential reading; for the declaration of Tityrus brings to mind a precedent in the book—Meliboeus' first exclamation at the Tityran scene: (E.i 2)

siluestrem tenui musam meditaris auena.

you work to make a woodland muse with slender oat.

Similarity strikes us at once—signs of generic continuity. Differences then obtrude—e.g. no longer 'woodland' but 'country'. What are we to infer about coherence in the general design of the book joining the first moments in the first and second halves,[5] but also about development and differentiation of poetic ideas? a bucolic 'woodland'? a georgic 'country'?

Our answers to these questions may be conditioned, too, by allusion to other texts. Commentaries remark that Tityrus' 'country muse' recalls the well-known passage where

---

[3] Clausen loc. cit. on E.i 2: "involved word order... suggestive of Hellenistic elegance"; Fedeli 1972.275-286, gives an exemplary documentation of stylistic idea through linguistic nuance.

[4] VS 1966.504, n. 38.

[5] Becker 1955.320.

Lucretius speaks of the simple and satisfying art of primitive man—*agrestis enim tum musa uigebat* (v 1398); and Meliboeus' mention of 'woodland muse' recalls the passage where Lucretius debunked pastoral mythology as a mere self-deceiving fiction by anxious rural folk—*fistula siluestrem ne cesset fundere musam* (iiii 589). The verbal similarities draw attention, but are the differences meaningful, and at what levels? Such questions can only be defined, let alone answered, by considering the four passages systematically, first each in its own immediate context, then Lucretius' two in his whole work, and Virgil's two in his, then finally the play of similarity and difference between both pairs. More than likely we will start with one set of working hypotheses about the meaning of these texts and end with another, finding it necessary to modify, as we read, our perceptions of the passages and of the design of Virgil's book. Does the book open not just by 'thanks to the Emperor' and its ideological antithesis but also by implying, for those who ponder texts, that this new Roman-heroic myth may be a deceptive, if comforting, fiction? Or does the new context counter Lucretius' critique of the anxious figments of mountain folk by anchoring its myth in history and Rome? But does the second half-book, then, revert to something less deliberately mythopoeic and mystifying, but also less consoling and efficacious, more rude? Is Virgil "clearly exploring methods of measuring myth against the bleaker realities of contemporary thought"? [6]

As if such considerations were not enough in the way of ideas about the status and nature of this poetry, we also know of course that Tityrus' poetic program forms part of the response to a famous Alexandrian poetics—the

[6] Damon 1961.286. For a warning against the reductive cast of mind that would seek refuge in only one of such multiple and contrasting implications, see Johnson 1977.1-22. Together they give the poetry an intellectual complexity and depth.

prologue added by Callimachus to his *Aitia* in his old age, justifying his life-long practice of slightness in style. The generic similarity between the programs is obvious; and just now we need not tarry with the specific differences, except to note one large fact of structure: Callimachus placed his program at the beginning (*sic insigniter*), but Virgil placed his echo of Callimachus in the middle (*minus insigniter*), although opening the second half-book. Here we have to draw our inferences for poetics from a difference in general designs: clearly Virgil is giving a special programmatic importance to the beginning of the second half by echoing such a famous program; [7] on the other hand, this also demotes the Callimachean idea from its original predominance; evidently Callimachus was not Virgil's primary authority in poetics. For us again, the theoretical (and practical) lesson is that we must attend to generic similarity and specific difference at every level, alert to *oppositio in imitando* from word and verse to the whole disposition of books. [8] The principle holds equally for Theocritus, whose first idyll underlies the last eclogue, [9] and whose retrospective summary of the bucolic mode (in this sense at least a last bucolic idyll) underlies Virgil's first. [10]

The modes of inference we have sketched thus far belong to conventional literary history. Others no doubt should be adduced. Yet even this modest concession to

[7] Clausen 1964.193.

[8] For the fundamental concept, *oppositio in imitando*, see G. Conte, "Memoria dei poeti e arte allusiva" *Strumenti Critici* 16 (1971) 325-333, especially pp. 330-332, and G. Giangrande, "The Utilisation of Homeric Variants by Apollonius Rhodius" *QUCC* 15 (1973) 75-76; also the examples from *epos* cited by Pfeiffer 1968.4, and by West 1966. on *Theog.* 1-2, with discussion and the added instance of Virgil, A.i 1, in VS 1975.52. For the related concepts, *aemulatio* and *retractatio*, and the modern discussion of Virgil's originality see Perutelli 1973.118, 136.

[9] VS 1967.494 discusses some differences.

[10] VS 1976.23-24.

systematics invites reproof from other readers, who insist on the real, material nature of this art: [11]

Disons tout de suite que nous relirons les *Bucoliques* avec le tempérament d'un Méridional épris de soleil, de plein air et de paysages vallonnés, sensible aux aspects de la campagne et des saisons, plutôt qu'avec l'acribie du philologue. Lire les *Bucoliques*, c'est aussi et d'abord les vivre. Rien de mieux pour cela que de s'en réciter des passages *patulae recubans sub tegmine fagi*: avouons l'avoir fait plus d'une fois, au pied des Pyrénées.

Then, too, as that fine reader and teacher of readers, Reuben A. Brower, would remark, we ought not to forget "the music of the verse." Nor should we forget the drama, the interplay and pathos of rustic character. However much we are forced to acknowledge its limited and subordinate role in larger designs, [12] it stands with the image of the country and the music as an immediate and material impression.

Altogether these instances of the most diverse readings suggest that yet some further synthesis may be required, that would integrate what might be called the analytic (or historical) and the esthetic modes so that a reader comes to know what and where this is as poetry in and through those other—the more immediate—feelings:

...Score this anecdote
Invented for its pith, not doctrinal
In form though in design...

Virgil may well have been able to assume such a habit of mind in his best readers. He does not, then, it has been argued, "formulate...teaching about poetry apart from poems. He belongs to an age which could see that the poem is the teaching and the teaching is the poem. It is we who belong to an abstracting age, who must abstract the teaching." [13]

[11] Soubiran 1972.42.
[12] Cf. nn. 2.10, 11, 47.
[13] Beyers 1962.42.

Yet the difference may lie not so much between his age
and ours as between one cast of mind or training and
another within any age. Most will see only 'thanks to the
Emperor' and will do well to stand and cheer with the
rest, or turn and frown. [14] But a few, always, can be counted
on to see that the "anecdote" or rustic tale "invented for its
pith, ...doctrinal...in design" reflects also on the nature and
status of the work. Such readers must suspect that a story
like that of Tityrus does serve to lionize the 'Emperor' as
hero-god, but also serves itself of the hero to lionize bucolic
art. The "anecdote" must be allegorical in both ideology and
poetics. It follows then, for such readers, that if the eclogues
"seem deliberately to tease and confuse, with their Arcadian
shepherds on the banks of Mincio, their Tityrus who goes
to Rome to win his freedom and returns with permission
to stay on his farm—one and the same thing, that is, accord-
ing to the poet," [15] the design that flaunts the unities and
sets reality "at defiance" must not be purely ideological: in
poetics, could Virgil afford to let his bucolic personage loll
in umbratile play or get freed by a conventional master if
the bucolic mode was to get new impetus and authority
from Rome and merit its heroic frame? Can Virgil, setting
out on his poetic course, be compared to another hero:

How many poems he denied himself
In his observant progress, lesser things
Than the relentless contact he desired.

[14] Tacitus, *Dial.* 13: "Malo securum et quietum Vergilii secessum,
in quo tamen neque apud diuum Augustum gratia caruit neque apud
populum Romanum notitia. Testes Augusti epistulae, testis ipse po-
pulus, qui auditis in theatro Vergilii uersibus surrexit uniuersus et
forte praesentem spectantemque Vergilium ueneratus est sic quasi
Augustum." H. T. Rowell suggested to me that actors might well
interpolate lines on observing the poet's presence. Hardie 1970.1124
too easily assumes this must have been a performance of the *Bucolics.*
Among those who frowned, Pollio: Cicero, *ad fam.* 10.31.2-3; Sue-
tonius, *Diuus Aug.* 43; cf. Syme 1939.291, 445, 448.

[15] Skutsch 1969.167.

A history of such a mode of reading the *Bucolics* would require a separate study, which we cannot even begin to outline here, although it should not overlook Desport, [16] or Damon, [17] or Gerald Fitzgerald and his influence on the contemporary poetic reinterpretation of the eclogue book as one design. [18] The first assumption would appear to be, however, that every element in the work has import for poetics. This indicates a solution to a common scholarly aporia: [19]

Scholars have been finding statements of poetics piecemeal in various *Eclogues* and in *Idylls*. The tendency has been to speak of a poetics in, say, the first or seventh... ninth or fourth, sixth... as if poetics could be the property of one or another.... This is criticism by a principle of divide and conquer. In fact, every... (piece) contains a poetics, which is to say that it reflects on its own nature as poetry... own peculiar way of shaping and knowing; some also reflect their relation to others and even a quality of the whole. Pastoral poetry is symbolist in the sense that, far from representing country matters, it uses country matters to represent a new kind of art. [20]

Such a principle, of course, requires the corollary, which was necessary, too, in other modes of inference, that when

[16] Desport 1952.10: "Ce qu'il s'agit d'étudier, donc, ... c'est la poésie parlant d'elle-même, la poésie interpretant la poésie." On poetic self-interpretation, see also Pfeiffer 1968.1-4, 125. Desport unfortunately failed to see that Virgil's work is dialectical. She reduced everything to Orphic ideas at the expense of the opposite—the Arcadian (cf. nn. 1.55, 57).

[17] Damon 1961.261ff.

[18] G. F. Fitzgerald, *Elements of Unity in the Sixth Eclogue: Some Notes on Vergil's Literary Method* (1953, Harvard Coll. Libr., unpublished), also cited by Elder 1961.124, n. 40; and for the poetic reinterpretation of the *Bucolics* influenced by Fitzgerald, see VS 1978.

[19] VS 1967.492-93.

[20] "Symbolist": C. M. Bowra, *The Heritage of Symbolism* (New York 1961, reprint of 1943 edition) 31, writes of Valéry's *Les Pas*, "The steps belong not to a human mistress but to poetry, the poetic

images, situations, or characters recur, their similarities and differences provide an important index of sense. In this way, as we have argued above, Arcadian images yield an idea of general coherence and development in the book, from the challenge to 'Sicilian Muses' to pull themselves together for the ultimate contest with Pan (E.iiii 1-3, 58-59), through the teasing and confusing memory of Arcadians near Mantua with Sicilian Daphnis (E.vii), to the final Arcadian mise-en-scène (E.x).[21] In particular, the contest of the displaced Arcadians, with its echoes of previous eclogues, emerges as an imaginative device for recalling and sorting out the terms of a fundamental opposition that recurs in progressive transformations in the book.[22]

Both the principle, "every piece its own poetics," and the idea of comprehensive design, "poetics of gradually realized, carefully proportioned, and deeply felt relations... among poems,"[23] would lead us to look for a poetics in the first eclogue, something important, as befits the first place in a structure (*sic insigniter*) and especially in a new work.[24] But the effort to reintegrate matter and idea has to take up at the point where the natural setting is most memorable, the drama moving and reknowned, political allegory notorious.[25]

One recent sample begins by inferring that the famous 'beech' of Tityrus, which led Soubiran to seek out shade, is a "conventional image...literary reminiscence" of the "tradi-

---

impulse, for which the poet waits." Evidently Wallace Stevens' "The Comedian as the Letter C," quoted above, must be read as symbolist. In a deeper sense, such poetic self-reflection cannot be confined to one time or group. It is a perennial, half-hidden secret of the art.

[21] VS 1967.493-94.
[22] Op. cit. 501-04.
[23] Op. cit. 493.
[24] Pöschl 1964.10-11.
[25] VS 1970b.887; and nn. 2.15-17.

tional disposition of the mode in which Virgil was about to write," and the contrast between it and Meliboeus' plight is then construed as a sign of the "need for reinterpreting the tradition." [26] It follows, then, that the autobiography of Tityrus must be an index: [27]

As an old slave who has found a new life of freedom and Roman citizenship, Tityrus is analogous to the *Eclogues*, a Roman renaissance of the bucolic mode. His former life of inertia with its wasted love for Galatea and fruitless trips to country towns represents a dull bondage to convention, an isolation from reality that can be found in the literary history of pastoral itself.

Or again, continuing:

No sooner has he heralded the instauration of a bucolic order than the revelations of Meliboeus show the same order swept away.

Here before we can venture on poetics, we face problems with inference of a simpler order. Meliboeus, we remember, evoked a complex civic, georgic, and bucolic system expropriated in the background—a complete imaginative alternative to the foreground, middle ground and background of Tityrus: the two bridged only in the utterance of the 'god'. [28] Thus we can hardly speak of the "same order swept away." Again, we must accept, with Skutsch, Klingner and others, [29] the inconsistency that Tityrus went to Rome for freedom, was told to go back to work 'as before' if not harder, and speaks of permission 'to play'. The inference,

[26] Leach 1975.119.

[27] Op. cit. 130.

[28] Cf. n. 2.11, 18.

[29] Skutsch 1969.167, quoted in n. 4.15; F. Klingner, *Hermes* 62 (1927) 129; but Pöschl 1964.37-38 writes of "die Beschlagnahme" of Tityrus, reading-in the poet's autobiography in the manner of the scholiasts.

then, for poetics may have to be slightly different, self-irony if anything more acute, if Tityrus did not become a *libertus* by a special rite. It will be very well to appreciate that the bucolic mode was 'without art' (cf. *inertem,* i 27) and could not get up *peculium* (i 32) until it looked to Rome from love; but it will not do to gloss over the precise terms of the transaction: the imperative to stay within the bucolic mode *(ut ante boues)* addressed categorically as to slaves, with only an exhortation for *auxesis;* [30] the resultant permission, by the god's leave, to play, but the burden of frequent sacrifice. [31] If the *religio* of Tityrus does indeed represent in rustic fiction the etiology of a "Roman renaissance of the bucolic mode," Rome seems to get and impose as much as give (or are we to imagine also Tityrus and Amaryllis battening on the flesh of monthly *abbacchio,* leaving Octavian with the bones of political contention ill concealed by ideological fat?): the god of Callimachus in the *Aitia*-prologue was much more discreet, interesting himself in the fatness of one victim not a whole herd, and more courteous (the rudeness of the Roman deity's charge to 'boys' more nearly resembles that of the Muses on Helicon rebuking Hesiod when his poetic career began [32]). In the imaginative hierarchy of the eclogue, too, *impius barbarus/seruus/ciuis/deus,* there seems to be room for only one citizen, Meliboeus (a full order lost), and for a slave, aspiring but kept in place. The images of unwilling flight and of subservient, uxorious old age dissimulate the audacity of the debut and emphasize the lowliness of the mode.

Whatever the rewards of inference of this kind, the risks are manifest. The play of allegory in poetics seems to be limited only by each reader's fund of historical

[30] Cf. n. 2.33.
[31] Cf. n. 2.6.
[32] Hanslik 1955.16-17.

information and antiquarian lore: *Veiouis,* or *manumissio
censu,* Octavian's march on Rome (and Tityrus'), or Pro-
metheus' tricking Zeus. Other controls are wanted: not only
regard for what the text does contain, but also more realis-
tic appraisal of the dynamics of political allegory (what
broad strokes of a message could come across in perfor-
mance),[33] and more measured attentiveness to the role of
such a message in the design of the book. "Roman renais-
sance of bucolic" sounds both too much and too little,
between the uncertain gain and certain loss of citizenship,
bucolic steading at the cost of other modes. We want a
more precise estimate of the import of such figures: their
function in the intrinsic order of the book; what they imply
about its relations to the literary past and Virgil's fullest
poetic designs.

[33] Cf. n. 2.15-17.

Chapter 5
A NEW DESIGN FOR *EPOS*

After poetry, the next most general background for the design of the *Bucolics* is the tradition of the *epos* from Homer down, in which the bucolic takes its place as a particular type or mode. From the present looking back through European literature, we perceive an eclogue tradition within a pastoral genre; but these are later terms and perspectives with their own history, which appropriates but an appearance of an idea from Virgil's book.[1] The very word pastoral suggests the unfolding of that history in the Latin-European west. Bucolic points back to the Greek and to origins long since dignified by myth.

Carefully the first Bucolic works out the hypothesis of the 'beech' and Tityrus' love, the antithesis of the vineyards and 'sweet plowlands' lost to Meliboeus, and the elusive synthesis of the god's generic 'as before' (i 45), a potential only hinted in 'rest with me' (i 79). This hierarchy ascending through dialectic has its ideological grip, giving the poetry that public presence it so evidently enjoyed, fulfilling then, too, perhaps a poet's "need for communion with his

---

[1] Alpers 1972.352-371 discusses the "eclogue tradition" within pastoral, but assumes that it is dead. No doubt Robert Frost would have demurred; and see VS 1978. The "bucolic tradition" had suffered its first death and was handed over to scholars and commentators in the first half of the first century B.C.: see VS 1976. 27-37. Then Virgil (perhaps prompted by a scholar, cf. n. 5.65) reclaimed it and turned it inside out. Death notices for genres are always premature.

society" through intelligible myths. [2] In poetics, in the tradition of the *epos* (poetry in dactylic hexameters), such a hierarchy at once brings to mind the development of Virgil's work: *Bucolics, Georgics,* and *Aeneid—pascua, rura, duces.*

Accustomed as we have been to think that Virgil wrote in three distinct genres, pastoral, didactic, and epic, are we authorized now by the three-part pattern in the first eclogue to suppose that Virgil coveted three genres from the start? Or are we merely committing the anachronism of reading the pattern of the life back into an early text where it cannot belong? "No" is the answer in each case, for reasons we can now explore.

It is well known that the idea of a three part hierarchy did not originate with Virgil. It was already a commonplace in literary history and rhetoric when he began to write. Thus no bar exists a priori to his adapting it for his designs from the start. It had arisen most probably in the Hellenistic theoreticians of rhetoric. Theophrastus distinguished between stylistic extremes: the poetical diction of Gorgias, the plain of Lysias, and a third, between. [3] But even before him Plato, in the *Phaedrus,* represented three styles in three successive speeches: first that of 'Lysias' (plain and

[2] R. Wellek and A. Warren, *Theory of Literature* (New York 1956) 181, cite Yeats, who admired the symbolist Mallarmé yet felt the need for myth. Virgil succeeded in being both hermetic and resoundingly public. The remark in the Donatan life is well known: "Bucolica eo successu edidit, ut in scena quoque per cantores crebro pronuntiarentur" (91 Hardie); cf. Tacitus' report, n. 4.14, and nn. 2.15-16; "crebro" presupposes not merely popular appeal but official encouragement (cf. n. 2.17 on use of the theater for propaganda by the Caesarian party). The *Bucolics* with their brevity, variety, topicality, must have created Virgil's personal legend in his own time; we have no evidence that the *Georgics* served or were suited as crowd-pleasers; the *Aeneid* was posthumous: see Hardie 1970. 1124, 1127; VS 1970b.887; and Hardie 1966.xv, xx.

[3] Grube 1965.107-09.

inchoate, as well as ethically perverse), then that labelled in retrospect of 'Phaedrus' (244A, referring back to the first speech delivered by Socrates, head veiled, still perverse in content, but ordered in style, chiasmic in plan), and finally that styled of 'Stesichorus' (244A, anticipating Socrates' second speech, ethically correct, enthused, full, varied, a diapason of styles). Of course, too, before Plato, Aristophanes implies, at least, a hierarchy of three, with Aeschylus and Euripides as the extremes and Sophocles between by default.

Apart from the *Phaedrus*, the idea of a three part hierarchy appears to arise through a process of positing two extremes, then a mean.[4] We find this pattern, for example, still in Virgil's contemporary, Dionysius of Halicarnassus, whose sources were Hellenistic, and who speaks of a diction that is 'extraordinary' and 'outstanding', of one that is 'light' and 'humble', and of one that is 'mingled' and 'combined' from these two (*de Dem.* 1, 3). Or again, Dionysius mentions a 'character' which is 'thin', one which is 'sublime', and a third which is between (id. 5, 13). At another point Dionysius shows us that such categorizing had a parallel in music: in discussing characters or differences of style, which metaphorically can be called 'austere' or 'flowery', he doubts how a third could come into being, since here 'it is not as in Music, that the middle is halfway between the extremes' (*peri synth. onomat.* 21 Schaeffer 1808).

By contrast with rhetorical theory, Alexandrian poetics has left little trace of an idea of three part hierarchy. The predominant conception is bipartite and bipolar, reflecting the situation in *epos* where Homer and Hesiod had long been perceived as representative of contrasting styles or modes. This polarity of types within the genre may have been articulated by Hesiod himself in the prologue to the

---

[4] G. L. Hendrickson, "The Origin and Meaning of the Ancient Characters of Style," *AJP* 26 (1905) 290.

Theogony, where the Muses' rude utterance declares that they know how to say false things resembling actual ones, but when they wish they can also tell the truth. [5] But if not in Hesiod, the perception of his work as a type in contrast with that of Homer may go back to the sixth century, if that is where the poetic "Contest of Homer and Hesiod" began to take form. [6]

The pattern, then, of bi-polarity, appears in the poetics of Callimachus, generalized and abstracted as a principle of style. [7] In the original introduction to the *Aitia*, Callimachus laid claim to the stylistic authority of Hesiod (fr. 2 Pf.). In the prologue added at the end of his life, he emphasized in retrospect that he had always kept to the slight, had never ventured grand, continuous works (sc. the Homeric type: fr. 1 Pf.). At the end of the *Aitia*, however, Callimachus does appear to distinguish two levels within the general area of his slight style; for he recalls, in the epilogue, his earlier description of Hesiod meeting the Muses by Hippocrene (fr. 2 Pf.), which he imagined as near the top of Helicon; [8] then he closes with what must be an allusion to his iambs, which followed next in his collected works: [9] *Mouseon pezon epeimi nomon*. In an allusion to poetry, the iambs, *pezon* cannot mean 'prose', [10] while in contrast with a poetics of the peak it can have a meaning which it

---

[5] E.g. Koster 1970.9, and now the important further analysis by Pucci 1977.8-16, esp. n. 11, p. 36; but not West 1966. on *Theog.* 25.

[6] Pfeiffer 1968.11; 43; 50, nn. 4, 5; West 1966.40, 47.

[7] Pfeiffer 1968.137 notes the parallel with Aristophanes, including the term *lepton*, and denies that the two poets were influenced by rhetorical theory, thus correcting E. Reitzenstein, "Zur Stiltheorie des Kallimachos," *Festschrift R. Reitzenstein* (Leipzig 1931) 40. See also D. L. Clayman, "The Origins of Greek Literary Criticism and the Aitia Prologue," *WS* 90 (1977) 27-34.

[8] Pfeiffer 1951. ad loc.

[9] Pfeiffer 1965.125.

[10] C. A. Trypanis, *Callimachus* (Cambridge, Mass., 1958) 87, errs.

had in Homer and Pindar, 'at the foot of the mountain', [11] no doubt here also with the connotations of common or lower class (e.g. foot soldier as opposed to knight). This suits the traditional character of iambs, which Aristotle called the common meter as opposed to the heroic (*Rhet.* 3.7.4). The literary heirs of iamb, too, comedy and satire, were to be called *pedestris* by Horace (S.2.17; A.P. 95). In short, Callimachus uses the topography of Helicon metaphorically to suggest a difference in poetic levels within his own work. [12] In the immediate context the metaphor distinguishes between two genres, both falling within the area of slight style, [13] while the stylistic area associated with Homer remains in the background, excluded by the *Aitia*-prologue. From here it would be only a step to take these genres as themselves stylistic types, and to posit iambic and Homeric as extremes, with Hesiodic in between. [14]

The contrast of Hesiod and Homer also shaped the poetics of Theocritus, well before Callimachus composed his

[11] *LSJ, s.v. pezon,* II, citing Il.2.824, 20.59; Pindar, P.11.36, etc.
[12] C. M. Dawson, "The Iambi of Callimachus," *YCS* 11 (1950) 148, "He is leaving the mountain pastures in which he, like Hesiod, was inspired by the Muses and is entering a lowlier field." But Dawson translates, "I shall enter the pasturage of the Muses where one goes on foot," as if there were some other means for getting to the other, and ignores the sense, 'at the foot of the mountain'.
[13] VS 1976-1977.330-331 on E.vi 64-65 and Propertius, *Eleg.* 2.10.25-26.
[14] Cf. the Varronian classification discussed below, pp. 111-12. Dawson (n. 5.12 above) 5 observes on Callimachus' *Iambs* that "it is as a collection of poems, as a carefully planned and organized book, I believe, that the work will have its greatest significance"; D. L. Clayman, "Callimachus' Thirteenth Iamb: The Last Word," *Hermes* 104 (1976) 35 elaborates: "Callimachus then has recalled in Iamb 13 many of the themes and ideas about the Alexandrian literary scene which he introduces in the first Iamb and develops in the subsequent poems ... defense of his own concept of poetry as a product of craft as well as inspiration ... distinct and coherent group ... with a true prologue ... and a true conclusion."

final reply to his critics. [15] It would be too simple to accept the common assumption that Callimachus initiated the Alexandrian use of Hesiod as a stylistic authority and thus necessarily showed Theocritus the way. [16] But we need to approach Theocritus' poetics with caution. More than Callimachus he placed himself in the tradition of Homer and Hesiod and invited comparison directly with them; for he wrote by far the greatest portion of his work in dactylic hexameter, and the epic allusions and transformations abound. [17] Besides this implicit testimony, Quintilian classed him with Aratus and Apollonius among the writers of *epos*, led by Homer. [18] Within this ample generic frame, however, Theocritus experimented in various directions, mingling his *epos* with attributes drawn from other genres. [19] Perhaps the most characteristic of these generic mixes was the use of Doric dialect in 12 poems, bringing a feature of choral and tragic lyric and Syracusan mime to *epos*. In turn, within this Doric group, it has been argued, he further distinguished some poems by more frequent use of Homeric forms and words: the poems, in order of ascending frequency, are Idd. 3, 1, 4, 2, 6, 7, all belonging to the first seven in our vulgate editions. [20] These seven share, then, the stylistic mannerism, unusually frequent diaeresis at the end of the fourth foot, which ancient critics called 'bucolic' and iden-

[15] Cf. VS 1975.62, n. 77.

[16] Gow 1952.xxiii, n. 3: "The views which Callimachus was prominent in defending need not have originated with him. He and Theocritus may have derived them independently from (for instance) Philitas"; cf. VS 1975.49, n. 18 and 58, n. 61.

[17] E.g. Fabiano 1971.passim; Serrao 1971.91-108; VS 1969.945-46; Di Benedetto 1956.48-60.

[18] Quintilian 10.1.55; VS 1976.19-20; Koster 1970.22-24.

[19] On generic mingling as characteristically Alexandrian, see Rossi 1971.84; and for stylistic mixing in Theocritus, with the tension of working in and against generic norms, Fabiano 1971.524-26, 529, 537.

[20] Di Benedetto 1956.53.

tified as a feature of bucolic genre. [21] Recognized as charac-
teristic of Theocritean hexameter, by contrast with the style

[21] In the following table, where the total number of lines differs
from the last figure in Gow 1952, the different total (given in
parentheses) reflects the following changes: omit Id.i 108 (omitted
by mss KPQWA¹G¹); omit Id.ii 61 (omitted by Pap. 3, K, Gow);
omit Id.vi 41 (so K, Gow); omit Id.xiv 60 (lacunose at this posi-
tion); add *Ep. Bion.* 69a, 92a (refrains). Ionic idylls are shown in
italic type. (Id.viii, hexameters only.) The count of "word ends"
follows the criteria of P. Maas, *Greek Metre* (Oxford 1962) 84-85:
"...we count as a 'word'...the whole group formed by an im-
portant part of a sentence (i.e. noun, verb, etc.) together with any
prepositives...and postpositives...that go with it"; "A preposition
placed between adjective and substantive loses something of its pre-
positional nature."

Id.	Total Lines	$\frac{8}{\cup\cup}\vert$	$\underline{8}\vert$	Total Word-ends	Per-cent
i	(151)	121	1	122	81%
ii	(165)	128	1	129	78%
iii	54	45		45	83%
iv	63	49		49	78%
v	150	133	1	134	89%
vi	(45)	35		35	78%
vii	157	117		117	74%
x	58	32	2	34	59%
xi	81	39	6	45	56%
xiii	*74*	*40*	*1*	*41*	*55%*
xiv	(69)	45	1	46	67%
xv	149	54	13	67	44%
xvi	*109*	*46*	*1*	*47*	*43%*
xvii	*137*	*47*	*5*	*52*	*38%*
xviii	58	28	5	33	57%
xxii	*223*	*96*	*7*	*103*	*46%*
	1743	1055	44	1099	
		61%	2.5%	63%	
(viii)	(78)	46	2	48	62%
(ix)	36	14	2	16	45%
Ep. Bion.	(128)	97	1	98	78%

of others, [22] the bucolic diaeresis now appears more specifically a mannerism of the group of poems that also share the intensive use of epic language, [23] and are also interrelated by many thematic and verbal links. [24] In what sense, if any, this set of poems ever formed a poetic book, we cannot say because of the accidents of their transmission, tenuous and contradictory, unlike that of the *Bucolics*, although perhaps not quite so random as has been supposed. [25]

Whatever their status as a book, the group do emerge as the product of a single and concerted poetic undertaking. This, in turn, has allowed scholars to recognize in the seventh idyll signs of retrospection, affirmation of accomplishment, and definition of the bucolic group as a distinc-

[22] E. G. O'Neill, Jr., "The Localization of Metrical Word Types in the Greek Hexameter: Homer, Hesiod, and Alexandrians," *YCS* 8 (1942) provides the raw material (based on a 1000 line sample, p. 107) for this table in his own tables 1, 2, 3, 6, 8, 10, 11, 14, 16, 17, 18; he discusses (p. 167) the history of study of the "bucolic bridge" (avoidance of word-end after monosyllabic eighth element) and "bucolic diaeresis" (word-end at position eight); cf. also P. Maas op. cit. (n. 5.21) 93-95, who notes the distinctiveness of Idd.1-7 in this respect. Unlike Maas, O'Neill counts as a "word" every separately printed element. Applying O'Neill's criterion to the sample in n. 5.21 increases percentages on an average of 2 to 4 points, excepting Id.11 where the increase is 14 points (from 56% to 70%). The following is the resume derived from O'Neill:

	Il.	Od.	Hes.	Arat.	Call.	Ap.	Theocr.
$\frac{8\mid}{8\mid}$	494	494	488	599	657	604	710
	123	96	101	70	11	20	52
Total	617	590	589	669	668	624	762
	62%	59%	59%	58%	67%	62%	76%

[23] Cf. n. 5.20.

[24] A listing in G. Lawall, *Theocritus' Coan Pastorals: A Poetry Book* (Washington 1967) 136-138; cf. VS 1970a.

[25] VS 1976.31-34, 42, n. 81.

tive new poetic mode,[26] 'bucolic singing', which takes its place as a subspecies of the Hesiodic rather than Homeric species of *epos*.[27] Nothing suggests that Theocritus here was following Callimachus. A close examination of his poetics points rather to his own work, epigram, and the tradition of *epos* itself as his primary authority and concern.

The story of the seventh idyll is familiar, how the narrator, Simichidas, a sometime cowherd, remembers walking out from town to a harvest feast, only to meet, along the way, the goatherd Lycidas, a favorite of the Muses: Lycidas praised the poetic accomplishment of Simichidas, who modestly replied that he did not aspire to compete with Philetas and Sikelidas (usually identified as Asclepiades). At this, Lycidas, pleased, promised Simichidas a rabbit stick (gift from the Muses) and denounced those who emulate the bulk of Homer.

In poetics, three things at least can be inferred. The references to Philetas, and to Cos, as well as Simichidas' song of love in an urban setting not only recall urban motifs and poetic forms in other idylls of the group but also seem to suggest affinities between this 'bucolic song' (Id.vii 49) and epigram.[28] Philetas, if anyone, not Callimachus, would appear to be the formative figure.

At the same time, the narrative of the journey and meeting recalls a pattern of encounter scenes in Homer, particularly the meeting of Odysseus and Eumaeus with Melantheus the goatherd: this use, with evident adaptations, of the Homeric type has been interpreted as showing by example a properly selective and restrained employment of Homer, as opposed to the gross emulation that is expressly condemned through the poetics of Lycidas.[29]

[26] Serrao 1971.52.

[27] VS 1976.23-24, elaborating on Serrao 1971.38 et passim.

[28] VS 1976.23.

[29] U. Ott, "Theokrits Thalysien und Ihre literarischen Vorbilder," *RhM* 115 (1972) 142-45.

In itself such an "appropriate" use of Homer might seem to associate Theocritus with the stylistic authority of Hesiod; but Theocritus also makes this specific claim by alluding to the initiation on Helicon, where the Muses not only spoke rather rudely but also gave Hesiod a staff. Puelma was the first, so far as I know, to point out a generic similarity between Hesiod, Theocritus (Id. 7), and Callimachus (fr. 1, 2, cf. 112 Pf.). [30] Serrao rightly insisted on the specific differences by which Theocritus distinguished his own 'bucolic song' from its Hesiodic precedent. [31] Lycidas, for example, stands at one remove from Muses. He transmits their gift; and he is anything but severe and well scrubbed, as they were, in Helicon's streams.

Altogether Theocritus gives greatest emphasis to the contrast between slight and great, between modest and excessively ambitious, all the while demonstrating how the 'bucolic' can appropriate from established forms. Modesty dissimulates emulation. Here, too, as in Callimachus, it is only in retrospect that we can trace out a three part hierarchy, although here there is no necessity to abstract from genre to style or mode. Within *epos* Theocritus imagines the extremes of great and slight: those who would build as high as Homer, but then his own 'cowherd singing'. Between them is the shadowy trace of Hesiod, the authority for a form of *epos* less than Homeric, himself more however than a bucolic mode that receives its sanction second hand from the Muses—a hunter's stick not a prophet's laurel rod. When Theocritus uses Hesiod elsewhere, it is the *Works and Days*, setting a work ethic over against bucolic romanticism, in a poem which stands somewhat apart from the bucolic group. [32]

[30] M. Puelma-Piwonka, "Die Dichter-begegnung in Theokrits Thalysien," *MHelv* 17 (1960) 144-164.
[31] Serrao 1971.11-68, cf. VS 1975.48-51.
[32] VS 1975.52 on Id.x.

In general, then, the contrast between Hesiod and Homer, and the dualism it implies, would appear to be the fundamental model in Alexandrian poetics. Only rhetorical theory, whether or not influenced by philosophy or music, went beyond the schema of the opposing extremes to posit a mean. We cannot say who first applied the three part schema to poetry. Our first evidence comes from Varro, in a passage that shows how adaptable such an idea could be, how readily employed wherever a ranking is desired, and, by implication, how much of a commonplace: (Aul. Gell. 6.14)

Et in carmine et in soluta oratione genera dicendi probabilia sunt tria, quae Graeci *characteres* uocant nominaque eis fecerunt *hadron, ischnon, meson*. Nos quoque, quem primum posuimus, uberem uocamus, secundum gracilem, tertium mediocrem.

Both in poetry and in prose there are three accepted kinds of speaking, which the Greeks call 'characters' and give the names of 'stout', 'thin', and 'middle'. We, too, call the one we put first the 'full', the second the 'thin', and the third the 'middle'.

Varro goes on to specify the virtues of each character, and the related vices. He then asserts that the true exemplars of the three in Latin are Pacuvius for 'full', Lucilius for 'thin', and Terence for 'middle'; but already from antiquity the three had been handed down by Homer in three speakers: the 'grand' in Ulysses, 'compressed' in Menelaus, and the 'mingled' and 'measured' in Nestor; and he closes by reporting that the same *tripertita uarietas* had been observed in the three Greek philosophers who came as ambassadors to the Senate in 156 B.C.: when they spoke before a great assembly of men, it was a cause for *admiratio* (according to the historians Polybius and Rutilius) that each philosopher had his own *genus* of eloquence.

Here we have ranking by modes of speaking in one genre (philosophy), and of writers in different genres (tragedy, satire, comedy), and of personae in one poet.

But even without Varro, the *auctor ad Herennium* (IV, 8, 11) and more fully Cicero (e.g. *Orator* 69-112) show the familiarity of the tripartite scheme in rhetoric in Virgil's formative years. What Varro shows is an application of the scheme to poetry. Altogether, then, we should be interested but not surprised to find evidence of *tripertita uarietas* in the *Bucolics*, nor need we posit Varro as a source for an idea so versatile and so commonplace, still less fear we have been merely induced by the later works to imagine it in the first.

With regard, now, to our other question, whether Virgil could have planned from the start to work in three genres, we have seen already the elements of an answer. He could well have planned to work in three styles or modes, as the ancient commentators say; [33] he would hardly have thought of the bucolic, georgic, and heroic as distinct genres since all were written in the dactylic hexameter and were classed as a single genre by the criterion of metrical form: a criterion implicit in the practice of a poet like Theocritus and articulated already by Alexandrian critics, [34] whose approach still appears in Quintilian, as we have seen. Returning to that passage for a moment (10.1.55), we can note that Quintilian added Apollonius, Aratus, and Theocritus to the canon of writers of *epos* (starting with Homer) because, he says, the Alexandrian critics had not included the living in their lists. We may wonder if Quintilian's choice of just these three, arranging them in what looks like a descending hierarchy of styles, betrays his own interest in Virgil and their relation to Virgil's three works. Nothing in Alexandrian poetics would dictate this order or associate these three authors in this way.

If Quintilian provides evidence of the metrical criterion for genre in Alexandrian criticism and its persistence well

[33] VS 1975.45-47.
[34] Cf. n. 5.18.

beyond Virgil's time, Horace shows its presence in Rome
in Virgil's own circle, indeed applied to Virgil's work. The
tenth satire of the first book reflects on the history of
satire and its nature in this new version. In the course
of his poetics, Horace says that Quirinus came to him in
a dream and bade him write Latin not Greek (S.1.10.31-
35). For a 'footling Muse', the play of allusion is complex.
The image of a god's advice recalls no doubt the *Aitia*-
prologue, but the dream, then, Callimachus' own transport
to Helicon (fr. 2 Pf.). Yet the polemical shift to a Roman
authority may bring to mind Ennius' earlier programmatic
intrusion of Homer into the Hesiodic-Callimachean frame,
by way of justifying his own heroic Roman *epos*. [35] It seems
probable, too, that Horace, by placing his version of the
poetic *aition* at the end of his book, invites comparison
with the different placement of the different versions in
Callimachus and Virgil, and thus also calls attention to
the arrangement of his poems and their claim to status as
a book, like the *Bucolics*, of ten. [36]

Having thus established satire as distinctively Roman,
Horace goes on to characterize it as slight by contrast with
more prepossessing literary cousins. While others make
swollen mythological or historical works, *haec ego ludo*
(37), 'I play at these', not of the sort to compete before
a judge or return again and again to the stage. Then, having
taken his distances, he goes on to compliment those who
do write well in, presumably, the near-by genres he has

---

[35] For the anti-Callimachean use of Callimachus' dream, see S. Ma-
riotti, *Lezioni su Ennio* (Pesaro 1951) 57; cf. Horace, *Epist.* 2.1.
50-51:

> Ennius et sapiens et fortis et alter Homerus,
> ut critici dicunt, leuiter curare uidetur
> quo promissa cadant et somnia Pythagorea.

[36] Cf. nn. 4.6-10 and 1.23. I am grateful to Dr. J. E. G. Zetzel
for permitting me to read his unpublished paper on Satires I and the
Bucolics and to Dr. Matthew Santirocco for conversations.

just set apart: he praises writers of comedy, tragedy, and *epos*. For the generic affinity of satire with writing for the theater, we have Horace's own testimony that Lucilius owed everything to the satiric voice of old comedy (S.1.4. 1-6) and we remember Varro's collocation (Pacuvius, Lucilius, Terence; but, when Horace denies that he wrote to be ogled again and again, one can only ask what he would have thought of the clamorous success of the *Bucolics*: *in scena quoque crebro per cantores*).

On the note of praise for satire's more ambitious kin (a gracious *recusatio*), he mentions comedy by Fundanius, then tragedy by Pollio (*regum facta canit*, 42), from which he passes directly to heroic *epos*, then down to the *Bucolics*, and finally to satire, which thus stands at the bottom of a descending hierarchy of "different kinds of *epos*": [37] (S.1.10.43-48)

...forte epos acer
ut nemo Varius ducit, molle atque facetum
Vergilio adnuerunt gaudentes rure Camenae:
hoc erat, experto frustra Varrone Atacino
atque quibusdam aliis, melius quod scribere possem,
inventore minor...

...Varius brave as no one else marshalls the strong *epos*, the gentle and deft the Camenae taking delight in country granted Virgil: this one was what I could write, better than Varro of Atax, who tried in vain, and some others, though less than the founder...

At the top, the generic term, *epos*, comes second, following the specific differentiating attribute. The changing specific terms then lead off each of the successive lower ranks, where the parallel construction continues to imply the generic idea (*molle*, sc. *epos*; and *hoc*, sc. *epos*). The writer of heroic *epos* is described in terms drawn from his matter

---

[37] So E. Fraenkel, *Horace* (Oxford 1957) 130; for the three part schema in Propertius, see VS 1974.116ff.

(*acer, ducit*). Then, by contrast with *forte, molle* suggests the peaceful, amorous matter as well as smooth manner of the *Bucolics*. In a gentle paradox, divinities who take pleasure in country things are said to have granted qualities that an earlier generation of poets had reserved for urbane verse. [38] The very image of rural goddesses authorizing poetry recalls Hesiod's initiation, while the shift from Muses to Camenae marks a specific, Italo-Roman difference (cf. E.iii 59), as a comparable shift had done at the beginning of Roman letters. [39] Horace perceives the *Bucolics* as a form of epos, Hesiodic rather than Homeric, following the Alexandrian dualism. Then below the Hesiodic he places his own *epos*. After his earlier allusion to the prologue of the *Aitia*, we well may wonder if here he has the epilogue in mind, with the iambs (a satiric genre, linked to comedy) below a Hesiodic mode; [40] in any case he has realized, in classifying modes of *epos*, the idea of *tripertita uarietas* that was at most implicit in Callimachus.

The evidence of Horace, Quintilian, and Theocritus makes it reasonable to suppose that Virgil, too, conceived of the bucolic as a form of *epos*. When he carefully distinguished the bucolic, the georgic, and the historico-mythic themes in the first eclogue, he might well, then, have been thinking in terms of three possibilities within the range of *epos*. This alone would be a departure from the poetics of post-Theocritean bucolic, which merely set the Theocri-

---

[38] W. Clausen, in a forthcoming study which he has generously shared, will note that "Horace associates with the country the very quality (*facetum*) that Catullus denied to it" (Clausen cites Catullus, C.22.14, *idem infaceto est infacetior rure*; and C.36.19, *pleni ruris et inficetiarum*). In a different vein, Horace himself could take country as the type of crudity: Epist. 2.1.160, *manent uestigia ruris* (cf. E.iiii 13).

[39] Livius Andronicus began his translation of the Odyssey by replacing the Greek *Mousa* with *Camena*.

[40] Cf. nn. 5.9-14, and Horace, S.2.6.17. *Musa pedestris* for satire.

tean against the Homeric as two contrasting types. [41] But if done by design, in a deliberate reappraisal of *epos*, it ought to deal with the seventh idyll, where Theocritus prepared, as it were, the material for a three part conception by defining the bucolic as a sub-species of the Hesiodic species of the genus. Theocritus placed the bucolic, by implication, at the bottom of a descending hierarchy that could easily be perceived, too, as the end of an historical descent. Hence Virgil, in return to the same moment, would have the opportunity to articulate the idea of hierarchy but reverse it, projecting a new development back to the top. For ambitions of such scope, Roman history and above all ideological myth would be essential. 'Tityrus' might have wanted freedom. His maker needed a 'god'.

The 'god' we have in the first eclogue. But scholars have seen a programmatic response to the seventh idyll only in the ninth eclogue, the less prominent companion to the first. We are missing the crucial link between Virgil's first and Theocritus' "last" that might be expected to establish the design of the book.

A. *Growth through Contrast: the Tityran Bucolic Mode* (*E.i + ii + iii + iiii*)

As we approach the first eclogues with an eye to their moment in poetics between prior *epos* and the work that ensues, we need to remember, too, the figure such texts made in the eyes of readers far more practiced, who sought and found a useful discipline of language, which orchestrated feelings and articulated ideas that we now seek for less utilitarian reasons. Something on the order of their views concerning the individual force of words and the collective force to be attained through forms of disposition needs to

[41] VS 1976.27.

inform any effort to reintegrate the *Bucolics* as a moving
yet theoretical design: (Badius on E.i 1-5)

Singula enim uocabula emphasim quandam ac uim propriae signi-
ficationis habent: et cum stylus sit exilis ac gracilis, nihil tamen
artis praetermissum quod ad excitandam miserationem faciat.
Nam statim in principio utitur contentione, qui color rhetoricus
habens fieri quotiens sententiae inter se contendunt, ac fere
contrariae sunt, multum elucidationis atque ornatus adfert. hic
autem totum principium in contentione est... nihil autem magis
contendunt quam hunc recubantem sub tegmine phagi cantilenis
indulgere, at illum profugum a patria, ignarum quo se recipiant:
sarcinulis ac misera pecude infeliciter depressum: sub fasce inge-
miscere.
Est praeterea hic (ut Landinus adnotauit) expolitio: quia eadem
de re saepius dicit.
Est et repetitio: nam nos in principio clausulae repetitur.
Est ad hoc interpretatio, quae saepe affert magnum augmentum
rei: nam interpretatur, fines patriae esse dulcia arua, quae res
mouet commiserationem.
Est quoque cum dicit, tu recubans, meditaris, euocatio etiam
pueris nota.

Individual words, to be sure, have a certain sense by implication
and the force of their own meaning; and, although the style is
meagre and plain, yet nothing is left undone that would make
for arousal of pity.
For instance straightway at the start he employs contrast. This
coloring in oratory occurs whenever statements contend among
themselves and are virtually antithetical. It adds much clarifica-
tion and embellishment. Here in fact the whole start consists
in contrast.... And indeed nothing contrasts more than that one
lying back should indulge in ditties beneath the cover of a
beech, but the other, exiled from his country, not knowing
where to betake himself, unluckily weighed down with poor
little bundles and pitiful ewe, should groan beneath a burden.
Here besides, as Landino noted, there is elaboration: because
he dwells in different ways on the same matter.
There is also anaphora: for "we" is repeated at the start of the
phrase.
Next to this there is explanation, which always adds a great
increase in matter: for it is explained that the "bounds of his
country" are "sweet plowlands," a matter that stirs pity.

There is, too, when he says "you lying back... work up," evocation, well known even to school boys.

The analysis comes from a teacher eager that his pupils shall know the poet's abundance and find occupation for their own exuberance. Nevertheless it may serve as a reminder of the energy in particular artifice with which this language grows and builds: [42] the hints of resolute contrivance in the least details augur well for the larger inquiry into the role of the first eclogues between tradition and future work.

1. E.i—*Outline of New Order vs. Old (Rome)*: the form is dramatic. [43] The goatherd—'Meliboeus'—is portrayed as speaking directly to the shepherd-cowherd—'Tityrus'. In the dramatic fiction, Meliboeus exclaims at the contrast between his own forced movement out and Ti-

---

[42] Yet Servius could write (2.4, 4.10 Th.-H.): "personae hic rusticae sunt et simplicitate gaudentes a quibus nihil altum debet requiri ... unde nihil in his urbanum, nihil declamatorium invenitur, sed ex re rustica sunt omnia negotia, comparationes, et si qua alia." But Servius reasons from an abstract idea of genre not from the text. Only a telling rhetoric could have won and held the crowd (cf. n. 4.14). For a related critique of Servius, finely documented from E.i, see Fedeli 1972.275 ff. Where Servius notes vaguely (E.i 4), "nos patriam fugimus plus est quam si diceret relinquimus," Renaissance critics (Landino, Badius) brought the fine-tuned force of Virgil's language into focus: the shift from *linquimus* (3), itself neutral (though underlined here by use of *simplex pro composito*, Fedeli), to *fugimus* (4), charged with despair (and political overtones), brought great *augmentum*, auxesis: see the fuller elaboration on the rhetoric of these lines in VS 1970b.896-904, and above, Chapter 2.B, "Growth of Contrasting Images."

[43] The discussion of each eclogue begins with a brief summary of the situation, while an introductory note presents (a) selected names, (b) some literary precedents, and (c) a sketch of linear and concentric structuring in the piece.

   (a) *NAMES.* Servius 4.4-10 says that most names of personae in the *Bucolics* are put together from rustic things, e.g. 'Meliboeus', *hoti melei autô tôn boôn*, 'because he takes care of cows', and

tyrus' apparent immunity to the effects of force from
without; but Tityrus explains that he has already moved
out by his volition, and has returned by the authority of
an outside force—'god' at Rome. Meliboeus both marvels
and laments; but Tityrus invites him to spend at least the
night.

The story of Tityrus' trip to Rome posits an outline
for poetics as well as ideology, for it recalls and transforms
the myths of poetics from the seventh idyll and Hesiod.
Tityrus is shown as a cowherd-shepherd who travelled from
country to city (and back), and who met an ambiguously
divine-human figure that spoke to him in an authoritative
way. This plot, in general outline, resembles that of Theo-
critus' cowherd-narrator, who told of traveling between

'Tityrus', which means 'bell wether' in Spartan. He cites similar
names in comedy. The etymological tradition is ancient and per-
vasive: e.g. Pfeiffer 1968.4-5; Robinson-Fluck 1937.1-2; and Wendel
1900.passim.
   TITYRUS. Theocritus, Id.iii 2-4; vii 72-78. It has multiple mean-
ings and associations — with Dionysus, animals, birds, music: thus
Silen, satyr, billy goat, bell wether (Schol. Theocr. Id.iii 2, Servius);
bird, reed, or pipe (Hesychius); cf. *tityristes*, 'piper', and *titis*, 'small
bird' or female sexual organ. For possible paronomastic associations
with Latin, cf. *titus, turtur* (E.i 58). Perret ad loc., observes, "sobri-
quet, plutôt que nom véritable." Cf. "Billy, Buck." Others liken
its sound to Id.i 1, *hady ti to psithyrisma kai ha pitys*: thus Skutsch
1956.200.
   MELIBOEUS. Not Theocr. Wendel 1900.49 cites the Suda for
a Meliboeus *georgos* who reared Oidipous, and would have this
Virgil's source. The name's meaning cannot be that stated by Servius
(quoted above) since Meliboeus is a goatherd, not cowherd (E.i 12,
74; cf. vii 7, 9). Conington ad loc. questions Servius, points to an
appropriate analogy with Greek *meli*, 'honey' (cf. Id.i 128-129, 146;
Hesiod, *Theog.* 84, 97; and a rich tradition which associates *meli*
with *melos*, 'song'), but still considers significant the other Servian
analogy with cattle (*bóas*). More appropriate to the persona of a
singer (see E.i 77) would seem an analogy with sounds or cries
(*boás*); cf. *meliboas*, 'sweet singing', Euripides, fr. 773.34 *LSJ*; and

city and country and of meeting an ambiguously divine-human figure which spoke in an authoritative manner; and both stories have elements in common with Hesiod's ac-

Lucretius' association of *meli*, 'honey', with *melos*, 'song', *meliores*, 'better', and *Meliboea*, a place, ii 500-509.

AMARYLLIS (i 5, 30, 36). Theocritus, Id.iii 1, 6, 22; iiii 36, 38. Identified as diminutive by Gow 1952.II 65, who relates it to *amaryssein*, 'to sparkle, dart glances'; cf. *LSJ* s.v. and Badius ad loc.; also Plato's similarly appropriate name for a lover, *Phaidros*, in the dialogue which exalts sight as the chief erotic sense. Since the adjective which Virgil attaches to *Amaryllis* has visual connotations, he may intend it to complement or explicate the Greek root: for other examples of this practice, see D. O. Ross Jr., "*Uriosque apertos*: A Catullan Gloss" *Mnemosyne* 26 (1973) 60-62. Paronomastic relation in Latin: *amor*, etc. Scholiasts read it as an allegory for Rome.

GALATEA (i 30, 31). Theocritus, Id.vi 6; xi 8, 13, 19, 63, 76; but also earlier literary tradition and cult (Gow II.118); (Moschus) *Epitaph. Bion.* 58, 61. Cf. *gala*, 'milk'; the nymph is called 'white . . . whiter than curds' in a rustic compliment, Id.xi 19. Cf. Flintoff 1976.16-17.

(b) *SELECTED PRECEDENTS.* Tityrus' journey and *aition* ~ Simichidas' journey and encounter, Id.vii (see nn. 5.44-45 below); Tityrus' ideal locus, E.i 51-58 ~ Id.vii 136-142; Tityrus as implicit Daphnis (cowherd) figure, E.i 38-39 ~ Id.i 71-75, cf. iiii 12; and Putnam 1969.41, Pöschl 1964.40. For others, see Posch 1969.19; also nn. 5.48, 59 below; and C. Hosius, *Bucolics* (Bonn 1915). Reference to Posch and Hosius will not be repeated, but is presumed, for the other eclogues.

(c) *STRUCTURE. Linear by increments*: 18 verses (1-18), Meliboeus/Tityrus, Meliboeus' present; 27 verses (19-45), Tityrus' past, from slavery to Rome, *aition*; 18 verses (46-63), Tityrus' ideal past as future; 20 verses (64-83), Meliboeus' future and past, Tityrus with Meliboeus in present. Cf. n. 1.42, above.

Concentric; focussing on 'god' at Rome (i 40-44, *aition*): 5/5/29/5+1/28+5/5; cf. the similar structure in E.ii, n. 5.60 below; and on E.i, Skutsch 1969.157. Meliboeus' last five lines (74-78) form a distinct group that focusses down from the civic and georgic registers to the bucolic, to Meliboeus' own poetics ('songs' lost), and to the actual gesture toward exile.

count of his start in poetry, meeting the Muses while he shepherded on Helicon.

We have seen that Theocritus was making conscious use of Hesiod's myth to define the status of 'bucolic song'; [44] and how specific differences in the stories give the bucolic a unique character within the general area of Hesiodic *epos*: not only the contrast noted between severe, virginal and well-washed Muses and a genial, lecherous, stinking goatherd, but especially the fact that Lycidas approves poetic work already done rather than initiating a neophyte. [45] The claim to generic continuity but specific identity returns, then, in the first eclogue. The direction of travel changes. Theocritus' narrator moved from city to country. Also, the spirit of the meeting alters from familiar, bantering equality with erotic overtones to a slave's experience of something like an epiphany: the 'god' no longer a figure of bucolic or poetic myth but a new Roman ideological hero. [46]

In poetics, Theocritus' version of the story was suited to confirm the invention of a new and original mode of *epos*: an experienced cowherd (taught by nymphs on the hills, another Hesiodic echo, Id.i 95) returns to the country to celebrate a harvest festival and meets approval from a palpable rural denizen. [47] Consequently we can expect the story of Tityrus to reflect a different moment in the history of the mode: [48] the past of Tityrus appears as poor, subject to erotic bondage, without force (sc. art, *inertem*, i 27). Hence the desire for freedom, imagined in the rustic drama as coming late in life, may well be an index in poetics of

[44] VS 1975.48-60; Serrao 1971.16-39; cf. n. 5.31.

[45] VS 1975.50; Serrao 1971.37.

[46] By contrast with Virgil's *deus*, Theocritus alludes to Ptolemy II Philadelphus as a rather vague, distant Zeus: Id.vii, 93, cf. VS 1975.61, n. 70, and 59-60, n. 100.

[47] VS 1975.69; Serrao 1971.11, 48; Rossi 1971.93, n. 81; cf. nn. 5.28-31 above.

[48] Cf. nn. 4.26, 27 and discussion there.

the restricted and artificial state of the bucolic mode, reduced after Theocritus to mannerism, then recently criticized by Lucretius as being a mere mystification and echoic fiction. [49] With this unsatisfactory generic past, the story of Tityrus marks a break; whether or not he becomes a Roman citizen, there is a new dispensation for expansiveness in the bucolic (i 45), [50] hence something beyond the confines of Greek mannerism and Theocritus. [51]

Changing the direction of travel and the character of the city were radical departures, as the dramatic fiction underlines through the wonder of Meliboeus and the explanations of Tityrus: so, too, authority derived from an historical figure through a new and controversial ideological myth that provides the basis for regenerating traditional mythology and epic forms. [52] Choosing the seventh idyll and transforming its myth must be the work of a conscious and ambitious artist. Not some Callimachean elegy or short epic or bucolic mannerism but Theocritus' own declaration of status recommends itself to Virgil, not, however, like Theocritus to confirm a position at the bottom of the

[49] Cf. n. 4.6 and, for mannerism in bucolic, VS 1976.25-27. Damon 1961.281-86 noted the irony implicit in evoking Lucretius' *siluestris musa* (E.i 2 ~ Lucr.iiii 589), yet Virgil's *imitatio* may also imply *oppositio* (cf. n. 4.8), for against the hint of Lucretius' critique of pastoral he sets Tityrus' *aition* (i 6-7), which echoes and transforms Lucretius' image of an idyllic rural life (*otia dia*, v 1387) and of *Epicurus* as a saving god (*deus ille fuit, deus, inclute Memmi*, v 8); Virgil's *deus* is an active, historical, and public figure rather than a philosopher of retirement: see B. Farrington, "Vergil and Lucretius" *AClass* 1 (1958) 45 ff.

[50] Cf. n. 4.28.

[51] VS 1975.69.

[52] Thus overcoming the degeneration of mythology and implicitly also the "obsolescence of epic" which Otis 1964.1-40 diagnosed. The importance of Otis' view of change and possible reversal in tradition, as opposed to the static-idealist conception of Eliot, is underlined by Perutelli 1973.131-35; see also n. 5.60 for a dynamic idea of tradition.

stylistic hierarchy but to prepare for new growth, back up in the direction of history and higher epic modes. The implication of Virgil's audacity is twofold. Not only does he claim for himself the role of second founder in the bucolic mode, by reinterpreting Theocritus' myth of origin for himself as none of the Greek bucolic mannerists had done, but he also reopens the question of the relations between bucolic and other modes of *epos*, since growth once undertaken need not necessarily be confined to the boundaries of Theocritean bucolic, which in any case the first eclogue has already grown beyond. [53]

The need to sketch a general outline for the whole book does not allow us to linger to reconstruct step-by-step the dramatic development of Tityrus' *aition* or dwell on a number of particular allusions and transformations. For example, the name 'Tityrus' itself may also suggest a relation of identity/difference with the seventh idyll, which mentioned a Tityrus as the potential singer of a complex song. [54] Then, too, Meliboeus' praise of Tityrus' ideal bucolic locus also bears a significant relation to the seventh idyll, to Theocritus' account of the ideal country locus where his cowherd-narrator finally went. [55] In the dramatic fiction of the eclogue, it is the intense nostalgia of exile — loss of place — which gives force and intricacy to this particular Theocritean interpretation. [56]

The import of 'Meliboeus' for poetics would also merit study. He, too, speaks of travel, and more complex than Tityrus'. The name is new and etymologically appropriate to the dramatic-poetic character, [57] though the generic category, goatherd, was Theocritean and represented by the

[53] VS 1975.70; cf. nn. 5.46, 48.
[54] See n. 43.
[55] See n. 43, s.v. *PRECEDENTS*.
[56] Segal 1965.240-41; and Badius ad loc., cf. VS 1970b.897.
[57] See n. 43, s.v. *MELIBOEUS*.

more authoritative of the two figures in the seventh idyll. [58]
Two points may be underlined: Meliboeus is the protagonist,
and begins the piece with political ideas of the late re-
public—the old order—and in language which recalls the
style and poetic ideas of late republican Roman poets —
the literary culture in which Virgil grew up, both neoteric
poetry and Lucretius, with his critique of the simple bucolic
mode; [59] but Meliboeus applies the neoteric and Lucretian
terms to Tityrus' art, and refers to his own art interrupted
in the background as singing 'songs'. [60] Also, Meliboeus'
language is the most wide-ranging and full, with its back-
ground of implicit civic order, georgic cultivation, and
pastoral art. Three modes are negated through the figure of

[58] Lycidas, the figure that is imagined confirming bucolic poetics
and condemning the wrong sort of emulation of Homer: VS 1969a.
945.
[59] For Lucretius, n. 5.48; word order, nn. 4.3, 4; *meditari*
suggests the careful workmanship and effort characteristic of the
Callimachean and neoteric idea: for these themes in Theocritus,
Callimachus, Philetas, Catullus, see VS 1975.58-59, n. 61. *Tenui* also
belongs to this poetic ideology, but *auena* is Virgil's Latin substitute
for the conventional Greek *calamo* (cf. E.i 10, Id.viii 24). We cannot
assume that a 'pipe' is meant or simply assume that *auena* belonged
to poetic language before Virgil; elsewhere (E.x 51-54) it is as-
sociated with writing; hence Tityrus may be imagined as writing
what he will sing to the woods, and *auena, calamo* (i 10) both imply
'pen': *ludere scribere* glosses Servius; and Tityrus, E.vi 1-12, is
imagined as a writer (*ludere*, vi 1; *meditabor*, vi 8; *praescripsit*,
vi 12). Meliboeus is a singer, see n. 5.43.c, 60.
[60] E.i 77, *carmina nulla canam*. The figure of 'Meliboeus' ex-
presses what Bayet 1967.189 called "l'ébranlement initial, à partir
duquel s'organisa la 1ère Bucolique." Such a figure is the instrument
of creative self-criticism: cf. R. Girard, "Tiresias and the Critic"
The Languages of Criticism and the Sciences of Man, ed. R. Macksey
(Baltimore 1970) 20: "I am personally convinced that truly great
works of art, literature, and thought stem, like Oedipus' own rein-
terpretation of the past, from a genius's ability to undertake and
carry out a radically destructive reinterpretation of his former in-
tellectual and spiritual structures." Cf. also Duckworth 1969.46,

exile, only to be reconstituted in new terms, no longer civic but mythic in the highest register.

2. E.ii—*Growth in New Bucolic-Georgic Terms* (*Love*): the form is mixed narrative and dramatic. The narrator, continuing the positive outline of Tityrus, as we have seen, spans the background and foreground, but not without an almost supercilious detachment from the erotic excitement and disordered utterance of the bucolic lover. [61]

quoting Hardie, *JPh* 30 (1907) 272, "The versification of the Eclogues might almost be regarded as a revolt, a protest or reaction against the verse rhythm of the preceding generation." Schmidt 1972.61, in characterizing Virgil's relation to Theocritus, quotes Tynjanov: "Jede literarische Nachfolge ist doch primär ein Kampf, die Zerstörung eines alten Ganzen und der neue Aufbau aus alten Elementen." Yet the new may also be viewed as a "stronger system" which subsumes and brings out latent implications in the works and tradition to which it replies; cf. VS 1970b.912-913. However Wormell 1969.6 can still conceive of the relation as "reproduction of a Greek original." On the question of conceptions of tradition, see also nn. 4.8, 5.52. Within the book, too, as we shall see, Virgil destroys one structure and rebuilds another from its traces: this is the idea of change as *uestigia irrita* (E.iiii 13-14).

[61] (a) *NAMES. CORYDON.* Theocritus, Id.iiii 1, v 6; (Erycius, A.P.6.96.1). Servius 18.11-12 compares the bird's name, *corydalis* (cf. the associations of 'Tityrus', note 5.43 above; and Id.vii 23); Virgil hints paronomastically at a Latin root, *corylos* (E.vii 63-64).

ALEXIS. Name of *pueri delicati* in Anacreon, Plato (A.P.7.100), Meleager (A.P.12.127): Wendel 1900.49; Robinson-Fluck 1937.47, 50. Here, too, however, Servius 18.12-13 implies a significant Greek root, 'boy who does not reply' (*a + lexis*).

THESTYLIS (ii 10, 43). Theocritus Id.ii 1, 19, 35, 59, the servant who brings ingredients and prepares magic spells; here the girl who prepares a refreshing herb salad for reapers (E.ii 10-11). Servius 19.17 appears to derive the name from *tithemi*, 'she sets food before farmers'.

AMARYLLIS (ii 14, 52). Cf. n. 5.43.a.

OTHERS. The image of a "peopled peace" begins to fill out: *AMYNTAS* (ii 35, 39), cf. n. 5.84; *DAMOETAS* (ii 37, 39), cf. n. 5.65; *DAPHNIS* (ii 26), cf. n. 5.84; *IOLLAS* (ii 57), cf. E.iii

In turn, the lover, Corydon, whose eager attempt to draw the boy Alexis from the background provides the substance of the narrative, seems to continue both the energy and the poetics of Meliboeus as singer of 'songs'. [62] In and against

76, 79; *MENALCAS* (ii 15), cf. n. 5.65. For the number and repetition of names in Theocritus (51, only 10 repeated) and Virgil (34, 20 repeated), itself an index of interest in coherence, see Flintoff 1976.17.

(b) *SELECTED PRECEDENTS.* Plea by lover to an unresponsive beloved ~ plea by goatherd (Id.iii) and Polyphemus (Id.xi), but both to female objects (Schmidt Rev. Posch 1969.774 underlines differences); details of introduction (ii 1-5) ~ Callimachus' *Acontius*, Phanocles, *Boy Loves*, cited by Schmidt op. cit. 774; also Meleager (A.P.12.127) adduced by Leach 1975.148; for allusions to epigram in the plea itself, see Schmidt op. cit. 774-775; and for the tradition of Corydon's poetic aition, n. 5.63.

(c) *STRUCTURE. Linear-dynamic:* 5 verses (1-5), introduce disparity between foreground and background; 13 verses (6-18), elaborate on the disparity; 37 verses (19-55), actively seek to overcome the disparity, building up foreground, cajoling background, culminating in urgent plea to Alexis to enter a place of ideal nature and art; 13 verses (56-68), collapse, critique of plea; 5 verses (69-73), reflect on disparity between foreground and middle ground. Cf. n. 1.43 above.

Concentric, focussing on myth of origin of Corydon's pipe (ii 35-39): 5, 13+16+5+16+13+5 (i.e. 5, 29+5+29+5). Pöschl 1964.64 observes that E.i and E.ii have the same ground plan, though the relation is more calculated and thorough-going than he thinks (cf. n. 5.43, *STRUCTURE. Concentric*). In E.i we have 5/5/63+5/5 and in E.ii we find 5, 63+5, not to mention the centered five-line myths of origin in both pieces. Skutsch 1970.95-99 does not give due weight to the unity of the piece as we have it with its complex integration into the structure of the first four pieces (as well as responsion with E.i) when he argues that ii 45-55 are a later addition designed to make an "early" (cf. n. 1.4) eclogue fit the book's final scheme. If anything, one might be tempted to view ii 1-5 as added to establish a specific link with E.i (see nn. 2.21, 23 above); but all such chronological speculation is futile (see nn. 1.30, 31).

[62] E.g. *nihil mea carmina curas,* ii 6, where the background figure, Alexis, is imagined as negating the value of songs: compare

the dynamism of Corydon's song, however, we find a structural resemblance to the first eclogue—placement of a myth of origins at the center, except that this myth is overtly poetic and implies a simple, direct succession from an old to a new master in bucolic art. Hence we infer that Virgil here means to claim a direct relation between Theocritus and himself, excluding the poetry of the Greek bucolic manner. [63] He has already, at the center of the first eclogue, expressed the difference between his version of bucolic and Theocritus'; thus he can emphasize the generic continuity now. As noted in our study of ideology, Corydon's energetic singing amplifies both the bucolic foreground and the georgic middle ground of the positive outline. Here again a full study of poetics would retrace the erotic drama step-by-step and its transformations of the structure and substance of precedents in Theocritus and Hellenistic epigram. [64]

3. E.iii—*A Full Bucolic-Georgic Outline (Love)*: the form is dramatic. A testy and envious goatherd — 'Menal-

the negation of songs in the background, E.i 77, *carmina nulla canam* (discussed in n. 5.60), and the affirmation of songs in the background, E.iii 61, *illi mea carmina curae*, where Jove harks to them. In E.iiii, then, it is a question of whether the *puer* (*incrementum Iouis*) will resemble the unresponsive *puer* of E.ii or responsive Jove of E.iii. The song ends with an urgent plea: *incipe, parve puer . . . incipe, parve puer* (iiii 60, 62).

[63] *Te nunc habet ista secundum*, E.ii 38; cf. Klingner 1967.12-13. At Id.vi 43, Damoetas kisses Daphnis and gives him a pipe, receiving a flute. They both play. Virgil has turned this into a myth of musical tradition (cf. E.v 86-90). Virgil's ecphrasis of the pipe synthesizes and reinterprets Id.i 129 and (Theocritus) Id.viii 18-24; the former makes allusion to the myth of Pan as inventor of the pipe. Virgil has already sketched that myth (E.ii 32-33) as generic background to his specific myth of poetic continuity. His new version of the pipe also echoes Lucretius' account of the *otia dia* (*cicutis*, E.ii 36, Lucretius, v 1382-1383; cf. n. 5.48 above).

[64] See *PRECEDENTS*, n. 5.61. Galinsky 1965 (1968) 164 and E. W. Leach, "Nature and Art in Vergil's Second Eclogue," *AJP*

cas' — accosts 'Damoetas', calling him to account. The resulting quarrel verges toward artistic differences and leads to agreement on a match. 'Neighbor Palaemon', summoned not so much to separate out as to store up what they sing, sets the scene and invites them to start. They sing. He confirms both and any true lover as worthy of a living prize. [65]

Here the *persona* of 'Menalcas' comes to the foreground

87 (1966) 433, find Corydon's cure less certain that that of Polyphemus (Id.xi); but the issue may be not so much "cure" as employment of passion, cf. Spofford 1969.35. If anything "contains" passion here, it is not nature (not close of day, cf. E.i 82-83), since Corydon still burns (ii 66-68), but an idea of responsible and shaping art, *detexere, indiget usus* (ii 71, 72). Both Pöschl and Leach op. cit. 431 attribute these ideas to the narrator (cf. n. 2.26); but what serves at this point in the development of the book is an idea of order in the middle ground or register and in the voice of the passionate singer (cf. nn. 5.60, 62): discipline cancelling out the disorders of Meliboeus and Corydon, but conceived in the middle ground, cf. the images of georgic order through E.ii.

[65] (a) NAMES. DAMOETAS. Theocritus, Id.vi 1, 20, 42, 44; E.ii 37, 39 (the dead former owner of the pipe). Gow II.120 cites Thessalian inscriptions for the name; and possible connection of its second element with *oisein*. First element, Doric, *dêmos*, 'people', *dèmos*, 'fat'? i.e. an aristocratic name degenerated (like Amyntas, Mopsus, Codrus) or a rustic sobriquet (Perret on Tityrus)?

MENALCAS (iii 13). (Theocritus), Id.viii, viiii; Hermesianax told of his love for Daphnis (Schol. Theocr. Id.viii 55; cf. Ath. 14.619c, quoted by Gow II.172); E.ii 15. Significance of the name is problematical (cf. the hypotheses for Damoetas): *men-* might suggest 'abiding', and the second element perhaps 'strength' or 'defence, help' (*alke*). Latin paronomasia: *mens? mencla?*

OTHERS. As befits the place and function of the piece, the fullest stock of names: *AEGON* (2), cf. Id.iiii 2, E.v 72; *ALCIMEDON* (37, 44); *AMYNTAS* (66, 74, 88), cf. E.ii 35, 39, and n. 84; *BAVIUS* (90); *DAMON* (17, 23), cf. E.viii 1 etc.; *DAPHNIS* (12), cf. E.ii 26 and n. 5.84; *DELIA* (67); *GALATEA* (64, 72), cf. E.i 30, 31 and n. 5.43; *IOLLAS* (76, 79), cf. ii 57; *MAEVIUS* (90); *MELIBOEUS* (1), cf. i 6 and n. 5.43; *MICON* (10); *NEAERA* (3), a hetaira-name, cf. Callimachus, fr. 43.15 Pf., with note;

for the first time— goatherd, figure of property, with some relation to 'Meliboeus', and reaching the foreground from a 'home' elsewhere. Virgil endows 'Menalcas' with cups that recall in their designs the subjects of the Hesiodic mode in *epos*, while the cups assigned to Damoetas (a more free-wheeling, energetic, and less propertied character) show Orpheus—woods in tow, recalling the legendary origins of

PALAEMON (56), sea god and perhaps, too, 'wrestler'; *PHYLLIS* (76, 78, 107), cf. n. 6.81; not to mention Venus, Camenae, Pierians, Orpheus, Conon, (*alter*,) Pollio, Lycisca, Jove.

(b) *SELECTED PRECEDENTS*. General plan, quarrel as prelude to competition ~ Id.v; opening sally ~ Id.iiii 1-2, 13; cups ~ Id.i 27-61; negotiations for prize ~ Id.viii 14-24, where the contestants fall back to the lesser prizes, which are identical rather than differentiated significantly in content as here (see n. 5.66. below). The number of lines in the contest (48) equals that in the contest proper of Id.viii (and of E.vii): see n. 1.21. Dr. John Vaughn argued (CASUS Conference on Virgil and his Influence, Oct. 1, 1977) that some of Virgil's departures from Theocritus in E.ii, iii reflect details of the commentary on Theocritus and treatise on Nestor's Cup by Asclepiades of Myrleia, who is discussed as the probable importer of Theocritus to Rome by VS 1976.35-36.

(c) *STRUCTURE. Linear dynamic*: 6 verses (1-6), tension in foreground fueled by envy of background; 14 verses (7-20), tension amplified in terms of sex, property; 7 verses (21-27), tension expressed in terms of musicality (climax of first half of quarrel); 21 verses (28-48), formal challenge to compete and negotiation of terms; 6 verses (49-54), contrast formalized, judge-repository summoned; 5 verses (55-59), judge orders contest; 48 verses (60-107), first half of contest (24 verses: 60-83, permutations of love), second half of contest (24 verses: 84-107, poetry beyond the foreground, growth, dangers in and on the borders of pastoral, diminution, envy, everywhere/nowhere — language reduced to cipher); 4 verses (108-111), tension maintained, both sides affirmed.

Concentric: in the whole piece, Palaemon's invitation to compete stands roughly at the center (iii 55-59). The quarrel is highly structured, e.g. 6+21+21+6, or, to show the transitional nature of iii 21-28, 6+14+7+21+6: all this despite the surface rudeness which Servius remarked: cf. Skutsch 1969.157.

the epos and its hymnic mode. [66] By the center of the piece, as we have seen, the gradual amplification of language through systematic contrasts has reached a point of elaborate synthesis and an expression of full bucolic-georgic order in the figure of Palaemon. At the similar juncture in the fifth idyll, a judge is summoned, but says nothing until after the contest. Thus Palaemon's utterance, with its generalizing and all-inclusive language, is a deliberate augmentation with respect to Theocritus. [67] We have considered its ideological implications already, but it thus also has importance for poetics, and this is confirmed by the appearance of a newly full and explicit terminology for the form of bucolic art itself, both *uariatio* and contrast—*alterna*, the Greek *amoebaea*. [68] What we are seeing is close co-ordination between the growth of images in language and the progress of theoretical reflection on the language itself.

At this point, as if to emphasize that the book has grown beyond the matter if not yet the formal semblance of Theocritus, the match opens with an allusion to Aratus, a Hesiodic mode of *epos* also implicit in the design of Menalcas' cups. [69] The formal exchanges of song then work through the permutations of love — fulfilled/frustrated, homo-

[66] Orpheus at the head of early lists of epic poets: West 1966.47, and Pfeiffer 1968.50, 164. For the cups as a suggestion of the scope reached by Virgil's pastoral, see Segal 1967.290. Wormell 1969.12-13 notes that they point beyond conventional pastoral limits toward the poetry of the *Georgics* and *Aeneid*. Virgil, in calling them 'beech' *fagina* (iii 37), would seem to imply a development in poetics: see n. 2.21 above. Mention of Conon as subject of their illustration (iii 40) is an evident allusion to Alexandrian-Callimachean (Catullan, *C.*66) poetics, so too Schmidt 1972.295.

[67] Compare Id.v 76; vii 135-146; and Id.viii 41; Bion, *Aposp.* 2.17. See also discussion, VS 1967.498-499.

[68] The term first enters the technical lexicon of bucolic genre in Id.viii 31, 61: cf. VS 1970a.22. Virgil refers to the Latin *Camenae* only here in all his works; cf. n. 5.40 above.

[69] See n. 5.65 above.

sexual/heterosexual — in a *uariatio per alterna* that fills out the mythic framework and exhausts the conventional erotic themes that were introduced in the first and second eclogues. The latter half of the exchange then looks to elements of authority and encouragement beyond the bucolic-georgic order and verges into preoccupation with boundaries, envy, and insufficiency.[70] In a full reconstruction of the poetics of the eclogue, these themes might perhaps be shown to reflect on the growth of the work itself to the limits of a traditional poetic mode.

The eclogue closes by returning to Palaemon, who synthesizes and generalizes about the positive force for poetry of love, which has been an ostensible cause of song in the second and third pieces. Palaemon's last line expressly identifies bucolic song with a natural element and rural task, thus making explicit a metaphor which has been implicit in the language at least since the center of the first piece.[71]

4. *E.iiii—Hint of New Heroic Myth: Total Epic Design (Rome: Fates)*: by and large, the fourth Bucolic is a directly sung narrative, with only a snatch of an utterance attributed to the Parcae (iiii 46). In structure, as we may recall, the eclogue has seven parts which coincide with the successive stages of its thematic development: 3-7-7-28-7-7-4. The import of this structure for poetics can perhaps best be

---

[70] Klingner 1967.56 sees a shift from opposition to complementarity in the exchanges after iii 84. On the riddles, Büchner 1955.1193.8-11 notes an essential quality, that the language brings together the largest and smallest things (*parua/magna*, the bucolic paradox, cf. E.iii 54; i 23); and Segal 1967.297-298 remarks the return to earlier motifs of the piece, especially of the cups; Schmidt 1972.296, n. 294, also notes that the riddles point to the beginning of the contest (hyacinth, Aratus). Segal 1967.304-308 discusses the anticipations of E.iiii, v, and vi. These several observations gain still more precise focus once we consider Asclepiades' treatise (n. 5.65.b).

[71] See Segal 1967.303-304, and nn. 5.51, 2.33 above.

suggested by taking the sections in order. First we have the reductive view of the bucolic mode in the first three eclogues as mere trees and groundling tamarisks, 'Sicilian Muses'—generic formulas which deliberately diminish the accomplishment of the first three pieces in their growth beyond Theocritus and the bucolic manner. Against this we have the standard of a Roman high style, 'consul' (1-3). [72]

Into the gap, then, between these two extremes of low

[72] The language summing up the bucolic mode is discussed in n. 2.32 above, excepting *Sicelides Musae* (iiii 1). Not Theocritean (cf. the discussion of Theocritus' 'Bucolic Muses' in VS 1976.22-24, cf. 26, and of *Sikelikai Moisai* as generic reference to Theocritus in the *Epitaph. Bion.*, p. 27), *Sicelides* is a rare word, though cast in the form of a patronym or toponym which is common for the names of Muses (Varro, LL 7.20). Its counterpart, however, masculine toponym or patronym, does occur at Id.vii 40, cited as an instance of a poetry Theocritus' narrator does not presume to surpass. In E.iiii, it marks the level that is to be surpassed. Virgil echoes Id.vii 44 at E.iiii 49: discussed by VS 1967.496.

(a) *NAMES*. Some signs of play on etymology and paronomasia, e.g. *Apollo* (10) and *Pollio* (12); or *amomum* as opposed to *fallax herba* (24-25); or the balanced line, "Orphei Calliopea Lino formosus Apollo" (57), where, by *apo koinou*, one attribute serves two deities, glossing the Greek root of the first (cf. examples given by Ross, cited in n. 5.43 above, s.v. Amaryllis).

(b) *SELECTED PRECEDENTS*. Praise of ruler, miracles of birth, prophecy flattering his rule ~ Idd.xvi, xvii (to Ptolemy); Callimachus, Hymn iiii (Delos, Ptolemy); Hesiod, *Theog.* 32, 38, Muses' gift of prophecy: see Williams 1968.274-277, Leach 1975. 228-29, and cf. VS 1975.52-54 on epic convention of the hymn in Theocritus and *Theogony*. Virgil departs from Hesiod by challenging Muses (of bucolic) rather than being instructed by Muses (of Helicon); cf. n. 2.32.

(c) *STRUCTURE*. The dynamic and linear development of the piece has been sketched in the text, also the articulation, 3+7+7+ 28+7+7+4. Each part may be further articulated, thus 3+4+ 3+4+3 (iiii 1-17), then 8+[5+6]+9 (iiii 18-45), and finally 2+(2+3):2+(3+2):2+2. Precedents for numerical construction appear in Theocritus, *Idd*.i, ii, iii, iiii, v, and viii: see VS 1967.495-497, and n. 6.22 below.

and high, come elements from the tradition of Hesiod and the other than bucolic modes of Hesiodic *epos*: cosmic cycle, Justice leaving human society, theogony (4-10). But against this generic identity stands the important specific difference that here the Hesiodic view of the decline of civilization from the beginning has been reversed on grounds of new historical belief: Justice returns, a new line descends from heaven. Among the poets who continued the tradition of Hesiodic pessimism, Virgil seems to have two of his Latin predecessors particularly in mind: Lucretius, who denied the possibility of renewal for this world, and Catullus, who gloomily saw the violence and passion of the heroic age as preface to moral decline to his own iron present. [73] Catullus imagined Apollo and Diana standing aloof from the wedding of Achilles' parents in the midst of the old heroic age; Virgil imagines them as presiding at the birth of his new hero. [74]

---

[73] Lucretius, ii 1153-1154, specifically denies that life on earth may derive from heaven, thus criticizing the Stoic allegory based on Homer, *Il.* 8.19, as Büchner 1955.1197, 8-12 observed; and in general Lucretius denies both divine intervention and that any particular world can renew itself or halt its natural course from growth to decay. Against this naturalistic and philosophical pessimism, Virgil sets historical optimism, with return, transformation, and a new political deity against Lucretius' philosophical hero-god (cf. n. 5.49 above).

Catullus, *C.* 64: short *epos* organized as etiology of unjust (iron age) present; treats heroic age as single causal chain of violent desire from Argo to Achilles (read *prima*, 64,11, as signal of *aition*), hence heroic past is viewed as containing the seeds of decline to the present. In poetics, this structure synthesizes major typologies of *epos* (*Argonautica* + *Iliad* + Hesiodic myth of decline) recapitulating history of the genre; Virgil, by incorporating and reversing such a structure, gains theoretical purchase on the whole genre : cf. Schmidt 1972.165, n. 174; VS 1968.508-09; VS 1966.350.

[74] Catullus, *C.*64.298-302; E.iiii 8-10. The ancient compilers of Virgilian *furta* had already noted a relation between *C.*64 and E.iiii, in the refrain of the Parcae (*C.*64.327 etc. ~ E.iiii 46; cf. Macro-

The more historicizing vision of future change which follows (11-17) goes beyond the traditional material of the Hesiodic modes of *epos* into the realm of Roman history which had belonged especially in Roman tradition to the Homericizing *epos* of Ennius. Virgil imagines the boy, fully grown, as a hero mingling with gods and heroes, in what looks like a deliberate recovery of an ideal that Catullus imagined as lost. [75]

In the center of the eclogue, the first of the three stages of growth draws on materials which suggest the bucolic mode (18-25), while in the second stage, both the natural miracles (26-30) and the remnants of old civilization (31-33) recall the other modes of Hesiodic *epos*. Then the brief, artfully contrived and pointed vignette of the violent age of heroes — 'Argo' to 'Achilles' (34-36) — recalls in both style and programmatic compression of the heroic idea the example of Catullus, which has already been important earlier in the eclogue. Virgil, continuing his critique and reversal of Catullus, imagines passage in time back from the iron age through the old, violent heroic age toward the full golden age when the new hero — the 'boy' fullgrown — will supplant the heroic example of a dreadful, violent Achilles. [76] The failure by the critics to attend to the divisions and progressive unfolding of Virgil's design, with its

---

bius, *Sat.* 6.1.41); and modern critics have often discussed the relation, e.g. E. K. Rand, "Catullus and the Augustans," *HSCP* 17 (1906) 21; Büchner 1955.1206; VS 1966.350; Putnam 1969.157-158; and Schmidt 1972.164-165. In certain details of style, E.iiii is much closer to Catullus, *C.*64 than to other eclogues: see Duckworth 1969.50-51 on dactyl-spondee texture, and VS 1968.506. Catullus by asserting that Apollo shunned Peleus' wedding corrects Il.24.56-63.

[75] Catullus, 64.384-408.

[76] Berg 1974.158-161 mistakenly equates Catullus' image of the heroic age with Virgil's new conception of the golden age. But the point of Virgil's *aemulatio* consists in reversing the Catullan-Hesiodic model of decline and in projecting a new heroism and golden-age hero-god superior to Achilles. In E.iiii 34-36, Virgil recalls Catullus'

reversal of Catullus, has made this passage unnecessarily an aporia of recent interpretation. With the vignette of old-fashioned heroism, Virgil exhausts the materials of both the Hesiodic and now also the Homericizing modes of *epos*, so that in the third stage he is called upon to imagine something new. This turns out to be partly negation of iron age elements which recall Hesiodic epic subjects and partly transformation of bucolic materials. [77]

The ensuing claim that the Parcae have authorized generations 'such as these' (46-47) echoes Catullus once again. The verbal similarity underlines the ideological reversal. Virgil's new heroic idea is not like the violent heroism of Achilles which Catullus imagined as a prelude to

conception of the heroic age, and the alliterative patterning of *C*.64.1-11:

alter . . .Tiphys// . . . Argo	iiii 34
. . . heroas// . . . altera bella	35
atque . . . Troiam// . . . Achilles	36

a scheme of the heroic age, conceived as running from Argo to Achilles; cf. the patterning of Catullus. *C* . . .//*A* . . .*P*, *A* . . .//*C* . . . *P*, *A* . . .//*C* . . .*P*, and *C* . . .//*A* . . .*P*, at 64.4-7; and Ap. Rhod. *Arg*. 1.1-4, *Archo* . . . *Argo*.

For a different estimate of Virgil's treatment of the return of the heroic age, see Putnam 1969.151-152 and Klingner 1967.80-82. Perret 1970.ad loc., however, sees retracing the Catullan steps of decline. Schmidt 1972.163-164 effectively answers recent critics of iiii 31-36. Coleman 1977.139-140 rightly underlines *temptare Thetin* (32) as a hint of violation that anticipates the themes of 34-36.

[77] E.iiii 37-45. Here note the key expression, *uirum te* (37), i.e. the *puer* imagined as having grown into a full hero, beyond and above *Achilles* (36). Cf. Schmidt 1972.164. In this full golden age, traces of Promethean civilization such as sea-faring, agriculture (iiii 30-33) would cease (iiii 38-41), or rather become functions of a willing and productive nature: *omnis feret omnia tellus* (iiii 39; cf. iii 55-57, 60-61, *omnis*, *omnia*); *sponte sua* (iiii 45; cf. E.iiii 21, 23; E.i 38-39; Lucretius, i 250-254, spring, and ii 1150-1159, the original fecundity of the world). Berg loc. cit. (n. 5.76) mistakenly sees iiii 34-36 as the climax of development.

the decline of civilization into the iron age. [78] The very comparison of Virgil's language with 'fates' must also imply epic vision and ambition in poetics. These are confirmed by the claim of the child's divine origin: i.e. imagined as a hero, *magnum Iouis incrementum* (49), 'great scion of Jove'. [79] But in our study of the ideological implications of this whole linguistic climax, we passed over the section which follows, in which the poet gives his explicit estimate of the import of his language and ideas in poetics (53-59). He expresses his desire to tell *facta* (54), the 'deeds' of the child, which as conceived and imagined thus far would consist in miraculous growth, but which in terms of poetics imply heroic epic in the Homeric mode. As if, then, to spell out the full import of this ambition, Virgil goes on to say that such a song would defeat all the powers of previous poetry, such as Orpheus and Linus, with their divine parents Apollo and Calliope. [80] Since Orpheus stood first in the older and legendary lists of the poets of *epos*, he might be expected to be the climactic figure in a challenge to the tradition, sufficing to imply that the whole range of *epos* could be mastered and outstripped by a new Roman his-

[78] See nn. 5.73-75.

[79] For the echo of Theocritus, Id.vii 40, see note 134 above. E. Norden, *Die Geburt des Kindes* (Leipzig 1924) 129, calls iiii 49 "der kunstreichste der ganzen Ekloge", and in his *Aeneis Buch VI* (repr.[2] Stuttgart 1957) 443-446, he cites it as an example of the way poets relate metrical form to content, comparing also Catullus, *C.*64.274, *increbescunt*. One of only three spondaic endings in the *Bucolics*, 33 in all Virgil. In a work constructed in modules of seven, this is the 49th verse (7 x 7).

[80] On Orpheus and Linus as founders of *epos*, Schmidt 1972.166, n. 177. Calliopea, who serves princes (Hesiod, *Theog.* 79-80); whom Lucretius invoked as *callida Musa*, in a paronomastic Latin etymology of her name (vi 93-94); here perhaps the Greek etymology is implied (see n. 5.72 above, s.v. *NAMES*); it is explicit in Propertius, 3.3.38. She appears weeping for her son, Orpheus, in *A.P.* 7.8.6, Antipater of Sidon (10 Gow-Page), quoted by Schmidt 204.

torical and mythological epic conception. [81] Instead, however, the climax of Virgil's poetic boast proves to be a challenge to Pan: (iiii 58-59)

Pan etiam, Arcadia mecum si iudice certet,
Pan etiam Arcadia dicat se iudice uictum.

Pan even, though Arcadia judged, if he would try with me,
Pan, though even Arcadia judged, would tell his own defeat.

Here we find a slight shift of emphasis within an unchanging verbal framework—from 'even Pan' to 'even Arcadia'. This has the effect of placing Arcadian myth at the climax in poetics. Arcadia is imagined as the ultimate arbiter of poetry in the imaginary golden age. As a judge, it would confirm poetic growth after the other growth is done. But since the age has been conceived as the return of a distant, ideal past through the agency of the growing 'child', Arcadian myth, at the climax of the list of poetic powers, is also imagined as the oldest and first, and thus Arcady as the original locus of the *epos*. This recalls the myth of bucolic origins which was implicit in the first idyll (Pan was summoned from Arcadia by the dying cowherd, Daphnis, to reclaim the pipe which was Pan's invention), a myth also sketched fleetingly in the second eclogue. However, in this context, the bucolic mode not only is traced back to an Arcadian origin, but also is imagined as the original mode of *epos* itself, more authoritative even than the Orphic hymn. Victory over Pan thus comes to imply, in terms of poetics, a new beginning in the entire tradition of *epos*. It is interesting that the idea of victory, which has been carefully excluded and suppressed from Virgil's ideologically tendentious version of change in society, here returns to become the predominant idea in his model of poetic change; and interesting, too, that Virgil chooses to characterize his own

---

[81] For Orpheus in the tradition of *epos*, see notes 5.66, 70, and cf. Ap. Rhod. *Arg.*i 492-518, cited in n. 6.8 below.

new poetics as a return to the very oldest poetic state, formally 'as before' but with audacious innovation. [82]

Just as the ideological development of the second, third, and fourth eclogues carries the positive outline to totality, matching and indeed far surpassing the scope of Meliboeus' negative, so too the development in poetics would appear to have projected new 'songs' far greater than the 'songs' imagined as precluded for Meliboeus by Roman change (i 77). Perhaps, too, even as the new ideological outline seems likely to determine Virgil's subsequent ideology, so the new myth of the origin of *epos* may be expected to predispose development in Virgilian poetics, including the recurrence of Arcadian elements in successive work. [83]

B. *Recapitulation: Myth of the Tityran Bucolic Mode*

E.v 1-84—*Daphnis as Bucolic-Georgic Hero*: reverts to dramatic form. 'Menalcas' is shown asking 'Mopsus' why the two have not settled in the shady wood. 'Mopsus' in turn proposes a 'dell'. He sings a freshly written song of Daphnis dead and mourned. 'Menalcas' replies with a famous old song of Daphnis deified and functioning as a rural god. Then with mutual esteem they exchange gifts. [84]

Not only the dramatic form, but also details of place

---

[82] It may be useful to compare Virgil's own model of change here with the conceptions of tradition which critics bring to him (cf. nn. 5.72, 60, 52, and 4.8); his *aemulatio* is explicit and ambitious, in theory comprising everything.

[83] For subsequent use of Arcadian material, see notes 6.43, 45. Schmidt 1972.164-172, sees in E.iiii Virgil's promise of an epic to come, and not in the manner of the epigonoi but with the seal of Homer himself: an astonishing step in the development of Roman poetry.

[84] (a) *NAMES. MENALCAS*. See n. 5.65.

MOPSUS. According to Wendel 1900.46-47, mention of Mopsus makes an evident allusion to the translation by Cornelius Gallus of Euphorion's poem on the Grynean grove, since a Mopsus defeated and the name Menalcas recall the third eclogue, as we have seen (v 1-3: iii 55). Yet the singers move from the shade, which is criticized as 'shifting' (5), to an *antrum*, 'dell' — a term which recalls the lost ideal pastoral locus in the background of Meliboeus (i 75). We are not, then, still simply in the foreground of Tityrus' bucolic.

After 'Menalcas' proposes poetic subjects which sound like a generic simplification of the first three eclogues, 'Mopsus' promises something freshly written down. Both

the seer Calchas there; cf. Servius on E.vi 72: "Gryneum nemus ... in quo luco aliquando Calchas et Mopsus dicuntur de peritia divinandi inter se habuisse certamen: et cum de pomorum arboris cuiusdam contenderent numero, stetit gloria Mopso; cuius rei dolore Calchas interiit. hoc autem Euphorionis continent carmina, quae Gallus transtulit in sermonem latinum." Hesiod, too, wrote of Mopsus defeating Calchas, fr. 278 Merkelbach-West. In E.v 88-90, Mopsus appears endowed with the staff of a seer-poet, recalling the Muses' gift of a staff and powers of seeing to Hesiod in *Theog.* 32, 38. These associations may be significant, in view of the relations between Mopsus' song and the vatic poetry of E.iiii (see notes 5.85, 86 below), which also has strong Hesiodic associations.

AMYNTAS (v 8, 15, 18). Theocritus, Id.vii 2, 132. Gow II.132, cites its Macedonian associations (and Amyntas I was an ancestor of Ptolemy, Gow II.331). Etymology: *amun* + *tes*, 'defender' or 'avenger', hence another aristocratic name fallen into bucolic use (cf. n. 5.65 above, s.v. *NAMES*). In the *Bucolics*, it has been used for the generic types of feckless competitor (ii 35, 39) and boy love (iii 66, 74, 84).

DAPHNIS. Theocritus, Id.i, vi, and earlier Sicilian tradition, for which see Gow II.1-2; (Theocritus), Id. viii, viiii; E.ii 26, iii 12. Name associated with *daphne*, 'laurel'.

OTHERS: *AEGON* (72), *LYCTIUS*, cf. iii 2; *ALCON* (11), generic subject; *ALPHESIBOEUS* (73), cf. n. 6.71; *ANTIGENES* (89), Id.vii 4; *CODRUS* (11), generic subject, cf. *nomina regum*, iii 106; *DAMOETAS* (72), cf. iii 1, ii 37; *PHYLLIS* (10), generic subject, cf. E.iii 76 etc. and n. 6.81; *STIMICHON* (55); and the quoted Corydon, Alexis, Meliboeus (86-87, cf. E.ii 1, iii 1).

(b) *SELECTED PRECEDENTS*. Bucolic dialogue framing songs and closing with an exchange of gifts in mutual esteem ~ Id.vi, cf. also Id.vii and Id.viii 4; first song, the lament for Daphnis after

this newness and writing, scratched on beech bark, are jarring and seem to imply recent imposition on the bucolic mode. [85] Mopsus' song of the mourning echoes and negates terms of the utopian bucolic and georgic order of the fourth eclogue. With respect to tradition, it recalls the post-Theocritean bucolic lament but integrates it into a generic typology as a sequel to the first idyll, which told of Daphnis' dying. [86] In turn, Menalcas' song draws on positive terms of both the first and the fourth eclogues, as we have seen, echoing such key themes of the Tityran outline as 'ease', new divine benefaction, natural rejoicing, and poetry in powerful rapport with nature. [87] For an image of joyous celebration in a stable bucolic-georgic order, the song also draws on the seventh idyll, as noted above. The function in

his death ~ in Theocritus we only find Daphnis dying, e.g. Id.i 64-145, vii 72-77, while the lament for a dead hero-poet is post Theocritean, e.g. *Epitaph. Bion.*, *Epitaph. Adon.*; second song, apotheosis and cult ~ cf. the festival of Lycidas, Id.vii 63-72.

(c) *STRUCTURE.* $19+25+11+25+10$. In the first 19 lines, the deliberate shift of locus from 'shade' to *antrum*, 'dell', cf. E.i 75, and a Greek word, Schmidt 1972.257. The second song is a climax: see remarks by Putnam 1969.181 on Menalcas' terms, *tollemus, ad astra feremus.*

[85] Observes Putnam 1969.170 aptly: "We are concerned with a contrast within the bounds of song, between simple, common themes that an Amyntas might sing (and a Menalcas at first suggest) and the grander subject that Menalcas senses Mopsus will utter, however hesitant his introduction." In Mopsus' language, *fagi* suggests generic material (E.i, ii, iii in the book: see n. 2.21) and *nuper* implies a fresh imposition (cf. *nuper*, iii 2), thus something beyond the Theocritean-Tityran range: what comes out is a reaction (*alterna*) to E.iiii in the form of post-Theocritean lament. On writing, see n. 5.59 and Callimachus, fr. 73 Pf.

[86] Putnam 1969.173-178 compares Mopsus' song and E.iiii; Schmidt 1972.204 suggests that Daphnis is drawn as an Orpheus figure; he compares *Epitaph. Bion.* 18 which calls the dead bucolic poet *dorios Orpheus.*

[87] Cf. n. 3.7.

poetics of the two songs seems thus to include some kind of recapitulation of the first four pieces, the figure of Daphnis more ample than any of their bucolic figures, though less than the figure of the child in the fourth eclogue, from which it draws so much of its added force.

C. Modulation

E.v 85-90—*Exchanging Properties*: from the songs with the retrospective consolidation of the gains of the Tityran mode within the limits of a bucolicism generously drawn ('as before' but with good increase, as the mandate stood, i 45), we come again to the close of the fifth eclogue and the beginning of the new half-book. The close now falls into place as a signal that looking back and reinterpreting within the book itself have become the means of going ahead; and the reflective reader gets 'Menalcas' as a guide to unity in the first half. [88]

At the same time, the pause to gather impressions, sort them out, and recompose also inaugurates the second half of the eclogue book. In our preoccupation with the past we must not forget the dramatic fiction of the exchange of gifts. Menalcas, the elder—imaginative product of development—yields the instrument of accomplished design: *hac cicuta* (v 85), 'this hemlock', a metonomy of matter standing for an imaginary object and synechdoche of one stalk standing for a whole syrinx. Such figurative language presupposes not a natural situation but the language of the poetic aition at the center of the second eclogue, *disparibus septem compacta cicutis / fistula* (ii 36-37), 'pipe put together with seven unequal hemlocks'. That was Corydon's prize possession in the dramatic fiction. Here the matter is mentioned abstractly, allusively, as a sign of order in the book: sameness against which to measure development

[88] Cf. n. 3.6.

(*haec eadem*, but Menalcas *maior,* E.v 4, 87), hence a function of design above and beyond the imagined consciousness of this or that persona. [89]

On the other hand Mopsus, the younger and more aggressive, with his Hesiodic and vatic associations, gives a staff worthy to be a love gift, *formosum* (v 90), 'comely' like the objects of love and favoring season in the previous pieces (i 5; ii 1, cf. v 86; iii 55), and bringing to mind, perhaps, the gift of the rabbit stick (Id. vii) or of the staff of prophetic song to Hesiod. [90]

We first hear of these properties only in the process of the exchange. What the new combination implies for poetics for the second half book remains to be inferred: a Menalcas with such a staff? A Mopsus with such a pipe? Staff perhaps for wandering, displacement as well as authoritative utterance? Pipe for continued but ever more energetic evocation and return? Or pen? Mopsus, who scratched new songs on the generic beech (v 14): in the fifth eclogue, like Tityrus in the first, Mopsus has the last word, may be expected to presage the immediate sequel in design.

---

[89] Cf. nn. 1.7, 8; 2.10, 12, 47; 3.6.
[90] VS 1970b.904-915, and n. 5.84, s.v. *MOPSUS.* Coleman 1977. 171 forgets that Hesiod stood behind Id.vii, and he wrongly evokes "Arcady" here: cf. n. 2.46.

Chapter 6

FROM DESIGN TO REALIZATION:
RETURN TO THE ORIGINS OF *EPOS*

Daphnis learned music from Pan, a scholiast tells us. [1] Pan was first who did not let the reeds lie artless. [2] The ultimate challenge for 'Sicilian Muses', the poet's vaunt in the total new design for *epos*, is the match in Arcadia with Pan. [3] Virgil does not dissimulate his ambition to be *maior inuentore*. He would make a new version of what he conceives to be the original mode of *epos*. [4] The problem, then, for the rest of the eclogue book is to get from the ebullient Tityran to an appropriately Arcadian bucolic, transforming the mode yet further in a show of return to the source.

A. *From Tityran toward Arcadian Myth (E.vi + / —vii + / — viii + / —viiii)*

Daphnis is the first obstacle. The image in the fifth eclogue draws on the amplified bucolic-georgic themes of the first and fourth pieces. [5] The ideological message remains implicit in the unprecedented rural god. Political allegory would have been patent to contemporaries, attuned by custom and necessity, [6] however much it escapes some

---

[1] Servius Auctus ad E.v 20.
[2] E.viii 24: "Panaque qui primus calamos non passus inertis."
[3] E.iiii 58-59, cf. nn. 5.81, 82, 83.
[4] Ibid. and for the idea of pastoral as the original form of civilization, succeeded later by farming, Varro, *de re rust.* 1.11.16; Donatus cited by Servius 3.28-4.1.
[5] Cf. nn. 1.6, 3.7.
[6] Cf. nn. 2.15, 16, 17; 4.14; 5.2.

scholars in their stalls. The myth of the first half-book is grounded in Roman history and ideology, fit and needed to reappraise the whole tradition of *epos* including its heroic mode, but overblown and in fine distracting for the purpose of remaking the bucolic. To be sure, in the theoretical design for *epos*, the heroic and Roman came first (*facta*, iiii 54); but the imagined origin precedes in realization; hence momentarily commitment to the upper modes must be suspended. As a consequence, in the second half-book, we may expect something like a reversal of the process of amplification that brought Daphnis to his egregious height. The figure of the hero of the Tityran mode will have to diminish step-by-step in a critique of the ambitions that made it swell. Finally, no doubt, it will have to vanish with the last vestiges of the Tityran mode. Pure Arcadian myth would have no place for the Sicilian pupil of Pan. A successful return to origins, Virgil's aim, would make Theocritus look like a belated entry who settled for a secondary hero. [7]

1. E.vi—*Sketch for a New Middle* Epos (*Without Rome*): again narrative form. The story begins with the personal revelations of a narrator-singer called by Apollo 'Tityre', who first sketches his own past ups and downs in poetry as the back-drop and justification for his present project, which is the report of an encounter in a 'dell', where (he says) miscellaneous sylvan figures provoked a wine-soaked Silenus to sing a song that proved so vast that only evening could bring it to a close. The narrator in fact seems to remember only bits and snatches of the

---

[7] The concept of "belatedness" is crucial in the view of the relations between "strong poets" taken by Harold Bloom, *Wallace Stevens: The Poems of our Climate* (Ithaca 1977), discussed by Frank Kermode, *New York Times Book Review* (June 12, 1977) 9, 44, who quotes: "What is pleasure for a strong poet, ultimately, if it is not the pleasure of priority in one's own invention?"

song himself, and proves to be an arbitrary and highly personal teller, whose report gives disproportionate emphasis to a few peripheral (some scandalous) subjects while skimming over highly significant moments in human civilization. [8]

The narrator's brief confession-program has caused much controversy and deals explicitly with poetics: (vi 1-12)

T:		
	prima Syracosio dignata est ludere uersu	1
	nostra neque erubuit siluas habitare Thalea;	2
	cum canerem reges et proelia, Cynthius aurem	3
	uellit et admonuit 'Pastorem, Tityre, pinguis	4
	pascere oportet ouis, deductum dicere carmen';	5
	nunc ego (namque super tibi erunt qui dicere laudes,	6
	Vare, tuas cupiant et tristia condere bella)	7
	agrestem tenui meditabor harundine musam:	8
	non iniussa cano; si quis tamen haec quoque, si quis	9

[8] (a) *NAMES. THALEA* (2). A muse, Hesiod, *Theog.* 77 (cf. *en thalies*, 65), and a grace, idem 909. With Virgil's *nostra ... Thalea* compare Theocritus, Id.xvi 6, 'our graces', i.e., his poetry; and for possible associations with Callimachus, Schmidt 1972.244-246. Cf. *thalysia*, Id.vii 3.

TITYRUS (4). For Dionysiac associations, which acquire particular relevance in this piece, see n. 6.43, s.v. *NAMES*. In the interim, the name Tityrus has three times been used for a goatherd in the foreground, subordinate to the singers (iii 20, 96; v 12; cf. the similar Tityrus, Id.iii 1-5), thus the amplified figure of E.i (shepherd, cowherd) has been left in abeyance. But the Tityrus of E.vi is related to E.i, not only by echoes of poetics (vi 1-2, 8) but also by shepherding (vi 4) in a reduction of the figure from association with the highest register of bucolic material, but in renewed association with the middle register (cf. nn. 6.10, 13, 14, 52).

VARUS (7-12). Virgil makes so much of this as a *nomen* pleasing to Apollo, that irony might almost be expected: 'bent, crooked; stretched; diverse'. *Nomina praescripta: libro* (Gell. 11.16.7); *consulum monimentis* (Tac., *Ann.* 3.57, cf. H.3.13); *perscripta* as authorities *senatus consulto* (Caesar, B.C. I 5.4, 6.5; Cicero, *fam.* 8.8.5-8).

MNASYLLUS (13). Wendel 1900.50 notes its appropriateness to its dramatic role. Otherwise, the figure is merely generic rustic.

AEGLE (20). 'Fetter' or 'gleam', cf. Amaryllis (above n. 6.43.a)

captus amore leget, te nostrae, Vare, myricae,   10
te nemus omne canet; nec Phoebo gratior ulla est   11
quam sibi quae Vari praescripsit pagina nomen.   12

T: First in Syracusan verse she deigned to play   1
    and our own Thalia did not blush to dwell in woods.   2
    When I sang kings and combats, Cynthius plucked   3
    my ear and warned, "A grazer, Tityrus, it behooves   4
    'fat' to graze sheep, 'fine-drawn' to tell song."   5
    Now I (for you'll have a surfeit, Varus, who'll
                                                    desire   6
    to tell your praise and set down gloomy wars)   7

and Galatea: and note Virgil's emphasis on seeing as erotic-poetic
stimulus, E.vi 21.

SILENUS (14). Perhaps *lenos,* 'wine vat', cf. vi 15, "inflatum
hesterno uenas ut semper Iaccho."

SCYLLA (74). Etymologized by Callimachus, fr. 288 Pf., from
skyllein, since she pulled her father's hair (Pfeiffer ad loc. refers to
fr. 231 for other etymologies in Callimachus). Virgil implies this
etymology with *uexasse* (76), but also hints at *skylakes* with *latran-
tibus* and *canibus.*

(b) *SELECTED PRECEDENTS.* A narrator discusses poetics in
a preface, then tells of a song sung by some more-than-human
figure ~ Theocritus, Id.xi; Callimachus, *Aitia* (prologue, then songs
by Muses); cf. also Hesiod, *Theogony,* where the proem (1-115) ends
with the invocation to the Muses to begin speaking, and the follow-
ing line might almost be taken as their reply. A. La Penna, "Esiodo
nella cultura e nella poesia di Virgilio" *Hésiode et son influence*
(Fondation Hardt VII 1960) 218 sees Hesiod and the Hesiodic
apocrypha as the principal source for the work, following Ribbeck,
Römische Dichtung II².28, and giving exhaustive examples. He also
discusses the other modern theories. For evidence of Alexandrian
intermediaries in the tradition, see nn. 6.10, 14, 15, 22, 24.

(c) *STRUCTURE.* 5+3+4: 14, 55: 5. Recent texts wrongly
begin a paragraph at vi 31, *namque canebat* .... But Virgil ex-
pressly signals the beginning of Silenus' song with *incipit ipse*
(vi 26, cf. F. Skutsch, *Gallus und Vergil,* Leipzig 1906, 131 cited
by Schmidt 256, n. 165). Thus indent at vi 27, *tum uero* ..., rather
than in vi 31, and place semi-colon after *Orphea,* vi 30. In the
account of the song, the most general language comes first (vi 31-40)
followed by particular cases.

will work to make a country Muse with slender
                               reed: 8
what's forbidden I don't sing. Yet if someone reads
                          these, too,   9
if someone, caught by love, you our tamarisks, Varus,   10
you all a grove will sing. Nor to Phoebus is any page
                        more graced   11
than one that's graved its very top with Varus' name.   12

The narrator shows a strong sense of temporal and stylistic distinctions. He spells out three moments in his poetic career — 'first' (1-2), 'when' (3-5), and 'now' (6-8) — and associates each with a different kind of poetics: first had been simple bucolic play in woods, with a suggestion of love and light verse; then was an attempt at heroic song, but repressed by Apollo; so now a program of work in slight style on country art. This third moment seems to fall between the stylistic extremes of the first two, for it is less than heroic song, and yet more than just a relapse to simple bucolic dalliance (e.g. 'work', 8, not 'play', 1). What precisely it is, and how different from the first moment, remains to be seen.

The dramatic fiction of a *biographia litteraria* implies in poetics a continuation of the retrospective summary which began with the end of the fifth eclogue. [9] Verbal echoes confirm this. 'Play' here (vi 1) recalls the ideal poetics of Tityrus (i 10). 'Syracusan' even more specifically than 'Sicilian' (iiii 1) implies a Theocritean bucolic mode. Deigning to 'dwell in woods' recalls Corydon's attempt to attract Alexis from the background to dwell in a humble habitat (ii 29) while woods are the generic locus of the first three pieces (e.g. i 5), and an established symbol for simple bucolic (iiii 3). It looks as if the bucolic

---

[9] Soubiran 1972.44: "Comme une conclusion, les rappels de II, 1 et III, 1 en V, 86 sq. et, au début de *B*.VI, le prologue de style callimachéen qui lui aussi évoque des églogues antérieures"; cf. VS 1967.504; Galinsky 1965 (1968) 177.

foreground of the first half-book were being summed up
and reduced to its simplest, most generic terms for the
sake of contrast with the background, which here is char-
acterized by generic terms for high style — 'kings and
combats' — which in turn exaggerate the content of the
background in the first half-book. Between these genericized
and overdrawn extremes, then, we find the poetic project
expressed in different terms: not 'woods' but 'country
(fields)', not 'play' but 'work'; in other words, something
other than a simple, sylvan bucolic and which may in
retrospect be associated with the material of the middle
ground of the first half-book, with the georgic and the
short epic subjects of the remaining Hesiodic modes of
epos. [10]

We have seen, however, that the narrator along with
this sense of distinct subjects (and styles) has been en-
dowed with a strong sense of sequence through time
— 'first', 'when', and 'now' — and this implies not merely

[10] In forming this middle poetic program, Virgil has recombined
elements of the two initial, differentiated accounts of Tityrus' bucolic
mode (E.i 2/10), and has altered the force of the terms not only
by repetition and permutation but by assigning them to different
moments of a marked temporal sequence, where before they were
simultaneous alternatives in the imagination (perhaps complementary
ideas of poetic art):

E.i 2, M: siluestrem tenui musam meditaris auena (abAvB)

10, T: ludere quae uellem calamo permisit agresti

E.vi 1, 2, T: . . . ludere . . ./ . . . siluas

E.vi 8, T: agrestem tenui meditabor harundine musam (abvBA)

In E.i 2, *siluestrem . . . musam* was Meliboeus' term for Tityrus' art,
and it seemed positive enough by contrast with exile and loss of
song; yet it also was an allusion to Lucretius' critique of the bucolic
mode as echoic fiction (see n. 5.48 above). That allusion now is
recalled and its irony reinforced by allusion to Lucretius' image of
an idyllic, natural music (v 1398, *agrestis . . . musa*). In the concept

a static over-view of the three registers or subject areas of the first half-book but also a linear view of the development of the book. We saw something comparable at the beginning of the fourth eclogue, which summarized the three preceding works as simple, sylvan bucolic by contrast with 'consular' poetic growth; and the close of the fifth eclogue has just remembered two earlier pieces in their order in the book. 'First play', then, will refer to the first three pieces. The show of heroic song must refer to the fourth eclogue, and Apollo's severe reaction, imposing a canon of stylistic limitation, will reflect the withdrawal from the heroic-historical background which took place in the fifth piece.

Much more should be said about the dramatic fiction and its import for poetics: Apollo's warning in the form of a Roman gesture; [11] the artful dodging of responsibility for the background (which is represented now conveniently

of *siluestris musa*, man imposes art on nature (*doces*, E.i 5); while nature taught man the *agrestis musa* (Lucr. v 1382-1383, *zephyri . . . agrestis docuere*). The former idea of poetics was particularly appropriate to the first half-book, which constructed an ideological and poetic myth, imposing it; the latter may be more appropriate to the second half-book, which seems driven and preoccupied by love. Note, incidentally, that the tenuous Latin coinage, *auena* (i 2), disappears, so too the Greek *calamo*, replaced by Latin *harundine*, which is well established (unlike *auena*) as a serviceable material in divers crafts. Word order in E.vi 8 takes a rarer, more symmetrical pattern (cf. n. 5.59 above). *Tenui* is a constant: we are still dealing with slight, i.e. Hesiodic, style, which now seems to be conceived as having two modes within it, one (*ludere*, *siluas*) prior and less than the other: cf. VS 1977a.107-108; VS 1976-1977.331.

[11] Arnaldi 1938.46: "*Vellit*: mi prese l'orecchio, mi tirò leggermente per l'orecchio, ch'era pei Romani un modo simbolico, comunemente accettato, di ricordare o consacrare (è il caso di Orazio, *Sat.* I, 9, 77, dove l'avversario del suo seccatore se l'accaparra per testimonio, toccandogli appunto l'orecchio) un impegno." The pointed alliteration, then, and etymological force of *pastorem . . . pinguis pascere* (4-5) not only "bucolicize" Callimachus' *thyos . . . hoti pachi-*

by no 'boy' or 'god' but only by his agent, Varus) just after assiduous courtship of the background in the first through the fourth eclogues. The very recurrence of 'Tityrus' must have considerable import for poetics. The figure which linked background and foreground in the first Bucolic, receiving the divine commands that initiated the ambitious poetics of the first half-book,[12] and then recurred as a simple part of the bucolic foreground,[13] here returns at the beginning of the second half-book and again reports having received divine orders; only that this new *responsum* reverses the expansive implications of the first. Virgil thus gives us a second causal myth modifying the import of the first and appropriate to a different moment in the eclogue book. The stylistic expansion of the first four pieces has been accomplished; the fifth eclogue has already withdrawn from the background and matter of high style, though drawing on the language and energetic scope. Here renunciation of the historical and heroic background — high style and Roman matter — becomes explicit. The god's command allows for some expansiveness still in bucolic material (in fact we are still to see the growth of the Arcadian image in the book) but imposes a definite withdrawal from stylistic ambition like that of the bucolic mode of Tityrus (we can also expect to see a progressive critique of poetic ambition).

A good deal has been made of the generic resemblance between the story of Apollo's intervention here and in the

ston, but also recall the image of Hesiod shepherding on Helicon (*Theog.* 23), cf. the echo of Hesiod's initiation also at E.i 44-45.

[12] Cf. nn. 4.5, 28; 6.51.

[13] Flintoff 1976.19 suggests that 'Tityrus' is addressed in terms appropriate to a slave at E.iii 20, v 12, viiii 23 (subordinated to Menalcas, an owner); the figure was given a slave's history in E.i (cf. nn. 2.9, 4.27). As a figure closely linked with generic tradition, 'Tityrus' might well be subordinated to the figure of continuity and development in the book, Menalcas. Cf. n. 6.8, s.v. Tityrus.

prologue to Callimachus' *Aitia*, but the specific differences
have been neglected, above all the fact that Virgil uses
the myth to begin the second half of his book, as a counter
to the poetics of the first half. [14] Also, Callimachus imag-
ined Apollo giving courteous advice to Callimachus himself
at the very start. Virgil has Apollo admonish a fictional
persona shown as already practiced in verse. [15] Moreover,
Callimachus distinguishes between two alternatives, the
slight and the great, with Hesiod and Homer as the
exemplary figures; [16] but Virgil in the biography of 'Tityrus',
and recollecting his own practice in the book, presents the
three alternatives we have seen: simple, which he associates
with Theocritus; [17] grand, which conventionally he associates
with heroic song; and between these two extremes the
middle that he calls 'country muse' and associates, through the
figure of Apollo's advice but to a shepherd, with both
Callimachus and Hesiod. [18] What we are seeing is the
articulation in *epos* of *tripertita uarietas*, replacing the Cal-
limachean duality, confirming the evidence for distinction

[14] Cf. nn. 4.6, 8. Schmidt 1972.251 reads the Callimachean echo
as a program for all the eclogue book (E.i 1-10 are mere description);
cf. similar views in Clausen 1964.195, Elder 1961.120-21, Otis 1964.
33-34. But in the context of the eclogue book, this poetic *aition*
modifies that of E.i 45, still *pasco*, but sheep not cattle, fullness,
but instead of an imperative to expand ('breed' or 'raise' bulls) a
restriction on song. Cf. nn. 4.5, 8 on the principles of interpretation
here, and for the import of the reduction to 'sheep', n. 6.8a, s.v.
Tityrus, and n. 6.52 below.

[15] Schmidt 1972.251 notes that Apollo intervened *protiston* in
Callimachus' *aition*, only at a second moment in that of 'Tityrus'.
Prima (E.vi 1) signals a beginning in the book in the bucolic mode,
followed by *maiora*, then a strategic retreat to the intermediate
register. In E.i, the 'god' is imagined intervening at the end of
a long career; Id.vii, Lycidas confirms youthful accomplishment;
Theogony, the Muses *protiston*; cf. nn. 5.30, 31.

[16] Cf. n. 5.7.

[17] Bucolic *epos*: cf. nn. 5.26, 27.

[18] And Lucretius: cf. nn. 5.3, 4, 33, and 6.10.

between modes in the preceding pieces, pointing to Virgil's
later work. [19] But enough theory, seems to say the narrator:
pergite Pierides (vi 13), 'Hesiodic-Callimachean Muses, get
along with the work!' [20]

One would like to dwell on the details of the ensuing
dramatic fiction, for they are rich in hints of a retrospective
poetics of the book: not only the implication that love,
not Rome, will be the principal issue from now on, but
especially the picture of Silenus — the old Bacchic singer,
his binge just over, sprawled in his 'dell', wine still in

[19] For the original sequence, slight/great: middle, see nn. 5.3, 4,
33. In E.vi 1-8, the poetry of Tityrus is imagined as passing from
humble start to high reach (both past), and then to something also
low (*tenui*) but "more" than the first category. Cf. E.iiii 1-7, where
we find the stylistic succession low (Sicilian), high (*consul*), middle
(Hesiodic-Lucretian elements). If we accept this theoretical structure,
and its relation to the system of images of foreground, middle ground,
and background in E.i-v, we can hardly agree with the ancient
scholiasts and such recent critics as Schmidt 1972.239 who take
prima (vi 1) as Virgil's claim to have been first with bucolic in
Latin: that reading wrenches *prima* out of the temporal-stylistic
sequence, *prima . . . cum . . . nunc*. Schmidt himself, in a useful cri-
tique of recent work on E.vi (pp. 261-281), argues that Virgil is
dealing with a "poetic space" that falls between the heroic epic
(excluded, vi 3-12) and erotic elegy (left behind, vi 64-65). From
this analysis it would seem natural to pass to the view that Virgil
himself divided the area of Alexandrian slight style (Hesiodic:
Theocritean, Callimachean) into low and middle, a division only
implicit in Id.vii (or the *Aitia + Iambs*) and one that he applies
both to his own work (E.vi 1-2/6-8) and to that of Gallus (vi 64-73):
cf. VS 1976-1977.332.

[20] *Pierides*: Hesiod, *Erga* 1, *Theog.* 53; Lucr. iiii 1-25, n.b. *pergo*
(7); but also Theocr. Id.xi 3, E.iii 85 (from the "Orphic" Damoetas
for Pollio: *uitulam lectori pascite uestro*, in juxtaposition of the
prize of E.iii with the *consul* addressed in E.iiii; cf. Damoetas' *ab
Ioue principium Musae*, iii 60). Leach 1975.260 does not distinguish
between *Sicelides Musae* (iiii 1), told that the bucolic (Theocritean)
mode does not suit 'all', and *Pierides*, told to get on with the
'country muse' (sc. the Hesiodic-Callimachean mode of *epos* just ar-
ticulated).

his veins; and the problem, how to extract song from such a case; the etymological appropriateness of the conspirators who wake him and draw him out ('Loud Noise'?, 'Reminder', 'Gleam'); then the song itself, which is imagined as so impressive and immense that the narrator makes no attempt even to report its first words, but instead amplifies by describing the dynamic effects of the *incipit* on nature, with an implicit challenge to Apollo and Orpheus (29-30); and only then offers a summary of the matter, dwelling especially on selected parts which appear to strike him most (31-81), although clearly at a loss to remember and quote directly more than a few choice snatches (47-60, 69-73). [21] The challenge to Apollo and Orpheus recalls the boast of the fourth eclogue that the song of the growth of the 'boy' would defeat them (iiii 55-57), and implies in poetics that the 'song' of Silenus is conceived as a replay of the scope and energy of the fourth (though without the historical and heroic background). In other words, we have a natural history imagined apart from the idea of Roman destiny — 'fates' (iiii 47). The sketch of song draws language of natural growth and development from the fourth eclogue, Apollonius, and Lucretius in an articulated and eclectic account of cosmic generation. [22] But

---

[21] The practice of summarizing briefly the contents of a song while praising its miraculous effects has a precedent in the proem to the *Theogony*, e.g. 36-52, 69-71, where Olympus and the dwellings of the gods echo the Muses, earth cries out around, and a lovely sound arises from their feet. The convention serves to suggest an idea of perfect and all-encompassing language; cf. Plato's distinction between the high style of divine discourse and low style of human discourse, *Phaedrus* 246a 4-6, and n. 6.22 below, for parallels in Theocritus and Apollonius.

[22] Compare *omnia* (vi 33 ~ iiii 39, 52), *mundi* (vi 34 ~ iiii 9, 50), *concreuerit* (vi 34 ~ *incrementum*, iiii 49), *paulatim* (vi 36 ~ iiii 28, cf. iiii 1; a typically Lucretian word), *siluae primum surgere* (vi 39 ~ iiii 3, 8, 9); also contrast *ignaros* (vi 40) with *nec discet mentiri* (iiii 42). The report of Silenus' singing has a formal parallel

the ensuing account of human civilization shows life ruled for the most part by transforming passions, with stories or fragments which recall the varieties of learned and erotic *epos* as practiced by Catullus, Calvus, Callimachus, and Theocritus.[23] Passion also is shown as a locally positive force in the form of etiological poetry, recalling Apollonius,

in Ap. Rhod., *Arg.* 1.496-511, where Orpheus sings a cosmology to calm the quarrelsome Argonauts, and Theocritus, Id.vii 72-82, where Tityrus would sing to entertain Lycidas: see Schmidt 1972. 272; cf. the precedent of *Theog.* 108-112; Orpheus as founder of *epos*, n. 5.80; Lucretian coloring in the passage, Perret 1970.70-71, and Schmidt 1972.267-68, warning rightly that Lucretian language and Epicurean philosophy are not the same thing.

[23] E.vi 41-42, told allusively, with epic *hysteron proteron*, flood mentioned before golden age (cf. iiii 6), punishment of Prometheus before crime (cf. iiii 31; Catullus, *C*.64.295, *extenuata gerens ueteris uestigia poenae*).

E.vi 43-44, Hylas, the subject of Ap. Rhod., *Arg.* 1.1207-1272, and Theocritus, Id.xiii; but Virgil fixes on the detail of the anguished outcry at loss, treats it in a way which recalls the emphasis given *Varus* (vi 9-12), and makes it a story of the origin of human utterance: 'Hyla Hyla', agitated and expressive rhythm; cf. the etymological associations with *hylao* (Greek), an animal's cry. Catullus, *C*.64, omitted this part of the Argonautic legend, but he did follow Apollonius in comparing the myths of the Argo and Crete (*Arg.* 3.997-1007, 1074-1076, 1105-1107); and Virgil passes from Argonaut Hylas to Cretan Pasiphaë. Here he alludes to Calvus' *Io, a uirgo infelix* (vi 47) — neoteric epyllion — and recalls Corydon's reflectiveness, *quae te dementia cepit* (vi 47, ii 69); then uses the myth of Proitus' daughters, an Arcadian legend drawn from Callimachus, *Artemis* (H. 3) 233-236, as a foil for Pasiphaë's lust. Then, at the emotional high point of the narrative (where 'Tityrus' is moved to quote directly from Silenus a direct outcry of Pasiphaë, vi 55-60), Virgil alludes to another etiology-etymology from the Artemis Hymn. He pictures Pasiphaë as a huntress, seeking to close in and capture the bull and evoking Cretan Nymphs, *Claudite Nymphae, Dictaeae Nymphae, nemorum iam claudite saltus*. Callimachus, shortly before the Proitus myth, had derived the Cretan names *Diktynna* and *diktaion* from *diktua*, 'nets' (H.3.190-200), those of fishermen who saved a fleeing, falling nymph. But nets

Callimachus, Gallus, Euphorion, Hesiod. [24] By and large, however, human passion appears unredeemed by any idea of historical growth or purpose. The pattern of degeneration in human society after an initial burst of natural generation recalls the Hesiodic idea of decline, which was reversed in the ideological myth of the fourth eclogue; as a result, the song of Silenus seems a deliberate reversion to something intellectually prior or aside from the ideological (historical-heroic) vision of the first half-book (an ironic reconstruction of a world 'as before' and without Rome). [25]

serve also in hunting (E.iii 75, v 60). Hence the learned point here of the desperate invocation to enclose and catch. Virgil also reinforces the outcry with an echo of Catullus' account of the consequences of Pasiphaë's craze (vi 58 ~ C.64.113); cf. his *aemulatio* of Catullus in E.iiii, nn. 5.73, 74, 76.

[24] Having confused traditional time sequence (vi 41-42, see n. 6.23), the narrative now uses marked temporal terms for material that had no temporal link in tradition (*tum*, 61, *tum*, 62, *tum* 64). First another Arcadian legend which also appeared in the Hymn to Artemis, though Callimachus mentioned Atalanta as virgin huntress (H.3.215-224) and Virgil focusses on an erotic detail (cf. Catullus, C.2.11-13), wonder as the cause of transformation. Then another transformation, told by Ap. Rhod., *Arg.* 4.595-611; but Virgil substitutes *Phaethontiades* for *Heliades* — the cause of grief expressed in the name rather than simple patronym.

E.vi 64-73: *errantem id est amantem*, Philargyrius (ap. Servius III 1.120), cf. vi 4, 52, 58. In the narrator's selection from Silenus' materials, the story of Gallus' wandering (64) balances that of Pasiphaë (52), cf. Putnam 1969.212. A Hesiodic tradition and force in poetry redeem Gallus from wandering and claim him for constructive work: in poetics, Virgil thus distinguishes two levels in Gallus' work (cf. n. 6.19), one characterized by the myth of the poet as lover, the other by the myth of the poet as initiate: cf. VS 1976-1977.330-332 which argues that the difference must be between elegy (of unspecifiable, most probably mixed content) and the one etiological *epos*; see also Schmidt 1972.273-280.

[25] Otis 1964.136-140 makes essential points on the differences between E.iiii and E.vi: e.g. "6 is hurried, varied, plaintive, curtly allusive; 4 is solemn, continuous, full of epic anaphora and phraseology" (p. 137); unfortunately Otis tended to think of E.vi as prior

To that ambitious project of a new start in history, society, and *epos*, this responds with myths of primordial, anti-social and passionate origins; [26] in other words a step away from Tityran myth, and all overheard and transmitted by Eurotas, a 'broad' stream but no doubt slight at its Arcadian source. [27] Was this 'Mopsus' with the retrospective 'hemlock'?

2. E.vii—*For New Bucolic, Sifting Out Arcadian and Tityran*: continues mixed narrative form. The narrator remembers having chanced upon a definite and dynamic situation in bucolic, that had taken shape before he arrived. A central and authoritative figure—the Sicilian cowherd Daphnis—provided the context for two perfectly matched

to E.iiii, or of the two as merely complementary and contemporary (e.g. p. 140); hence he misses the significance of E.vi as an ironic response, and withdrawal from positions asserted in E.iiii. He sees the reversal (also in the entire second half-book, cf. n. 1.46 above), but does not deal with it (e.g. p. 143, "So Virgil had developed ... from a neoteric and Theocritean to at least a potentially Augustan poet", as if the potentially Augustan part came last).

[26] Origins, passion, and a passion for etymology as a key to origins characterize E.vi. Its causal chains are complex, on the one hand, 'Tityrus' with a past, summoned to Apollo's disposition, on the other, Silenus' past of celebration and elusiveness, collapse, then the enacting drama of capture and seduction, drawing out the past (a *carmen* thus *deductum*), then at the end the discovery of Apollo as the ultimate source (*meditante*), working up song in frustrated love for Hyacinth, song committed to laurels, other object of Apollo's love: see n. 6.27.

[27] E.vi 82-83: omnia quae quondam Phoebo meditante beatus
audiit Eurotas iussitque ediscere lauros

All that once, as Phoebus worked it up, gladdened
Eurotas heard and bid the laurels learn.

Their suffering was Eurotas' pleasure; song at Eurotas recalls Hyacinth, but see also Callimachus, fr. 699 Pf., citing Ps.-Probus on E.vi 82 (p. 347.6): "Eurotas amnis, ut ait Callimachus, in flumina serpit per Laconum fines. fontes agit ex monte Maenalio, confunditur Alpheo rursusque discedit."

but differentiated figures—goatherd Corydon and shepherd Thyrsis—Arcadians both and both prompt to contend. The narrator's goats had strayed there. Daphnis addressed him as 'Meliboeus' and invited him to stop for a bit. It was a north Italian riverbank. There was a great contest. He preferred to neglect work elsewhere to listen to their play. They began to remember alternates:

C.:   (21-24) poetics of limitation.
Th.:   (25-28) poetics of growth.
C.:   (29-32) modest offer to chaste goddess (Diana).
Th.:   (33-36) churlish, boastful offer to Priapus.
C.:   (37-40) gentle invitation to beloved Phyllis.
Th.:   (41-44) harshly priapic protestation to beloved.
C.:   (45-48) prayer for natural shelter against start of summer heat.
Th.:   (49-52) boast of man-made shelter against winter cold.
C.:   (53-56) autumn abundance: 'but if' Alexis left, rivers would run dry.
Th.:   (57-60) summer drought: with Phyllis' coming, grove will green, rain will pour.
C.:   (61-64) each plant dearest to its deity: Phyllis loves *corylos*. While she does, they will not give way to other plants.
Th.:   (65-68) each tree loveliest in own setting: 'but if', Lycidas, you came oftener, each tree would give way to you, even in its setting.

This Meliboeus remembers, and that Thyrsis, beaten, competed in vain. From that time Corydon, only Corydon, has been everything to him. [28]

[28] (a) NAMES. CORYDON. E.ii; Idd.iiii, v; (A.P. 6.96) cf. n. 5.61.

THYRSIS. Theocritus, Id.i 19, 65, 146, shepherd, singer of the song about dying Daphnis; cf. *thyrsos*, the bacchic wand.

DAPHNIS. E.v, iii, ii; cf. n. 5.84.

MELIBOEUS. E.v 87, iii 1, i 6; cf. n. 5.43, 60 above.

OTHERS. ALCIDES (59), cf. E.iiii 49, 61; ALCIPPE (14), Id.v 132; ALEXIS (55), E.ii 1, etc.; CODRUS (22, 26), E.v 11 (*iurgia*); DELIA (29), cf. mortal girl, E.iii 67; GALATEA (37), here 'of Nereus', cf. mortal girl, E.iii 64, 72, i 30, 31; HYBLA (37),

Ecloga haec paene tota Theocriti, says Servius (82.7
Th.-H.); and we can almost hear the sigh of relief that
here at last, following three exceptions, is another piece
that conforms to the norms of simple bucolic (*proprie bu-
colicon*). After the ambitious subjects of E.iiii, v, and vi,
and the concomitant shift of locus to a more privileged
position, [29] here again is the shade of a tree, recalling that
first image of the Tityran bucolic mode; here, too, a figure
seated and familiar names as well as the usual goats and
sheep and poetic emulation, not to mention even an arrival
of Meliboeus from the background as before. This, at least,
is all Virgilian Theocritus. Servius had reason to be assured.

At the same time, of course, as more reflective readers
are well aware, these signs of simple return to the Tityran
scene are all complicated by specific differences: (E.vii 1-20)

M.:	Forte sub arguta consederat ilice Daphnis,	1
	compulerantque greges Corydon et Thyrsis in unum,	2
	Thyrsis ouis, Corydon distentas lacte capellas,	3

cf. E.i 34; *IACCHUS* (61), E.vi 15; *IUPPITER* (60), E.iiii 49, iii
60; *LIBER* (58); *LYCIDAS* (67), Id.vii 13; *MICON* (30), E.iii 10;
PHYLLIS (59, 63), E.v 10, iii 76, 78, 107; *PHOEBUS* (22, 62, 64),
E.vi 11, 29, 66, 82, E.v 9, iii 62; *PRIAPUS* (15), Id.i 81; *VENUS*
(62), E.iii 68 (metaphorically of a mortal, cf. *mihi . . . deus,* E.i 6,
mihi . . . Apollo, iii 104). After E.iii, most populous, but a signi-
ficantly different selection of types.

(b) *SELECTED PRECEDENTS.* Single narrator tells of a con-
test in which there was a victor ~ (Theocritus), Id.viii; cf. Id.vi,
without a victor. Separate stanzas in the contest also recall *topoi*
of epigram, e.g. vii 29-32 and A.P.6, the numerous dedications to
Pan, or vii 33-6 and dedications to Priapus, especially A.P.6.300,
which promises a greater offering to follow, if the property grows.
E.vii 4 resembles Erycius A.P.6.96, but of course even more Id.viii
3-4; and the Arcadian theme in any case has its own autonomous
development in the eclogue book.

(c) *STRUCTURE.* 5+8+7, "(4/4)x6", 2. The contest has 48
lines, as in E.iii, but distributed into four-line stanzas; cf. nn. 1.21,
5.65.

[29] *Antrum,* E.v 6, vi 13: remarked as a sign of thematic pro-

ambo florentes aetatibus, Arcades ambo,   4
et cantare pares, et respondere parati.   5
huc mihi, dum teneras defendo a frigore myrtos,   6
uir gregis ipse caper deerrauerat; atque ego Daphnim   7
aspicio. ille ubi me contra uidet, 'ocius' inquit   8
'huc ades, o Meliboee; caper tibi saluus et haedi;   9
et, si quid cessare potes, requiesce sub umbra.   10
huc ipsi potum uenient per prata iuuenci,   11
hic uiridis tenera praetexit harundine ripas   12
Mincius, eque sacra resonant examina quercu.'   13
quid facerem? neque ego Alcippen nec Phyllida
    habebam   14
depulsos a lacte domi quae clauderet agnos,   15
et certamen erat, Corydon cum Thyrside, magnum;   16
posthabui tamen illorum mea seria ludo.   17
alternis igitur contendere uersibus ambo   18
coepere, alternos Musae meminisse uolebant.   19
hos Corydon, illos referebat in ordine Thyrsis.   20

M.: By chance beneath a rustling holm-oak Daphnis had
    settled,   1
and Corydon and Thyrsis had driven their troops
    into one: 2
Thyrsis sheep, Corydon goats stretched full with milk,   3
both blooming in age, Arcadians both,   4
both equal at reciting and ready to respond.   5
Here, while I was protecting tender myrtles against
    cold,   6
my man-of-troop on his own, buck, had strayed on
    down; but I   7
spy Daphnis. He in turn, when he sees me, "Quickly,"
    says,   8
"Come here, Meliboeus, your buck is safe and your
    kids;   9
and, if you can slack off a bit, rest beneath shade.   10
Here young bulls will come on their own through
    meadows to drink.   11
Here Mincius is weaving its banks green with tender
    reed,   12
and swarms of bees sound back from sacred oak."   13
What should I do? I didn't have a Phyllis or Alcippe   14
back home to pen up lambs just weaned from milk,   15

> and here was a contest, Corydon with Thyrsis, a
> great one;   16
> yet I put my serious matters second to their play.   17
> Thereupon both commenced to strive in alternate
>   verses; 18
> they wanted to remember Muse's alternates.   19
> These Corydon, those Thyrsis in order began
>   recounting.   20

In the first place, 'chance' is the express cause, [30] not the 'god' at Rome (i), love (ii), envy (iii), overt poetic ambition (iiii), or self-esteem (v). And the tree, now, is musical, [31] and no longer the Tityran beech but *ilex* (evergreen, cf. *frigore*, 6: hints of shifting seasons?). This Daphnis is not in the background (whether type of beauty, ii 26; envied hunter, iii 12; hero of the Tityran mode, v), but is reduced from the dimensions of the Tityran hero and marks a locus among singers. [32] There is not the possessive discrimination between properties (E.iii) but promiscuous mingling (*in unum*, 2); and we have not the implicitly Sicilian or Italian herdsmen of the Tityran mode (e.g. Corydon, *meae Siculis*, ii 21; Thyrsis, from Etna, Id.i 65), nor an old Tityrus, but blooming youths and the first Arcadians in the book. As for Meliboeus, instead of a moving protagonist in drama, interrupting 'play' in the foreground (i 10), fleeing from negated bucolic, georgic,

gression by Frischer 1975.50-52, who forgets, however, that it marked the lost bucolic locus of Meliboeus (i 75). Cf. n. 6.84.c.

[30] 'Chance' excludes the earlier terms of progress and design in art, e.g. *maiora canamus* (iiii 1), *prima, cum canerem reges, uellit, oportet, meditabor* (vi 1, 3-5, 8), as well as claims to historical occasion and authority (i 45, iiii 11), or favoring season (iii 55-57).

[31] Cf. Id.i 1, quoted in relation to the sound of E.i 1 in n. 5.43a, s.v. Tityrus.

[32] Daphnis, the figure greater than in E.ii, iii, less than in E.v, its importance showing traces of that *auxesis*, discussed in both personal and thematic terms by Frischer 1975. 13, 50-51; Berg 1974. 122-23; cf. n. 1.6.

civic order in the background, we have a calm narrator. He remembers a moment's distraction from an ordered pastoral (perhaps also georgic) background into a foreground where he overheard without disrupting, indeed encouraged 'play', which thus is represented here for the first time in the book and is characterized as 'memory of alternates' (19).

Even these few details, and there are many more, [33] allow some inferences for poetics, especially when we consider the context in the book. If a concept like 'chance' (1) seems calculated to counter, even annul, the pressing causalities of the Tityran mode, other changes recall the amplification of bucolic imagery in the three 'greater' pieces. For example, *ilex* (1), first occurred in the curiously inverted bucolic idyl of E.vi (54). [34] 'Daphnis' was not amplified into a commanding figure until E.v. [35] *Distentas lacte* (3), prosperous troop of Corydon, recalls the bucolic miracles of the incipient golden age (iiii 21); *ambo . . . ambo* (4) echoes the self-satisfaction in art of the matured Menalcas, *boni . . . ambo* (v 1). *Arcades* (4) takes up the idea of Arcadian preeminence in poetics (iiii 58-59); [36] that cattle come to drink without a herder's attention (*huc ipsi*, 11), recalls the spontaneity of nature, another bucolic miracle. [37] In short, 'by chance' (1) suspends all the causes, propagating and propagated, the complex middle ground and background of the Tityran mode, and leaves only the

[33] Putnam 1969.222-230 shows the elaborate pains with which Virgil combined traces of previous pieces to form this one; also Frischer 1975.43-73, adding Theocritean parallels.

[34] Frischer 1975.46-47.

[35] Cf. n. 6.32.

[36] Cartault 1897.182 notes that E.iiii 58-59 makes E.vii 4 more intelligible.

[37] *Ipsae* (iiii 21), *ipsa* (iiii 23), *ipse* (iiii 43); not obviating work but expressing natural sympathy for the absent cowherd (i 38-39): *ipsae, ipsi, ipsa*. Cf. n. 3.7 for the similar language in E.v; also n. 5.77.

residue—an enriched and transformed bucolic locus, in which the only causes are imagined as inherent in the bucolic matter itself: attraction of musical shade, disposition to repose, readiness to differ in song, tendencies of beasts to water, weaving nature, echoing bees, the excitement of difference, the will to recall contrasting forms. It is as if the process of change imagined for the future in the fourth eclogue had been carried out in the language of the eclogue book: as if the traces of struggle and ambition—Tityran causes—had been cancelled or 'unthought' (*uestigia . . . irrita*, iiii 14, cf. 31) giving rise to a sweet dream of peace. This is a pure extract of the best of the bucolic as imagined in the first six poems (hence, too, it exemplifies *carmen deductum*, vi 5, 'song derived, drawn out fine from an inchoate mass', like strands from wool for yarn-spinning: *lana ... deducitur in tenuitatem*, Servius). Whatever was most characteristic there returns as a quintessence: the enchanced Daphnis, the idyllic Italian stream (the weaver), the quick Arcadians. The Arcadians are in action. The rest is context, Tityran bucolic material itself become a background for the advancing play of Arcadian myth.

These general inferences about the seventh eclogue can be confirmed and refined if we consider the fictional means by which Virgil reforms, as it were, his troops for the final assault on Arcadian myth. As in the sixth eclogue, he uses the representational form of mixed narrative, [38] but now for the narrative persona we have Meliboeus. The name recalls, of course, the first eclogue and the dramatic entry, thus at this moment in the book it also suggests a deliberate sequel and alternative to the sixth piece. There Virgil used the other persona from E.i as a means to revoke the positive and ambitious link between the bucolic and historical-heroic modes that had been forged at the beginning for the first half. The sixth made the

---

[38] Cf. n. 1.12.

effort to replay, reverse and reduce that growth to the terms of the middle mode: Hesiodic-Callimachean *epos*. Hence the sequel can be the further reduction to bucolic essence that we are seeing in the seventh. This is where 'Meliboeus' comes in. The original figure of relation between the bucolic and a complex, comprehensive order can serve in several ways.

Most generally, it does suggest the alternative to Tityrus (E.vi), thus raise expectation of a further step in the inner dialectic of the book (what had been a dramatic contrast between personae in a single piece becoming a contrast between pieces and modes). In particular, because 'Meliboeus' also brings to mind the whole crisis that generated the georgic, historical, and heroic outreach of the bucolic (the suffering that justified ambition), the new image of a peaceful background serves to counter that: this Meliboeus is engaged in regular work following the seasons (6) with planned and controlled development in the flocks (14-15), order disrupted only by whim. It is as if violent change had never (or not yet) taken place. Here is a harmless socio-political frame, in harmony with the idea of 'chance' as a general cause, to provide a background for Arcadian bucolic. To be sure 'chance' can be as devastating as Roman purpose; but, in the selective imagination, this is not the moment for that.

In the imaginative economy of the book, 'Meliboeus' also has the advantage of absence. The persona that fled (i 74), did not leave property (iii 1), became a song-title (v 87), has accrued no associations with the ups and downs of Tityran bucolic, the struggle towards higher modes. It has none of the thematic links with development and continuity of a 'Menalcas', or the recapitulative and synthetic functions of a 'Daphnis'. [39] Moreover, following the exclusion of the historical-heroic mode, it has been

---

[39] Names reused always invite comparison for similarity and

supplied with this newly pacific, but still complex background; thus it can serve in something like its original role as observer from outside,[40] but now to articulate the nature of the bucolic from a viewpoint in the mind where productive discipline not loss prevails. This new 'Meliboeus' can be imagined calmly perceiving the peculiar extract of Tityran bucolic as merely generic 'play' (17).

But for all this imaginative fitness, a persona like 'Meliboeus' cannot suffice for the delicate operation of fictionalizing a shift downward from the middle to the bucolic mode. Some cause has to be excogitated, for the dramatic fiction, that could distract a busy and prosperous worker from his round of chores. Once again Virgil needs an *aition* in poetics, yet it can no longer be a force from above or outside the bucolic mode, no *impius miles* or *deus*, now that *laudes* and *tristia bella* have been foreclosed (vi 6-7), and not a Callimachean Apollo, concerned with regular and productive bucolic work (vi 4-5). The cause has to be imagined plausibly within the country modes themselves precipitating a shift from work to play. Virgil's solution neatly divides the modes and effects the passage: in the dramatic fiction, while 'Meliboeus' was occupied with a putative georgic task (if protecting myrtles against

difference, and may accumulate significance for poetics, as we have seen (e.g. nn. 3.6, 7). On the risk, however, of imagining a realistic continuity in personal psychology, memory, experience and the like, see nn. 2.9, 10, 11, and 78. Such misapplied concreteness (fallacy of overpersonalization of fictional characters) in B.D. Dick, "Ancient Pastoral and the Pathetic Fallacy," *CompLit* 20 (1968) 27-44, has been reproved by Perutelli 1976.775, n. 34, as "un esempio in più della tendenza critica americana a psicologizzare ogni aspetto della poesia." Cf. n. 2.11; add Dick 1970. Perutelli remarks similarly on Leach 1975.42, 167 (p. 779, n. 53; and p. 787, n. 76: "la studiosa americana che si muove a suo agio, se si possono impostare problemi psicologici o, meglio ancora, psicanalitici") and Putnam 1969.371 ("ampie venature psicologistiche", p. 780, n. 54).

[40] Cf. nn. 2.47, 48, and Chapter 2.F, "A Total Design."

cold is not just an ironical, rustic euphemism for 'taking a snooze' in a bed of myrtle), bedding, then, the tender young plants with straw, a bucolic element followed its own bent: (7-8)

uir gregis ipse caper deerauerat. atque ego Daphnim
aspicio...

man-of-troop on his own, billy, had wandered in. But I spy Daphnis...

This, in bucolic terms, might be called a material cause. A moment's attention elsewhere and the leading bucolic matter gravitated to the ideal bucolic place, 'on his own', *ipse*, like other animals in that trace of golden age nature mentioned above. [41] The bucolic itself tends to reintegrate itself when freed of complex contingencies and conditions. Anamnesis is its best moment.

Style underlines import. In the verse, the metaphor begins, 'husband-of-herd', the leader, implying loss of the followers as well (cf. 9); then the theme of a golden age spontaneity, followed by the *interpretatio*, spelling out implication by means of a concrete term, 'billy' (cf. Meliboeus' similar rhetoric, E.i 3); finally the verb, the prefix "de-" suggesting perhaps not so much that the goat went away from the background as that its movement exhausted itself and ran its course precisely in the bucolic locus (*huc . . . deerrauerat*). This is the last pluperfect. It completes the narration of prior circumstances and trails off into an exemplary bucolic diaeresis, providing thus a stylistic analogue for the arrival of the goat in a generic locus. Virgil's language, as so often, becomes iconic. Abruptly the narrative shifts to historical present: *ego Daphnim*. The junction of background and foreground, of middle and bucolic modes, has been effected. Ellipsis veils search, the

[41] Cf. *ipsi* (vii 11) and n. 6.37; but note also *ipse*, the head or master, E.viiii 67.

groping for means of transition. Across the bucolic diaeresis appears Daphnis, the bucolic hero.

The treatment of *uir gregis*, placed so emphatically and glossed, brings to mind the scholiasts, who give 'lead goat' as one of the meanings of the name 'Tityrus'. If Virgil recalls a Theocritean commentary and pursues his active interest in the 'origins' of names,[42] here he may be implying that it was a *tityrus* that drew 'Meliboeus' once again into bucolic. In the development of the book, this would be an ironical reenactment and reduction of the crisis of the first eclogue, a distilled and utterly decontaminated etiology for the new bucolic mode. The etymological figure would be a fitting vestige of Tityran poetics (cf. the etymologies of E.vi) that would contribute to, indeed exemplify, the process of extraction and reduction which seems to be underway ('Tityrus' *deductus*, E. vi, and now fully *irritus*).

Dramatizing a return to bucolic is only a first step. Virgil still has to give the observer cause to stay. To be sure, the place is furnished with the best of ease from all the Tityran mode, as we have seen (add *requiesce*, of course, 10, and E.i 79); but, in the dramatic fiction as Virgil conceives it, the thing that captivates Meliboeus is not rest but *negotium*—the busyness of the Arcadians about poetic difference. It cannot be emphasized too often that these are the first Arcadians in the book, thus Virgil's first opportunity to give substance to the idea of Arcadian preeminence introduced so fleetingly in the fourth eclogue and not so full of literary resonance for his first hearers as for us.[43] First a generic detail. These are herdsmen (2); but following the new, unexpected, and still somewhat empty term, *Arca-*

---

[42] Cf. n. 5.43a. s.v. Tityrus, and n. 5.65.b for the commentary. Wendel 1920.152 traces the gloss, *tityrus, tragos* to Theon. Coleman 1977.210 adduces Id.viii 49.

[43] It seems recherché to adduce Polybius when we have Pan in Id.i (cf. n. 6.82), with a hint of his invention of the pipe. And if not Theocritus, why not Callimachus? In addition to the Arcadian

des (4), we get an *interpretatio*, filling in specific qualities, telling us what 'Arcadian' means in this work: (5) [44]

et cantare pares et respondere parati.

both equal at reciting and ready to respond.

The image is that of outstanding and eager competitors in poetry. It recalls the earlier association of Arcadia with competition and provides a plausible motive for 'Meliboeus': [45] with such singers, the contest can only be a 'great' one (16), a valid excuse to postpone work. *Magnum* was a characteristic theme of the Tityran mode in its preoccupation with the gap between great and slight and the dynamics of getting across it; [46] here it, too, has been reduced and assigned to a bucolic element—emulative contrast—which thus is singled out as worthy from the viewpoint of higher modes.

Here we cannot trace out the final links in the causal chain: Virgil imagines Meliboeus' decision as the immediate cause for the contest, giving the singers the stimulus to begin (*igitur*, 18); but the ultimate causes are veiled in chance (1) and in ambiguity: whose was the will to remember alternates that was carried out? [47]

---

material in other works (nn. 23, 24, 27 above, and Call. frr. 652, 802 Pf. with notes), the very *Aitia*-prologue itself mentioned that Arcadian speciality the production of asses (fr. 1.43 Pf. with diegesis).

[44] *Cantare* may suggest repetition as opposed to *canere*, production of song: e.g. *canamus* (iiii 1), a new song; *canerem* (vi 3), and *canebat* (vi 31); yet *cantabunt* (v 72), performance; *cantari* (v 54), praise; *cantabitis* (x 31), reproduction of Gallus' *Amores*, retelling; cf. *dicite* (iii 55, viii 63), *dicemus* (v 50), *dicamus* (x 6), all of telling songs already composed, and *deductum dicere carmen* (vi 5).

[45] E.iiii 58-59, *Pan, Arcadia, certet, dicat, uictum*; cf. n. 6.28.

[46] *Magna* (i 23, 47); *maiora* (iiii 1); cf. *maior*, E.v 4.

[47] Ambiguity is due to both the Latin and the transmission: if *uolebant* (19) with MSS, then either Corydon and Thyrsis (*Musae*, genitive singular) or 'Muses' (*Musae*, nominative plural) 'willed';

By structuring the narrative thus as recollection of recollection of alternation, Virgil might increase the imaginative distance between the narrative present and the Tityran mode. For besides the imagined viewpoint of the narrator from outside, [48] he has, within the bucolic mode itself, the traditional formula of the amoebaean contest. It might allow him to sum up ideological development and modal progression in the form of a simple thematic opposition. That something like this must be the function of the Arcadians can be inferred in the first instance from the character we have just observed: marked differentiation, forced unification of generic material (2); asserted equalness and promptness in reciting or performing (5, cf. *referebat*, 20). Both are conceived as drawing equally on the book, equally Virgilian both; [49] and representing an inherent and irreducible differentiation within the work [50]

'Corydon' has an explicit relation to the book (E.ii 1, 69, v 86). The generic continuity, as always, underlines specific difference: Sicilian has become Arcadian. It might be tempting to assume that here, just once, the same person does come back, the wiser for his 'disorderly' and 'empty' courtship of Alexis; but are we to suppose a precocious pattern of immigration from south to north, or perhaps an itinerant athlete of song, turning up for the Daphnic games on Mincius' bank as Hesiod once crossed over to Euboea? [51] In addition to the name, the occupation estab-

or if *uolebam*, "multi" ap. Servius, then Meliboeus 'wanted', giving further point to *igitur*: the observer provoked the competition.

[48] Cf. the imagined viewpoint of higher order looking down on bucolic, E.ii 1-5, iiii 1-3, vi 1-2: only here (and for ostensibly different reasons in E.i) does the figure of higher order descend to the level of the bucolic.

[49] Pöschl 1964.108-109.

[50] VS 1967.501-04.

[51] But Frischer 1975.77: "Die unterschiede sind nur verständlich innerhalb des Rahmens einer einzig, einheitlichen Persönlichkeit." A

lishes links: goats of Meliboeus (E.i 12, 74) and Menalcas (E.iii 34, v 12).

'Thyrsis' has no such precedent in the book: in the first idyll, as noted above, the singer of Daphnis dying is so named. This does imply, however, an affinity with Mopsus (singer of Daphnis dead), the more energetic and aggressive younger comrade of Menalcas. The occupation, too, shepherding, recalls Tityrus (E.vi 5) as well as Damoetas (E.iii 3), a figure distinguished from the younger Menalcas by energy and initiative and by the decoration on his cups— Orpheus with woods following—as opposed to the cups of Menalcas, with their arts of measurement and georgic work in fields.

To be sure, Tityrus also began as a shepherd (his spendthrift past, E.i 21) before the god's bucolic command (i 45). So, too, Corydon's abundant property in Sicily included lambs as well as goats (ii 30); and in the amboebaean exchange of E.iii, in the moment when Tityran bucolic fills to overflowing and is about to reach beyond country limits, both personae assume all three workers'

framing, unitary conception is required, to be sure, within which to discern meaningful difference, but "Personality" sounds like a relic of dramatic criticism (VS 1976.29-30 on probable origins of this approach to bucolic) if not just "un esempio di più della tendenza critica americana": Perutelli, cited in n. 6.39. The appropriate conception is the unfolding poetics of the book (cf. Chapter 4, "Background"). A step away from naively personalizing interpretation had already been taken by Wülfing 1970.381: "Vergil will ja nicht Thyrsis als egozentrischen Charakter, sondern eine Gattung der Bukolik als derb und naiv hinstellen; deshalb ist die Formulierungsweise entscheidend und nicht die Person, die sprechend gedacht ist." From this poetics of genre, it is only a further step to reading "personality" as a sign of poetics in the book. Frischer omits Wülfing's important review of scholarship from his own review (p. 17) and seems to ignore the issues that it raises. As for Mincius, it does become the site for much greater imaginary poetic competition (G.iii 10-20).

roles: goatherd, shepherd, cowherd. But in retrospect E.vii simplifies and separates. The leading bucolic animals, cattle, come to the locus on their own (11), perhaps belonging to Meliboeus (along with goats and sheep, 9, 15, hence another hint of tripartite completeness associated with his figure) or simply returning to Daphnis, traditionally the cowherd. Corydon is reduced to the lowest level, goats, leaving Thyrsis in the middle,[52] so that we have a simple polarity between the lower and the middle within the matter of bucolic itself.

In the context of the book, Corydon as 'Arcadian' suggests a poetics of continuity, associated with the prominent figure of continuity and development, goatherd Menalcas.[53] On the other hand, Thyrsis 'Arcadian' appears to suggest divers figures of ambitious poetic force (something like a Dionysiac or Orphic tendency in the book) which recurs in contrast with figures of containment.[54]

---

[52] The hierarchy of types of pastoral work begins with Theocritus, Id.i, at least insofar as it is an imaginative scheme: nameless goatherd (subject to Pan), possessed of marvelous artifact (Homeric typology, reflection on craft); Sicilian shepherd, named (Thyrsis), sings famous song (desired 'hymn'); its subject, the cowherd, *boukolos*, Daphnis, hence it is 'bucolic song' (cf. VS 1976.23, 24). On the import for poetics of these three registers of rural material, VS 1970a.82ff.; cf. more generally on such interpretation of country things, nn. 4.13, 21 above. The hierarchy is denied, wrongly I believe, by E. A. Schmidt, "Hirtenhierarchie in der antiken Bukolik," *Philol.* 113 (1969) 183-200. Cf. the uses of the hierarchy discussed in nn. 6.8.a, 10, 13, 14, 15, 19.

[53] Cf. nn. 3.6, 2.47. The figure that 'Corydon' cuts in poetics, without regard for the book, is well delineated by Wülfing 1970. 382: "Corydon formuliert seine Dichtung als etwas, worüber er noch nicht verfügt, worum er wie ein Liebender wirbt, *noster amor.* Die Ich-Person ist in dieser Strophe gerade Ausdrucksmittel der Bescheidenheit: die Gunst der Musen will er als eine ihm zuteil gewordene Gabe verstehen, *mihi... concedite.*" Cf. *concede* (x 1) and poetic love (x 73) in the final narrator of the full Arcadia.

[54] VS 1967.501-04. Again Wülfing 1970.382 hits the mark on

These, then, are the terms of the polarity into which Virgil recasts the development of the Tityran mode. The actual rereading and critique comes in the contest itself, *certamen*, a noun formed on a verbal base with a suffix that suggests both a process and its result—trial, whether by force or art, and final sifting out. [55]

In keeping with the import of this elaborate preparatory exercise, the first speech attributed to the Arcadians concerns poetics and presents contrast—between modesty and ambition: an accurate recollection of the dialectic of the Tityran mode. The themes are intelligible immediately on the dramatic surface. They also allow further inferences on which we can only touch here. Corydon, for example, addresses *Nymphae Libethrides*, obscure waters, associated with Orpheus or with a minor spring in the Hesiodic territory: not incompatible associations in the aftermath of the sixth eclogue, which referred to Hesiod in Orphic terms. [56] But after what we have seen of programmatic changes worked in myths of poetics both by Virgil and others, [57] we may want to infer that Corydon's address unassumingly locates this version of bucolic in the generally Hesiodic range of slight style, yet on the periphery, as it

the character in itself: "Wie anders Thyrsis. Bei ihm kein Werben, sondern Aufforderung an die *pastores* . . . *Arcades*, ihn zu bekränzen; er verkündet seinen Rang und Anspruch in der dritten Person, *crescentem poetam, vati . . . futuro*. Keine Bitte an Musen, kein Empfinden des subjektiven Risikos. Er zieht nur Diesseitiges in Betracht, sein Publikum und die Missgunst eines, der sich vielleicht besser dünkt." This focus on the public fits the figure of the Tityran bucolic mode, with its emphasis on ideological myth: see n. 6.58.

[55] Cf. *certare, certum, cernere, cribrum, crimen*, and J. Perrot, *Les dérivés latins en* -men *et* -mentum (Paris 1961). Cf. the rather different contest near Octogesa: *erat in celeritate omne positum certamen* (Caesar, B.C. I 70).

[56] E.vi 70; cf. Frischer 1975.86, n. 89; Desport 1952.244-47.

[57] See nn. 5.31, 6.15.

were, not challenging Hesiod himself by invoking Pierians or imagining an ascent to Helicon's top (as in E.vi 13, 65, 69).

By contrast, Thyrsis' ambition has evident connections with the fourth eclogue, its language and its vatic character. [58] The word *uates* may also bring to mind the Muses' gift of prophetic language and the staff of Hesiod (and Hesiodic—Euphorionic—Gallan associations of Mopsus). [59] Thus shepherd Thyrsis' boast, as opposed to modest goatherd Corydon, would be a trace of full middle style (cf. again E.vi 4-5, 'A shepherd, Tityrus, it behooves "fat" to herd sheep', which implies full middle range in the Tityran mode and recalls Hesiod herding lambs). Ambitions like those of Thyrsis were appropriate at their original moments in the book. In retrospect, transmuted into a purely bucolic locus in the prospect of Arcadian myth, they begin to sound excessive and to look out of place.

The overtly theoretical character of this opener, not to dwell on the way it invents the first Arcadian dialogue in the book (if not in literature) by 'remembering' and revaluing previous eclogues, should be enough to warn even an uninitiated reader that the exchange to come must also be read as a retrospective poetics. We can expect to find again and again that the character of the Arcadians is merely designed to summon up for judgment in the context of this new polarity, by the newly conceived standard of a pure

---

[58] Thyrsis, vii 25-28, truculently refers to himself as a growing poet (*crescentem*, 25, cf. *incrementum*, iiii 49), calls for *baccar* to ward off the evil eye (27, recalling Virgil's sole other mention of this apotropaic plant, iiii 19), and boasts of becoming a *uates,* a word which Virgil will use of himself only at A.vii 41, but which Horace made bold to adopt already in the thirties (*Epd.* 16.66), and which here in retrospect reflects ironically on the evidently vatic character of E.iiii. Cf. also the ironic mention of *uates* at E.viiii 34, and Thyrsis' "public" orientation, n. 6.54.

[59] Cf. the vatic asociations of Mopsus, n. 5.84, with his staff (v 88-90).

and original bucolic, language and themes that characterized the Tityran mode: on the one hand, the constant striving for objects beyond, the variously dramatized passion for what lies outside the limits of nature and above the bucolic mode; on the other hand, a restrained and measured attitude that finds satisfaction with itself within natural (and bucolic) limits. [60] The exchanges proceed by a design for thematic completeness that seems almost certainly to exceed the imagined consciousness of these personae—the most patently theoretical constructs in the book. Certainly their themes do not arise from a supposed immediate environment, or they could not touch in turn on so many different seasons (in varieties of rhetorical form) each invoked as if it were the present of the quatrain: late spring on the verge of full summer's heat; bitter cold and snow; ripe autumn; late summer drought (with hope of early winter rain, or early spring, with returning green). Together these suggest a sketch of the whole natural cycle: song can 'remember' winter without being sung in winter; winter song can be 'remembered' for variety in any season. [61]

In the design, 'Thyrsis' again and again is made the

[60] Cf. nn. 6.39, 51, 53, 54; and, for the principle of interpretation, nn. 2.10, 11, and 31.

[61] On achieving completeness through contrast and variation, Pöschl 1964.150-151, cited in n. 1.55. Yet Frischer 1975.80-85 assumes that the exploration of human character is the purpose of the contest and that the contestants can be understood as two people, each asserting his own vision of the world, indeed Corydon by mentioning 'Abundant Autumn' (53-56), would be trying to induce a change of attitude in Thyrsis (pp. 120-121); such a change, if I read the argument correctly, would undo the summer drought (*aret ager*, 57), which Frischer (pp. 123-24) interprets as the consequence of Thyrsis' flawed character. The advertisement that this was 'recollection of alternation' (vii 19) and the design for completeness through *alternos* (*uariatio* and contrast) are forgotten in the rush of psychologizing and ethicizing determinism: cf. the notes cited in n. 6.60.

vehicle of the harsher, the more expansive, the defiant
theme. His god is Priapus, treated with an exaggeration that
goes beyond any possible excess of Tityrus: [62] coming after
the boast of vatic ambition, gold Priapus sounds like an
ironical reduction of the hope for a golden race. [63] His
address, then, to a beloved has a priapic impatience with
the subordination of sex to the rhythms of daily work
(41-44). Instead of natural shelter against one natural
extreme, his shelter is man-made against the opposite ex-
treme, 'here,' [64] and 'always a great blaze' (49-52). Instead
of autumn in rich woodland, it is drought in the fieldland,
or a great stream of fecundating rain in the grove, descent
of Jove himself (57-60). [65] Finally, instead of an oblique
compliment to a beloved imagined as introducing hierarchy
and enhancing a natural-mythic setting (where etymology
implies continuity between natural and human), [66] Thyrsis
is depicted as asserting that his beloved surpasses nature
at its best (65-68). [67] This is very much in the character

[62] See n. 2.6.

[63] E.vii 36: *si fetura gregem suppleuerit, aureus esto!* Cf. E.iiii
9: ... *toto surget gens aurea mundo.* Thyrsis' garden makes a rather
smaller paradise; *fetura* strikes a note of raw natural productivity
untransformed by mythic vision. Berg 1974.158-61, drawing uplifting
inferences from the theme of gold (E.iii, iiii, viii), forgets this lewd
glint. For a positive, but also reduced vestige of E.iiii (52 and 20,
60, 62) see E.vii 55, *omnia nunc rident* (Corydon's autumn).

[64] *Hic* (vii 49) cannot, of course, refer to the time and place
of the contest; clearly then this is remembered verse (vii 19): cf.
n. 6.61.

[65] Cf. the other two mentions of the Father of Gods and Lover
of Females: Damoetas (iii 60), *ab Ioue principium Musae, Iouis
omnia plena*; and (iiii 49) *cara deum suboles, magnum Iouis incre-
mentum.* Both belong to the expansive phase of Tityran myth (cf.
crescentem, vii 25, *plurimus*, vii 60, and nn. 6.63, 58).

[66] Corydon, *corylos*: Pöschl 1964.138.

[67] Skutsch 1971.28 remarks that Corydon "gracefully and dis-
creetly ... intimates that his Phyllis is a goddess to him" while in
Thyrsis' reply "not very elegantly the rivalry between bushes is

of the Tityran mode—fixing on the object beyond nature and bucolic limits (like Tityrus after *Libertas*, the first Corydon after Alexis, the fourth eclogue after the *consul* and the 'boy'). Thyrsis typifies the ambitious character of the mode from first to last. [68] Hence the announcement of his defeat only articulates what has been implicit, that the expansive and ambitious, even perhaps some civilizing and constructive, values of the Tityran mode cannot become part of the final Arcadian myth. [69] When 'Meliboeus' de-

echoed by one between tree and man, and senselessly the *dum* clause, conveying that the hazel owes its rank entirely to Phyllis' affection, is transformed into a condition qualifying the beauty of Lycidas" (whether senseless or not, the shift to *at si* completes the variation of structures initiated by Corydon's *at si*, 55. Corydon's future indicative, 63, echoed that of Thyrsis, 59). Leach 1975.199: "In contrast to Corydon's unified, emblematic nature, Thyrsis' is only a catalogue. He has divided the natural world into four separate locations and chosen, rather arbitrarily, one outstanding object in each. For Thyrsis the trees have no ideal associations, and his more practical aesthetic is ready to give a human figure precedence over nature. Thus the final stanzas bring the songs back to their beginnings with Corydon establishing a divine presence in nature while Thyrsis insists upon a more limited and human point of view."

[68] Having observed the consistency with which Virgil constructed the figure of Thyrsis to reflect the poetics of Tityran bucolic in the book, we cannot agree with Frischer 1975.130-133 (following Pöschl 1964.148-149), who sees a change of character in Thyrsis foreshadowed in the penultimate exchange and occurring in the last: "Thyrsis' letzter Beitrag verwirklicht also die Möglichkeit einer Haltungsänderung gegenüber der Welt und damit auch einem Wandel der Persönlichkeit." Still less, then, can we accept the further argument that this "change" represents an Epicurean conversion.

[69] Wülfing 1970.380 sketches scholarly views of the criteria for victory: (1) inferiority in art of the loser, (2) arbitrary assignment by the poet, or (3) affirmation of one idea over another in poetics, this last the most recent tendency. His own conclusion, that Thyrsis represents the position of Theocritean bucolic might be modified to read "the amplification of Theocritean bucolic in the Tityran mode": vatic poetics does not suggest Theocritus himself.

clares that from that moment 'Corydon, yes Corydon' has
been the apple of his eye (70), we may infer that the
poetics of Corydon will prevail in the new bucolic mode
that develops in the remainder of the book while larger
interests rest suspended in the background. Qualities and
attributes of Corydon will recur in the ensuing pieces in
the growing image of Arcadian bucolic. Against them,
returning in varied forms of contrast, will be further
vestiges of the poetics of Thyrsis in figures of passion,
defeat and loss: ambition no longer dominant and positive
as in the first half-book but revalued and rendered pro-
blematical in the Arcadian context, yet still enlivening and
moving art. [70]

3. E.viii—*Contrast of Arcadian and Tityran Modes
(Love)*: again continues mixed narrative. An unnamed nar-
rator proposes to tell of a symmetrical and powerful contest
that held nature spellbound, then briefly, after weighing
his own commitment to the bucolic by contrast with re-
sponsibilities to a prestigious background, he introduces
the contest. It comprised first Damon's Arcadian verses
of unrequited love that led to suicide, but then Alphesi-
boeus' insistent songs that worked to draw Daphnis from
the city. [71]

The interlude has passed. This narrator, like 'Meliboeus'

---

[70] Shepherd Thyrsis, between shepherd Tityrus (vi 4-5, cf. nn. 6.8,
11, 14) and Gallus surrounded by sheep (x 16); cf. also the rather
harsh language, and passion that overreaches natural and poetic con-
solation in seeking a human object (*concedite siluae*, x 63). Motifs of
loss and defeat link Thyrsis and Gallus with figures in E.viii and
viiii as well: *uictum* (vii 69); *uicti tristes, quoniam fors omnia uersat*
(viiii 5); *tristis at ille* (x 31); *omnia uincit amor* (x 69); cf. *omnia
uel medium fiat mare, uiuite siluae* (viii 58); and the motif of death
(viii 60) with *perii* (viii 41), *amore peribat* (x 10). All these figures
lose contact with natural (and bucolic) bounds because of some
compulsion from the background.

[71] (a) *NAMES. DAMON.* E.iii 17, 23, defeated by Damoetas in

sees bucolic practice as an enclave set apart from some more serious area of endeavor in the background, only here the difference is expressed overtly in terms of poetics: the narrator says that the background was decisive in giving a start and a rule to his poetry, and now accomplishment and prestige in the background threaten to draw him away from the bucolic foreground toward higher style (6-13). This acknowledgement of the background as providing a cause for bucolic art summarizes in retrospect the poetics of the Tityran bucolic mode, which grew by integrating

performing, but refused to pay the forfeit. Cf. *demoomai* (Doric, *dam-*), 'to sing a popular song', crowdpleaser.

ALPHESIBOEUS. Cf. Theocritus, Id.iii 45, *periphronos Alphesiboias*, cited by Wendel 1900.49, who suggests that Virgil invented Alphesiboeus on this basis, like Meliboeus from Meliboea. Name of an entertainer honoring divine Daphnis, E.v 73, *saltantis satyros imitabitur Alphesiboeus*. Cf. *alphano*, 'bring in, yield' and *alphesiboios*, Il.18.593, of maidens who bring in many oxen for their parents from their suitors.

NYSA (18). Mountain sacred to Dionysus; also means 'tree'.

MOPSUS (26). Cf. n. 5.84.

MOERIS (96), cf. E.viiii 1 and n. 6.77.

MAENALUS (21 etc.). Cf. *mainomai*, 'to rage; be mad; be inspired': suggested by G. Doig, "Vergil's Art and the Greek Language" *CJ* 64 (1968) 1-6.

TITYRUS (55). Cf. n. 6.8.

DAPHNIS (68 etc.). Cf. n. 6.28.

AMARYLLIS (77 etc.). Cf. n. 5.43, and E.ii 14, 52; iii 81. Coleman 1977.243 poses the question whether this may be the passionate female addressing herself (cf. E.i 36-39, 'Amaryllis' calling for her lover absent in the city, an allusion to Id.i 71-75, the mourning for Daphnis).

HYLAX (107). For etymology, see VS "The Origin of the Reading, *Hylax*, in Virgil, *Ecl.* 8, 107," *RFIC* 102 (1974) 311-13.

(b) *SELECTED PRECEDENTS.* "In (E.) VIII a variation of the theme of Idyll I is balanced against a pastoral adaptation of Idyll II," R. G. Coleman, "Vergil and the Pastoral," *PCA* 69 (1972) 32: Theocritus' two idylls with refrains. Cf. Id.iii, threat of suicide, and note on structure following. Coleman 1977.253-55 makes a suggestive comparison of the two songs.

Roman materials and higher stylistic ambition; [72] for a moment, the poet conceives of higher style in terms of tragedy, by contrast with the comic muse of a humbler bucolic (*Thalea*, vi 2); [73] and he promises to end his work as it

(c) *STRUCTURE*. Skutsch 1969.153-156. In general: 5, 8, 3 + (36+9) + 2 + (36+9), where each reported song has 36 lines, while the total of introduction plus refrains is 36 for a total of 36+36+36 = 108. Within each song, stanzas are arranged in three sequences of three each (one four-line, one three-line, and one five-line stanza in each sequence). Skutsch excludes viii 76, which breaks the symmetry, without offering an historical explanation for why it may have intruded itself (see n. 7.4 below, and discussion).

Precedents for calculated structure in Theocritus: Id.i, 63 lines of song, 88 of context and refrains (omitting i 108, cf. n. 5.21), distributed—14+49, "63 (+18)," 7 (i.e. 63, 63 (18), 7); Id.ii, stanzas and refrains, but simpler sequences than Virgil's; Id.iiii, 63 lines with marked internal articulations (VS 1970.67-83; VS 1967. 497); and Id.viii, 48 lines of song, 48 of context, where the whole poem divides into three successive sections of 32 lines: VS 1973/ 1974.198-99. Be it clear that my approach to number in Theocritus differs from that of J. Irigoin, "Les bucoliques de Théocrite. La composition du recueil," *QUCC* 19 (1975) 27-44.

[72] E.i 45, iiii 1-3, 53-59. It follows that the anonymous leader referred to in E.viii 6-13 must belong to the series of figures of authority in the background, i.e. *deus* (i 6), *dominus* (ii 2), *Aegon* (iii 2), Juppiter (iii 60-61, *principium Musae*), and *Iouis incrementum* (iiii 49). Where these have ideological overtones, they presuppose and idealize the figure of Julius Caesar's heir, which, in the *deus* and *iuuenis* of E.i did give a start to the new bucolic mode (cf. *a te principium*, viii 11, and *tua dicere facta*, viii 8, iiii 54). Hence those ancient and modern critics are right who see an allusion to Octavian here (Servius 93.1, and Bowersock 1971), rather than to Pollio, who has appeared as fellow poet, lover of the rustic muse, and favoring consul and leader (E.iii 84-89, iiii 11-14) but not a detached and prestigious cause.

[73] Cf. *ludere* (vi 1) and *seria ludo* (vii 17): after the positing of three registers suggesting three modes in the first half-book, E.vi 1-8 has ruled out the third and E.vii 1-20 has defined a polarity between simply two (*seria/ludo*). This bi-polar model remains the framework for the rest of the book. In consequence here it is possible

began, for the sake of the prestige of the background, i.e.
for the sake of higher style.[74] In other words, departure
from the foreground, with the abandonment of bucolic
poetry, is to be determined by the same kind of poetic
ambition which brought about the growth of the Tityran
bucolic mode in the first half-book; hence we may perhaps
expect to find that the actual process of leaving the bucolic
scene will be carried out and justified in the dramatic fiction
by use of motives and forces like those which served in

to express the contrast of modes in terms of tragic versus bucolic
(low or comic): (E.viii 9-10).

en erit ut liceat totum mihi ferre per orbem   9
sola Sophocleo tua carmina digna cothurno   10

Eh! will I be allowed to recount whole globe throughout
songs of you, worthy of only Sophoclean style?

Servius 93.8 writes, "ac si diceret: quamquam impar sit ingenium
meum laudibus tuis; nam tuae laudes merentur exprimi Sophocleo
tantum cothurno. Sophocles autem tragoediographus fuit altisonus."
In other words, Servius takes *tua carmina* to mean 'praises of you',
'songs about you'; and he treats *sola* as either adverbial ('only',
tantum) or perhaps as transferred by hypallage, agreeing in syntax
with *carmina* but in sense with *cothurno*: cf. A. Ernout and F. Thom-
as, *Syntaxe latine* (Paris 1953²) 166, "C'est le procédé poétique
connu sous le nom d'hypallage, mais qui était à l'origine un fait de
langue." They cite A.vi 268, *ibant obscuri sola sub nocte,* and G.iii
249. No need, then, to think in connection with this passage of
either Pollio's victory or his tragedies, still less of the defeat which
Augustus' tragedy befell (and which was adduced here from Suetonius,
Aug. 85 by Beroaldus, quoted by Badius). 'Sophoclean' as equivalent
to 'tragic', Cicero, *Fam.* 16.18.3.

    [74] The formula of beginning and ending, *a te ... tibi ...* (viii 11),
is traditional, e.g. Homer, Il.9.97, Hesiod, *Theog.* 34, Theocritus,
Id.xvii 1, with remarks and further examples in Gow II ad loc.
But here, if *principium* refers back to E.i and the beginning of the
whole bucolic experiment, *tibi desinam* seems to promise not so
much that the *deus* will be named at the end, but that the ex-
periment in bucolic will finally be terminated on his account,
leaving the poet free to advance to higher modes.

the first half-book for the construction of the Tityran mode: love, but especially Rome, but reversed in import and exploited now as negating rather than positive causes.

The narrative proper then tells of two contrasting songs, which restate in more extremely polarized form the distinction between poetic tendencies which was drawn in the seventh piece. The poetics of limitation reappears as Arcadian poetry, 'verse of Maenalus', and proves incapable of capturing an object of desire beyond the foreground or of containing the figure of passionate erotic singing, who is imagined as flinging himself out of the bucolic context with a suicidal leap. Unlike the language of the lovers in the second and third eclogues, where erotic amplification served to expand the language of the positive outline toward the dimensions of the fourth piece, here the erotic rhetoric gains force by perverting and negating some of the language of natural miracles from the fourth. [75] On the other hand, in the part the narrator leaves to the Muses (62-63), the forceful expansiveness and vatic ambition of Thyrsis are recast in the form of *carmina*, 'songs', imagined in their archaic sense as operative chants or charms, which appear to succeed in drawing an object of love, Daphnis, from the city. [76] Here again we have a link and a further withdrawal from the fourth eclogue; for the poetic idea of the *uates*, 'bard', was implicit in the fourth with the lofty connotations of 'prophet, teacher', though it became explicit only in the boastful poetics of Thyrsis echoing the fourth (vii 25-28), where it was tarnished by association with superstition about

[75] E.viii 27-28, 47-58, cf. C. Fantazzi, "Virgilian Pastoral and Roman Love Poetry," *AJP* 87 (1966) 181; and note the allusion to themes of tragedy (Medea), viii 47-50. Otis 1964.108-120 took Damon's song as the starting point for his study of Virgil's "subjective style."

[76] A. Richter, *La huitième Bucolique* (Paris 1970) 106-107, and Putnam 1969.256, 280, as well as Desport 1952.50 all underline Virgil's allusion to the primitive sense of *carmen*.

the evil eye. Here, then, the concept of *uates* is implied in a still more vulgar and material sense, along with the archaic sense of 'songs' as spells.

After the prologue, which reopens the problem of the prestige and attractiveness of the background, we have seen in fact a return to love as the motive in dramatic fiction, with contrary results: Arcadian verse realized as a context but not sufficient mediator and container for love (cf. Id.i), as opposed to songs realized as effective, but at the price of reducing song to its most primitive material force (cf. Id.ii). Arcadian 'verse' cannot hold out against the lure of the background; 'song' manages to draw an object from the urban background, in effect further reducing the figure of Daphnis from its mythic state.

9. E.viiii—*Dismantling the Tityran Mode (Rome)*: reverts to dramatic form. A young enthusiast — 'Lycidas' — marvels that the old goatherd — 'Moeris' — is on the way to the city. Moeris replies that a new owner has driven him and Menalcas out, though once the power of Menalcas' songs seemed to have saved the whole little place. Both quote from Menalcas' old songs, and Lycidas insists on something from Moeris, too; but the most either one can manage is the memory of a fragment. Old age, a silent unresponsive landscape where shade is being cut, and the threat of rain impede singing. [77]

In the context of a unified book of eclogues, the old

[77] (a) NAMES. MENALCAS. Cf. n. 5.84, 3.6, 2.47. Reversion to dramatic form itself also recalls E.v and iii, where Menalcas figures, and of course E.i. For the rest, mixed narrative is the rule.

LYCIDAS. Theocritus, Id.vii 13; cf. E.vii 67, a generic boy love. Cf. Greek *lykos*, 'wolf', and its Arcadian associations.

MOERIS. A werewolf and producer of *mala carmina* (i.e. an *improbus uates*), mentioned in viii 95-99. In Greek, the name means 'half', but is also associated with Moira, 'fate, lot'. Badius related it to Latin *maeror*, 'grief'.

question disappears, whether Virgil wrote the ninth "poem" before or after the first "poem." We are free to read the eclogue in relation to what precedes and what comes after in the book.

The first line suggests that the background, which seemed countered momentarily by the force of 'songs' (E. viii), has reasserted its old force: against the repeated refrain and the climax (viii 108), 'from the city', the ninth eclogue begins with motion 'to the city' (viiii 1). Also, instead of love as the imagined cause of outward movement in the dramatic fiction, we find military force and new rights of property: in short a negative version of Roman causality

(b) *SELECTED PRECEDENTS.* Journey to city ~ Tityrus' journey to Rome (E.i), but this journey is hopeless and appears to allow no return (cf. viiii 67): a simple reversal of the pattern of Id.vii after the complex use in E.i.

(c) *STRUCTURE. Concentric:* traces of concentric patterning return with the dramatic form: 1/5/10/13/7/(7/7)/5/10/2. The key word for poetics, *uates*, appears at the beginning of the central verse (34). This diagram supposes that Lycidas quotes Menalcas (17-22, "23-25"), Moeris quotes Menalcas (26, "27-29"), Moeris quotes himself (37-38, "39-43"), and Lycidas quotes Moeris (44-45, "46-50"); for a different attribution, Williams 1968.313, who derives all quotes from Menalcas; and Geymonat 1973.48, who has 46-50 spoken by Moeris together with 51-55.

Linear: from the sedentary situation of E.vii, we moved to the curious situation of E.viii 14-16, of the singer standing, leaning on a staff, at dawn (evening thus unlikely to intervene to close, cf. E.i 83, ii 66-67, vi 85-86), or of viii 64-108, where the singer appears anything but restfully sitting; now the speakers are moving, specific place expropriated and shade threatened; cf. Damon 1961.289, "The 'densas, umbrosa cacumina, fagos' of the second have become 'ueteres, iam fracta cacumina, fagos' in the ninth [cf. n. 2.21 on 'beech' as a figure of poetics], and in this shattered sylvan locale we find the one instance of true pastoral singers addressing a silent, unresonant nature (viiii 57-58)...*aequor*...connotation of flatness...terrain without echoes, one which wastes pastoral song as the *triuium* (iii 26)": in short, linear movement dispersing rather than cumulatively gathering.

following the negative version of love which appeared in the first song of the eighth piece. Both theme, then, and dramatic form would seem in general those of the beginning of the Tityran bucolic mode, but with marked specific differences. For one, the Tityran ideology seems in part suspended, and instead of the positive-conservative image of Roman force, 'Graze as before!' (i 45), we get something that was never expressed in so many words in the first piece, and that represents the negative-innovative moment of that same force: 'These are mine. Old cultivators, get off!' (viiii 4). This evokes Roman force as a Meliboeus might have experienced it, but with a directness that found no place in the careful ideological and poetic calculus of the first eclogue. There the negative force of revolution had its vivid image—*barbarus, impius miles*—but no voice. Speech was reserved to the positive figure of the 'god'. Here where the negative has a function, its expression is curiously limited. It comes, not from a prestigious figure in the background with general instructions to an entire class, but from a more colorless *possessor* acting in the foreground; *aduena* may be ominous in the context, but it is less emphatic than the previous terms for the new owner; and instead of expropriation in 'whole territories' (i 11-12), making the whole commonwealth flee, 'wretched citizens' (i 71-72), the loss is confined to a 'little territory' or 'dear little property' carefully limited in extent. [78] Instead of a specific new deity we get generic 'spear of Mars' (viiii 12). The ideological dissimulation speaks for itself; and it is not to detract from the moving predicament of Moeris, the nearly fatal discomfiture of Menalcas, if we infer that in poetics this

---

[78] E.viiii 2-3, ... *aduena nostri* / ... *possessor agelli*; cf. *fors omnia uersat* (5), generalizing but also masking real causality; then *omnia carminibus uestrum seruasse Menalcan* (10), where *omnia* is no longer a universal (e.g. iiii 52) but a carefully delimited bucolic space (n.b. the old, broken beeches, 9, discussed in n. 6.77).

is designed to suggest the end of a particular mode. 'Chance', so promising as an alternative to the surfeit of external causes in the Tityran mode (vii 1), here, without the external guarantees of a Tityrus, is imagined as overturning a bucolic order (*fors omnia uersat,* 5). This is the Tityran mode in extremis, without its heroic myth, with its remaining spokesman an old *uates* enslaved to the town. [79]

The absence of a narrator spanning foreground and background (unlike the sixth, seventh, and eighth pieces) has a counterpart in the dramatic fiction, which complains of the absence of Menalcas and the undoing of the effects of his songs after earlier success in mediating force. Since Menalcas was the principal figure of continuity in the first half-book (his song recapitulating in E.v confident themes of E.i and E.iiii), his absence here suggests for poetics an incapacity to deal again in bucolic-georgic terms with the elements of history and heroic epic that the first four eclogues had successfully co-ordinated in the growth of Tityran bucolic and that indeed gave the Tityran mode its vitality and force. That growth has already been accomplished. This is another moment, when two subordinate figures are departing for the background. One is old, broken down, disheartened, forced to go. Moeris' associations with Menalcas make him particularly the figure of the dismantling of the Tityran mode. But the protagonist in the drama is young, insouciant, urging song; he joins the journey with good will, humanity, etc., but especially in hope of hearing song. Lycidas' devotion to poetry, even in the face of mortal

---

[79] If we think of the entire book as a system of deferral (see n. 1.49 above), we see that the negative response to the assertive *aition* of E.i 45 was not only put off but broken up, first the reaction expressed in terms of poetics, Apollo's rebuke, E.vi 3-5, and now the ideological counterpart, viiii 4. Here, in the negative, *Roma* is not mentioned, but only the vaguer *urbs,* and Roman force is covered by *aduena possessor,* less ideologically explosive than the polarized terms, *deus* (++) / *impius miles, barbarus* (—).

ills, and his eagerness, make him a figure of the Arcadian poetic myth, which is growing in this portion of the book, even as the Tityran mode declines. The limits on his energy and ambition are made quite explicit at the center of the eclogue, when he claims that he, like Moeris, is a poet, and that all the grazers call him, too, like Moeris, a *uates,* 'bard' (viiii 34), but he remains diffident, modest, no competitor for certain poets of the city. With this Virgil concludes the critique of ambitious, vatic poetics that we have seen since the seventh eclogue in progressive reactions to the poetics of the fourth. [80] Both figures, for their different motives, are on the way to the background from an Italian foreground that lacks an idealizing myth. Since scholars often note that their journey makes an evidently programmatic reversal of the journey in the seventh idyll, it may be well to emphasize again that this allusion and reversal take on their full significance only in the context of the whole book, where they can be seen as a simple undoing of the more complex use of the seventh idyll that occurred in the first Bucolic and inaugurated the Tityran bucolic mode. This single movement back to the city and Menalcas' absence mark the final undoing of the Tityran mode.

B. *Recapitulation: Myth of the New Bucolic Mode*

The hero of the Tityran mode appears for the last time in the book in the ninth eclogue. More exactly, Lycidas recalls a bit of old song by Moeris. It chided Daphnis as a

---

[80] See nn. 6.77, s.v. Moeris, and 6.58. Significantly the two figures with whom Virgil links the term *uates* have characteristics of expansiveness (Thyrsis) and mortality (Moeris) which belong to the Dionysiac-Orphic strain in the book, since it includes both initiating, amplifying force, but then also decay: in short, a strain of natural poetics, rise and fall. For the implication that Moeris is a *uates,* see viiii 32-34: *et me fecere poetam ... sunt et mihi carmina ... me quoque dicunt uatem,* 'me too (sc. like you), they made a poet, ... I, too, have songs ... me, also (sc. like you) they call a

farmer who had not yet learned of Caesar's star. The ideological and the poetic figures are distinct, the erstwhile bucolic-georgic hero reduced to humble georgic guise and part of a fiction barely remembered. The demythicizing of Daphnis is complete. A new hero can take his place in the new bucolic myth.

E.x—*Arcadia as a Return to the Source:* mixed narrative form. A nameless narrator invokes the nymph Arethusa to grant an end to work—songs for Gallus such as Lycoris herself would read. He recalls that Arethusa was not always a fountain in Syracuse and he wishes her fresh waters an unmingled journey beneath the salt sea if only song begin. Then he tells of the grief of Arcadian mountains over Gallus perishing for love and of an encounter in which variegated figures, including Menalcas, Silvanus, Apollo, Pan, query and admonish Gallus, who in turn greets them all as Arcadians, masters of poetic performance, envies their self-contained and sufficient life, then proclaims his own restlessness and finally defeat by love. Following this rehearsal of the dissatisfaction of another, the narrator closes with a pronouncement of satisfaction for the poetry sung while sitting and weaving. Then, with his goats, too, satisfied, he gets up to leave the unhealthy, chill shadows of a now wintry bucolic scene. [81]

In the aftermath of the ninth eclogue, which virtually

bard', remarks by Lycidas that follow the invitation to Moeris to begin, if he has anything (sc. in his memory, 32).

[81] Winter images begin to appear as the book gets along: E.vii 6; (viii 14?); x 20, 46-49, 56-57, 75-77; cf. Soubiran 1972.54-71.

(a) *NAMES. ARETHUSA.* Theocritus, Id.i 117; Callimachus, fr. 407.45 Pf.; (Moschus), *Epitaph. Bion.* 10, 77; Moschus, *Aposp.* 3.2. Cf. *Syracosio,* E.vi 1, and *en de Syrakosioisi Theokritos, Epitaph. Bion.* 93.

GALLUS. E.vi 64-73, and cf. Mopsus, n. 5.84 above. Servius 118.2-4, "fuit poeta eximius; nam Euphorionem ut supra diximus transtulit in latinum sermonem et amorum suorum de Cytheride scripsit libros quattuor".

puts the Tityran mode to rout, the poet here is free to complete the construction of Arcadia, although he is also constrained to bring his entire bucolic enterprise to a close. We have already noted that he begins the piece with express reference to its function in the design of the book: 'this end of toil' (x 1). But he also invokes Arethusa in a way that bears on his creation of Arcadian myth. At first he appears only to be reminding us that Daphnis in the first idyll said farewell to her in Sicily before dying (x 1);

LYCORIS. Servius 66.15-17, "(E.vi) dicitur autem ingenti fauore a Vergilio esse recitata, adeo ut, cum eam postea Cytheris *meretrix* cantasset in theatro, quam in fine Lycoridem uocat . . ."; i.e. Gallus' poetic name for Cytheris, chosen with what irony? F. Skutsch *RE* VII (1900) 1346.29-31 associates the name with an epithet of Apollo (*Lykoreus*, Euphorion, fr. 80.3 Powell, cf. Callimachus, H.ii 19) and a peak of Parnassus. Within the *Bucolics*, cf. *Lycisca* (iii 18), *Lycidas* (n. 6.77 above), and *Lycaeus* (x 15), the Arcadian mountain, all associated with Greek *lykos*, in Latin, *lupa*, a *meretrix*.
   PHYLLIS (37, 41). E.iii 76, 78, 107; v 10 (her loves a conventional poetic subject); vii 14, 59, 63 (again a conventional bucolic love). Servius on E.v 10 associates the name with Greek *phylla* in an erotic etiology.
   AMYNTAS (37, 38, 41). E.ii 35, 39; iii 66, 74, 83; v 8, 15, 18; cf. n. 5.84 above.
   MENALCAS (20). Cf. n. 6.77 above.
   (b) *SELECTED PRECEDENTS.* Visit by assorted divinities to a poet dying because of love, and his reply (9-69) ~ Thyrsis' song of Daphnis, Id.i 64-145. For a thorough study of the different kinds of uses of literary precedents that Virgil makes here, see Kidd 1964. *Laborem* (1) has precedents in the poetics of slight style: e.g. *labor*, *meditari*, *cura*, Catullus C.62; cf. n. 5.59 and E.i 2, vi 8, 82; also Greek *ponos*, Id.vii 139 (cf. 51, 74, 85). For the complementary idea, *ludus*, see E.i 10, vi 1, vii 17 (n. 6.73).
   (c) *STRUCTURE.* 8+61+8, of which 39 in Gallus' speech, 38 of context. Cf. the 8-line sections on poetics at E.vi 1-8, vii 6-13, viii 6-13. More articulated, concentric analysis: 8+26, 2, 5, 2, 26+8; cf. E.i, ii and viiii, with notes 5.43.c, 5.61.c, and 6.77.c. The allusions to an Arcadian life, easily available love, Phyllis and Amyntas come at the exact center (37-41), cf. similar use of the name Amyntas framing the central five lines, E.ii 35-39.

but then the allusion to her passage under the bitter Dorian sea would remind a schooled reader that she began as a nymph in mainland Greece, in the region of Arcadia and Achaea, then fled the sexual advances of the river Alph and reappeared, an unsullied spring, in Syracuse. This in itself would provide a link in myth between Sicily and Arcadia, and between the Tityran and Arcadian myths; but Virgil is more pointed still. His prayer that a future passage beneath the Dorian waves may be unmingled implies that the narrative present of the eclogue, its dramatic or fictional date, is set prior to Arethusa's flight to Sicily while she was still on Arcadian ground. [82] In other words, Virgil has imagined his last effort in bucolic as pre-Sicilian, hence pre-Theocritean and also, within his own book, pre-Tityran—an arrival at the place of origin as conceived in the fourth eclogue. [83]

---

[82] Desport 1952.218, following Hubaux, sees a return by Arethusa to Arcadia; but they also believe in an Arcadian school of poetry to which pastoral returns. Such an hypothesis, along with those that refer to Polybius (n. 6.43) or other sources, is unnecessary. The truth is simple and well put by Wendel 1920.71-72, who says that the question about the *Ursprung* of Arcadian bucolic is the same as asking where Virgil learned the story of the invention of the syrinx by Pan, but this is a commonplace available in any handbook of mythology, and is also in Theocritus, Id.i 123 ff., where Virgil could have understood it even if he did not know the pattern poem, *Syrinx*; cf. Schmidt 1972.58, and VS 1967.491-492. For a useful summary and dismissal of other views ("tutti falliti in blocco"!) see G. Jachmann, "L'Arcadia come paesaggio bucolico" *Maia* 5 (1952) 170-171, but Jachmann traces it to post-Theocritean bucolic, rather than focussing on development of Arcadian elements in the book and in relation to Theocritus (cf. Cartault in n. 6.36). Virgil in the book gradually focusses down from *Sicelides* (iiii 1), a general allusion to Greek bucolic, to *Syracosio* (vi 1), specifically Theocritus, to *Arethusa* (x 1), specifically Id.i but also the mythological link to Arcadia. In some respects, Id.i seems to have defined and initiated the bucolic mode for Theocritus; cf. VS 1975.54-58; hence Virgil returns to it to complete his transformation of the mode.

[83] Cf. nn. 6.3, 4.

His passage from Tityran to Arcadian myth is thus prepared. Yet paradoxically, in a typical forcing of the imaginative dialectic, the recovery of the most distant mythical past is motivated in the poetic fiction by a need to make songs for a living contemporary Roman, songs that might even be recited by a courtesan and actress much in the public eye. In the Tityran mode, the myth was admittedly new and contemporary, an ideological and public presence. The content was old and private discontent. Here the Arcadian myth purports to be old (dissimulating novelty) and is certainly obscure, with a nearly private and hermetic significance. But now the content is public, not politics but gossip, equally intelligible and as avidly consumed by the crowd.

After this prelude, the narrative proper presents the reflective reader with other paradoxes. The prayer to Arethusa has cancelled, as it were, Theocritus from the history of bucolic, as if the Sicilian moment had not yet taken place. The seventh eclogue administered a defeat to Thyrsis, the nonconforming Arcadian. The seventh, eighth and ninth gradually diminished the figure of Daphnis from new god to backward churl. Yet traces of Thyrsis' song of Daphnis from Theocritus' first idyll provide the narrative frame. [84] Within it the persona of the elegist is assigned the role of bucolic hero: death through love, though not exactly a chaste Daphnis; and surrounded by, not herder of, sheep, not cows; and mourned not by the 'hill' and Sicilian Himera's oaks (Id.vii 74-75) but by 'tamarisks' (E.x 13, vi 10, iiii 2, cf. Id.i 13) and by Arcadian mountains while

[84] Id.i 66. For two divergent views of Virgil's address to the Naids, see Kidd 1964.58 and Putnam 1969.348. Kidd's suggestion that they must be imagined as in Arcadia is untenable. Their absence, by contrast with the active presence of the Muses, 'sisters', at E.vi 65-66, is Virgil's point, as part of his shift away from dealing with Gallus as poet-initiate in the tradition of Hesiod to dealing with Gallus as poet-lover (cf. n. 6.24).

lying stretched at the foot of a lonely crag, the latter a
reversal of the mountain joy when Daphnis rose to heaven,
and a displacement and reduction, too, from the figure
of 'Gallus' led by a Muse to Helicon's top (E. v and E. vi).
Not least among the paradoxes, Menalcas returns, drawn
to the dying lover from winter work in the background
(x 20): 'acorns', a traditional Arcadian food. The figure of
design in the Tityran mode, so markedly absent during the
dismemberment of the mode (in E.viiii), provides a further
index that for Virgil Arcadia mean a poetics of design
calculated and accomplished through retrospective rein-
terpretation and exploitation of one's own prior writing.
As also in the seventh eclogue, where remembering produced
Arcadian dialogue, so here not only Menalcas but the *myricae*
(as just noted), Silvanus (a most Italic Arcadian, and echo
of Bacchic Silenus), the very words of Pan all are vestiges
of the Tityran mode. [85] In poetics, if not in life, expropriation
and expulsion free material for new construction.

This miscellany of old language, borrowed or gleaned,
displaced, acquires the dignity and coherence of myth only
in the response of Gallus: (E.x 31-43)

tristis at ille 'tamen cantabitis, Arcades,' inquit	31
'montibus haec uestris; soli cantare periti	32
Arcades. o mihi tum quam molliter ossa quiescant,	33
uestra meos olim si fistula dicat amores!	34

[85] Hahn 1944.240-41 asks, "Did Vergil intend his final Eclogue
thus to knit together the features of all the preceding ones? ... It
would at least justify the sense of fulfillment even to repletion that
rings in both the opening and closing lines of the eclogue." Bayet
1967.167 points to Virgil's self echoes: E.i 64-66 ~ x 65; ii 15-18
~ x 38-39; v 24ff. ~ x 13ff.; vi 14ff. ~ x 24-27; vii 1-5 ~
x 31-33; viii 43ff. ~ x 29-30; cf. Kidd 1964.56. Note also the
structural and verbal parallels mentioned above, n. 6.81.c; and add
E.ii 63-68 ~ x 26-30 (vi 21-22); also E.i 64-66, ii 61-62 ~ x 62-69,
a relation which implies that by the end 'Gallus' (and no longer
the goatherd-singer) has become the figure of despairing and wide-
ranging language.

atque utinam ex uobis unus uestrique fuissem   35
aut custos gregis aut maturae uinitor uuae!   36
certe siue mihi Phyllis siue esset Amyntas   37
seu quicumque furor (quid tum, si fuscus Amyntas?   38
et nigrae uiolae sunt et uaccinia nigra),   39
mecum inter salices lenta sub uite iaceret;   40
serta mihi Phyllis legeret, cantaret Amyntas.   41
hic gelidi fontes, hic mollia prata, Lycori,   42
hic nemus; hic ipso tecum consumerer aeuo.   43

But gloomy he says, "Yet, Arcadians, you'll perform   31
amid your mountains these, uniquely skilled to perform,   32
Arcadians: Oh how softly then my bones would rest,   33
if your pipe would sometime tell my loves!   34
But, really, would I'd been one of you, and either   35
guard of a troop of yours or cutter of ripened grape!   36
Surely, whether for me Amyntas it were or Phyllis   37
or whatever rage (what then if Amyntas is swarthy?   38
Violets, too, are dark, and hyacinths are dark),   39
they'd lie with me among willows beneath a pliant vine: 40
Phyllis would pick wreaths for me, Amyntas would perform.   41
Here are springs cool, here meadows soft, Lycoris!   42
Here's a grove. Here I'd be spent with you just by time."   43

The image of Arcadia comes to fulfilment as an idea of
pure and unique poetic skill that is an object of poetic ad-
miration and desire: *soli cantare periti* (32), "you alone...,
Arcadians." Again with the irony of Virgilian dialectic, it is
the voice of the opposite extreme that articulates an ideal.
Hence, in the dramatic fiction, it may also be taken as
overstatement (so, too, Meliboeus elaborated on the Tityran
locus, E.i 51-58): *soli* may be a bit much: 'Gallus' is a
desperate case. The persona of the elegiac lover serves,
like other figures "from outside," as a means of recalling
and, for the last time, revaluing essentials from the book.
    The center of the second eclogue (ii 35-39: *...Amyn-
tas? ...fistula...Amyntas.*) returns as an expanded center
(x 35-43), the ethical, so to speak, *interpretatio* of the
Arcadian poetic ideal: first an ideal order of work, recall-
ing the frame but not the central etiology of the second

piece (x 35-36, cf. ii 69-73, where georgic work was opposed to bucolic disorder); then the central image of bucolic ease and erotic satisfaction (x 37-41, five lines framed by *certe...Amyntas, serta...Amyntas,* and recalling the similar framing at the center of E.ii, but rehabilitating Amyntas as an object of love); and finally the confrontation between pure bucolic locus and the elusive object of desire (cf. E.ii 45-55, E.viiii 39-43). From the imagined viewpoint of the outsider, and perhaps only from such a viewpoint (we compare Meliboeus, E.vii, and also 'neighbor' Palaemon, E.iii), the conflicts of Tityran bucolic can be reinterpreted, programmatically misread in retrospect, to produce an image of self-sufficiency and ordered work and play and love within bucolic confines, in short the full Arcadian myth.

'Gallus', then proves very useful as an imaginative device for making one last perfect extract of bucolic; but the persona of the elegiac lover has been conceived with some tones that are slightly dissonant in the idyl: e.g. 'rage' (38), what the beloved would be in elegy not in Arcadian satisfaction, or 'spent by time' (43), a note of mortality appropriate to elegy but not to timeless, unaging Arcadian myth.[86] Such themes, however, should also remind us that the figure of 'Gallus' itself has precedents in the book, in the Tityran mode with its figures of change, growth, passion, aging, death such as Moeris, or the lover in Damon's song, Thyrsis, Pasiphaë, Mopsus (Daphnis dead), or old Tityrus. These have been opposites, in dialectic, to Menalcan and Arcadian steadiness, confidence, modesty, apotheosis, and, of course, 'Gallus' brought up from wandering below Helicon and told to make a grove. The 'dying Gallus' is one final vestige of the Tityran mode in a last productive contrast with containing form.

In the dramatic fiction, as 'Gallus' yearns to enter the

---

[86] Putnam 1969.361-86 cites these and other parallels with the erotic vocabulary of Propertius.

song and life of Arcadia, the new bucolic itself for a moment thus becomes an object of desire from the standpoint of recurrent Tityran discontent, which is imagined, now, on the outside looking in and up: nice turnabout after so many bucolic desires for other objects. But after building to the vision of the pure essentials of bucolic place (42-43), the desire veers. Once again a perfect ecphrasis is imagined as designed with an eye for capturing not so much nature as the beauty beyond. Hence, too, again the ecphrasis is followed by emphatic articulation of the gap between the object and the effective means in hand: (E.x 44-69)

'nunc insanus amor duri me Martis in armis	44
tela inter media atque aduersos detinet hostis.	45
tu procul a patria (nec sit mihi credere tantum)	46
Alpinas, a! dura niues et frigora Rheni	47
me sine sola uides. a, te ne frigora laedant!	48
a, tibi ne teneras glacies secet aspera plantas!	49
ibo et Chalcidico quae sunt mihi condita uersu	50
carmina pastoris Siculi modulabor auena.	51
certum est in siluis inter spelaea ferarum	52
malle pati tenerisque meos incidere amores	53
arboribus: crescent illae, crescetis amores.	54
interea mixtis lustrabo Maenala Nymphis	55
aut acris uenabor apros. non me ulla uetabunt	56
frigora Parthenios canibus circumdare saltus.	57
iam mihi per rupes uideor lucosque sonantis	58
ire, libet Partho torquere Cydonia cornu	59
spicula—tamquam haec sit nostri medicina furoris,	60
aut deus ille malis hominum mitescere discat.	61
iam neque Hamadryades rursus nec carmina nobis	62
ipsa placent; ipsae rursus concedite siluae.	63
non illum nostri possunt mutare labores,	64
nec si frigoribus mediis Hebrumque bibamus	65
Sithoniasque niues hiemis subeamus aquosae,	66
nec si, cum moriens alta liber aret in ulmo,	67
Aethiopum uersemus ouis sub sidere Cancri.	68
omnia uincit Amor: et nos cedamus Amori.'	69

"Now mad love is keeping me in arms	44
of hard Mars amid spears and marshalled foes;	45

you far from fatherland (may I not believe so far!)   46
without me, alone, Ah! hard are viewing Alpine snows   47
and chills of river Rhine. Ah, you may chills not harm!   48
Ah, may jagged ice not tear your tender soles!   49
I'll go and songs, that I've set down in verse of Chalcis,   50
I will tune with a Sicilian grazer's oat: 51
it's decided to prefer to endure in woods   52
among wild beasts' dens and to carve my loves   53
on tender trees—they will grow; you, loves, will grow.   54
Meantimes I'll range Maenalus with mingling Nymphs   55
or hunt brute boars. Not any chill will hold me back   56
from laying siege with dogs to Virgin Mountain's glens.   57
Already now to myself I seem to go through crags   58
and sounding bosks, delight in shooting Parthian points   59
with Cretan bow: as if this would be our rage's cure   60
or that god learn to gentle grow with ills of men.   61
Already again now us neither Hamadryads nor songs   62
themselves please. Woods again yourselves give way!   63
Not our toils can change that god,   64
not if we should drink of Hebrus while it's chill   65
and go on up to a watery winter's Thracian snows,   66
nor if, when dying bark dries on tall elm,   67
we'd drive Ethiopians' sheep beneath Cancer's sign: 68
Love defeats all; let us, too, give way to Love.   69

In poetics, after 'Here...Here...Here...Here...' (42-43) of the Arcadian bucolic myth, 'now' (44) must introduce the lower and unsuccessful alternative that confesses estrangement and impotence. At the comparable juncture, after a brilliantly industrious ecphrasis in the second eclogue, 'Corydon' styled himself 'hick', spoiler of flowers and springs (*rusticus es*, ii 56), in a collapse from the moment of bucolic as high art (capable of granting *honos* to a plumb, ii 53) to bucolic as awkward, poor, and low. Here, in the persona of an elegiac poet, the collapse appears to be from momentary identification with Arcadian myth back to the mythless hopelessness of elegiac love. Is perhaps, then, Virgil having a little fun with Gallus, using his persona first to gather the flower of bucolic myth from the book (and make a center piece for the tenth eclogue as a whole to correspond

in structure but differ in import from the central etiologies
of E.i and E.ii, and confirm the poetics of E.viiii), then
portraying elegy in its own right as a desperate alter-
native? The figure of elegy is imagined soldiering: thus
even a *miles* enters a bucolic scene, no longer *impius*
but a pathetic victim and destined loser in the war with
Love (cf. 69). Verses brought over, Servius says, from
Gallus spell out the parallel between the elegiac situation
and that of the Tityran mode, the constant yearning for the
object in the background, here evoked with a sighing plan-
gent rhetoric that is so palpably elegiac that one suspects a
bucolic parody and toning up of the 'rather stiff' Gallus
(46-49). [87]

In the dramatic fiction, the soldier-lover, having stated
his cause for despair, abruptly decides to take arms against
his troubles and projects a complex campaign: setting old
songs to a new measure, inscribing loves, letting them be
and hunting, all to no avail. Details of the maneuver suggest
that it may be Virgil's way of reflecting and completing his
own manipulation of the poetry and figure of Gallus from
the first image of 'Gallus' wandering below Helicon (i.e. the
poet-lover of elegy), but then 'Gallus' as poet-initiate for
an etiological poem, to this expansion on the earlier hint
of love with a full spectacle of erotic defeat, which recalls
figures of trouble and passion from the Tityran mode.

First the project (50-54). 'Songs set down in verse of
Chalcis' (50-51) points to the etiological poem (E.vi 70-72).
Chalcidico...uersu not merely suggests the derivation from
Euphorion but the long Greek adjective combined with

---

[87] Our only evidence for the way in which an Augustan poet
actually handled a verse of Gallus shows complete stylistic and
psychological metamorphosis of a rather woodenly mannered orig-
inal: the transformation of Gallus (p. 99 Morel) by Ovid (*Heroides*
18.125-26, 19.142) was noted by S. Mariotti, "Intorno a Domizio
Marso," *Miscellanea Rostagni* (Torino 1963) 613, n. 88; cf. VS
1976-1977.327.

uersu gives the impression that a Greek form has kept
stored up a Latin poetic force (*carmina*, cf. E.ii, iii) that
now might be released. The verb, then, *modulabor* (51),
means 'I'll regulate' in accordance with a rule or rhythm,
or 'set to music', or perhaps simply 'play' (cf. Calpurnius
Siculus, E.4.63, *Hyblaea modulabile carmen auena*, 'song
that can be played on Hyblean oat'). Its only other oc-
currence in the book was in the poetics of Mopsus: (E.v
13-14)

Immo haec, in uiridi nuper quae cortice fagi
carmina descripsi et modulans alterna notaui

Instead these songs, that newly on green bark of beech
I've copied off and noted, setting to music contrasts...

Mopsus' song, we recall, consisted of direct contrasts with
themes of the fourth eclogue, which thus in effect were
being reduced to a more conventionally bucolic form ('beech',
as type material of the Tityran mode, was there still imagined
as 'green' not broken and old). Thus with *modulabor* in the
tenth eclogue we can perhaps expect some comparable
idea of reworking previous matter into bucolic: reformulat-
ing those *carmina* from that 'verse'. Here, however, instead
of the fresh bark (suggesting the new Tityran mode) Virgil
speaks of an instrument first: 'oat of Sicilian grazer' (51).
Once again we are constrained to read back into the density
of recollective poetic signs. What these elements seem to
imply is a Latin version (cf. the Latin *auena*, Greek *calamo*,
E.i 2, 10) of Theocritean bucolic, in other words, the
mixed character of the Tityran mode, imagined as accessible
to 'Gallus'. This is not the Arcadian *fistula* (x 34). It
had associations with Corydon's poetic etiology (*septem
compacta cicutis / fistula*, E.ii 36-37, the center of E.ii,
which also contributed to the center of E.x). And Corydon's
fistula, in turn, was linked with the poetics of Menalcas
(his *cicuta*, E.v 85, recalling Corydon's *cicutis fistula*); and

Menalcas, too, became Arcadian (x 20). No, 'Theocritean oat' is one of those anomalies that "tease and confuse," like Daphnis and Arcadian rivals beside Mincius, or Tityrus' ambiguous state, all of which show the Tityran peculiarity. Hence the idea of bringing such an instrument to bear on 'songs set down in Euphorionic verse' so as to regularize them in some way (interpret or transpose them into Tityran bucolic terms) could well reflect on Virgil's actual transformations of the figure of Gallus (and allusions to Gallus' poetry): from poet-lover barely hinted (E.vi 64, elegy as poetry of the lowest register) to poet-initiate (*in montis*, vi 65, etiological poetry as the full Hesiodic middle register) back down to the lowest register (*sub rupe*, x 14) and the figure of the poet-lover reinterpreted as a bucolic (Tityran: sc. Virgilian-Theocritean) hero. Theocritus, excluded from the Arcadian mythic frame, surfaces here as the elegiac persona is imagined casting about for a weapon against love. In poetics this spells out what the eclogue has been showing us in fact, that the bucolic analogue for the elegiac poet-lover is not Arcadian myth, which supposes erotic satisfaction, but the hero of the Tityran mode, not however the exalted, Virgilian version, but more as Theocritus left it, dying in combat with Love. The future tense in the resolve of 'Gallus' thus will cover what is already under way in the book: even as the figure of Daphnis has been reduced (*deductus, irritus*) from divinity, so 'Gallus' is being regularized, brought down from example of power on Helicon to figure of impotence in Arcadia, from initiate to lover, from middle to low style and substitute Theocritean.

The next verses imagine the execution of the project (52-54). The locus, 'woods with wild beasts' lairs', sounds like a generic bucolic place, indeed the genre (cf. E.i 5, iiii 3), but something more. The activity, 'suffer, endure', is that of the abandoned lover (cf. 44-49). And the 'woods' are to receive the actual 'Loves' inscribed; indeed growth is foreseen. But why preference? Is 'Gallus' imagined as preferring to 'suffer' rather than do something else in 'woods'? Or is he preferring to suffer in 'woods' rather than somewhere else? If the former, the inference for poetics suggests itself that the very etiological poem of Gallus is now to be interpreted in bucolic terms, the 'Grove' imagined as a 'wood' and appropriate context for love. The preference, then, to 'suffer in woods' and the resolve to 'carve loves on trees' would suggest a mingling of the middle and lower modes that Virgil so carefully distinguished in Gallus' poetry (E.vi 64-65). Through the medium of Tityran bucolic, even Apollo's grove would be imagined as an erotic context. The result, for the genre of erotic elegy, is *auxesis*: 'you, loves, will grow' but the promised growth of the trees should also suggest that mixing would not diminish the middle style.

After such a theoretical tour de force, a tried reader might be expected to expect that the ensuing interlude (*interea*, 55), while loves were growing, would be a rendering in Tityran (sc. Virgilian-Theocritean) style of the figure of the elegiac lover in the context of the 'Grove'. [88] But the interlude is set on Maenalus, the Arcadian backdrop for this eclogue (x 15), and this brings us back to the other alternative: 'Gallus' must be imagined simply as preferring to

---

[88] One could speculate about the content of the 'Grove'. That way lies Mopsus. From our study of the fifth eclogue we remember his contentiousness, with his song a negation of the fourth eclogue, and we recall from Servius that the victory by Mopsus over the seer Calchas (itself already a Hesiodic subject, as we noted, too) had figured in the poems on Apollo's grove. We have, then, the prophetic (vatic, Hesiodic) fourth, ambitiously contentious and the climax to poetic growth that is predicated on an oracular *responsum* (E.i 44-45); then negating and contentious Mopsus, recalling the subject of a (Hesiodic) poem; then 'Gallus' raised and initiated for that poem (about a prophetic grove); then vatic Thyrsis, defeated; spells, Moeris werewolf, weaver of *mala carmina*; Moeris, defeated *uates*; and now, *carmina* of the grove to Tityran measure. *Non omnia possumus omnes*, but here must be elements.

suffer in bucolic (*siluis*) rather than in the state of militant elegiac love. His decision to 'go and carve' (53) then adds the important explanation (*interpretatio*) that the 'songs' are 'Loves' to be superimposed on bucolic material (as the reuse of *modulabor* implied). For poetics this confirms what seemed probable, that in the language of 'Gallus' Virgil reflects obliquely and elliptically on what he himself has done in the book: first imagine a transfer of poetic force from erotic to etiological verse, and then, undoing that transfer in the imagination, bring Gallus' poetic force back to erotic (but now bucolic) form, as the last variation on Tityran force in the whole design.

In confirmation of these Tityran signs, the interlude itself (55-61) is composed of motifs that recall, only to go beyond, the figure of Daphnis from Id.i and that expand on earlier elements in Virgil's book. 'Ranging with a cohort of Nymphs' (55) recalls Theocritean Daphnis, accused by Priapus of longing to join the dances but holding back like a goatherd (*dyseros*, Id.i 85), and thus reminds us once again how different is the Virgilian lover. Then 'hunting boars' recalls Adonis (*absit omen*, E.x 19; Id.i 109-10) and introduces the predominant theme: hunting as alternative, cure for love. Hunting has been a recurrent motif in the book (ii 29; iii 74-75; vii 29-32). Daphnis was endowed with enviable arrows and bow (iii 12-13, that Menalcas broke). But the most conspicuous hunt was that of Pasiphaë for the bull, calling to the Nymphs to close off the glens (with nets) and seek the tracks of the beloved beast (E.vi 52-60). There she was imagined as a figure of desperate wandering (*tu nunc in montibus erras*, vi 52) by contrast with 'Gallus' brought up from 'wandering' to purposeful song. Here 'Gallus' is reduced to the state of seeking to close off glens (*saltus*, x 57, cf. vi 56) in an ironic reversal of roles. The violence with which he defies the cold (56-57) also recalls Thyrsis (vii 49-53), another figure imagined as susceptible to being distracted from nature (bucolic limits) by love (unlike Pasiphaë who was drawn fatally, monstrously into nature). Finally, the despair of Gallus, that none of this can cure love, recalls and queries Theocritus, who cited that "natural" Polyphemus in clinical evidence that there is 'no other medicine but Pierians for love' (Id. x i). Yet before these precedents, Euripides had shown hunting as the alternative to passion, and a passionate dream of hunting as one symptom of the erotic madness for which designing speech was no cure.[89] Perhaps then the 'comic muse' of the Tityran mode (cf. vi 2) here touches again a tragic note (cf. viii 10, 47-50).

Daphnis, Hippolytus, Adonis: the mythic analogues ordain departure from the woods. 'This god' (61), unlike that of Tityrus (E.i 5-6, thus also an ironic echo of E.v 64), forces the lover from the locus. The compound of Tityran bucolic and erotic elegy is resolved in the ensuing dramatic fiction (62-69). Even wanderings greater than those of Meliboeus would not alter Love. Love defeats all. *Omnia.* The total confidence of the fourth eclogue comes to this. The antitype of Virgil's Daphnis, this Theocritean trace, exhausts the challenges to Theocritus' major idylls and the variations in the Tityran mode leaving Arcadian myth.

The piece closes as it opened with eight lines: (70-77)

Haec sat erit, diuae, uestrum cecinisse poetam,	70
dum sedet et gracili fiscellam texit hibisco,	71
Pierides: uos haec facietis maxima Gallo,	72
Gallo, cuius amor tantum mihi crescit in horas	73
quantum uere nouo uiridis se subicit alnus.	74
surgamus: solet esse grauis cantantibus umbra,	75

[89] Perutelli 1976.779: *Hippolytus* 255 ff., suggested by B. Snell, *La cultura greca e le origini del pensiero europeo* (Torino 1963) 406. Gorgias claimed that words (rhetoric) might benefit the soul as medicines the body; against him Plato urged the counter-claim of philosophy: Grube 1965.19. For other relations between poetry and magic (both curative and harmful), see Desport 1952.258, n. 25: e.g. Call. *Epigr.* 16.

iuniperi grauis umbra; nocent et frugibus umbrae.   76
ite domum saturae, uenit Hesperus, ite capellae.   77

These it will be enough for your poet to have sung   70
while sitting and weaving with thin mallow a wicker form,   71
Pierian goddesses: these you will make very great for Gallus, 72
Gallus, for whom my love grows hour-by-hour as much   73
as an alder when spring is new pushes up green.   74
Let's get up: shade is usually harsh to performers,   75
juniper shade is harsh. Shadows harm crops, too.   76
Go home, goats, with enough! Vesper's coming. Go!   77

Virgil has good cause to be satisfied. Small wonder if he imagines his goatherd-narrator turning back from Arethusa to the Pierians, who assisted at the burgeoning of the Tityran mode (E.iii 85) and initiated this half-book (E.vi 13); but, after those expansive and quickening commands, curt *via*, he declares his own judgment of enough, a theme that resonates with the memory of other observers pronouncing on the bucolic scene: Meliboeus, *et tibi magna satis* (E.i 47), and Palaemon, *sat prata biberunt* (E.iii 111). His image, then, of the status of this observer, so interested yet detached, shows traces of the sedentary Daphnis (E.vii 1), the interrupted handicrafts of Corydon (E.ii 72), no doubt pressed cheese in molds of Tityrus (E.i 81), the arts of ideal nature (E.vii 12, viiii 42, cf. ii 49), the tool of pastoral work (E.ii 30), the generic slightness, but an unexampled object, summing it up: *fiscellam* (71), 'something of wicker, a basket, receptacle', such as could serve to collect or compact into form for keeping some rural raw materials; the word a suggestion of *fistula,* but more utilitarian, suited to taking stock of the *labor* within the play, perfect figure for the realized design of the whole. [90]

---

[90] Skutsch 1969.166 unaccountably sees merely an allusion to E.x as a "garland woven from a catalogue of Gallus' poetry"; better Hahn, quoted in n. 6.85. We have seen how 'Gallus' serves as a means of recasting the Arcadian and the Tityran traces from the book: cf. VS 1976-1977.333, and n. 6.70. On *labor*, n. 6.81.b.

'These few songs' (x 2-3), then, are to be 'most great' (72) for Gallus, the largest claim in the most private case. After this gentle imperative to the Pierians to supplement once more (cf. E.viii 63), comes its imagined motive, that of the whole work, a form of love that is generative by contrast with that which defeated Gallus. 'Hours' are the shortest unit of time in these delaying works. 'Growth' recovers a positive value it had lost in the critique of the Tityran mode (e.g. E.vii 25; x 54, where the implications are catastrophic for the lover), but enjoyed in the first four pieces (E.ii 67, iiii 49, *magnum Iouis incrementum*). Yet the simile of pressing natural exuberance seems rather pointedly quantified, its springtime freshness recalling colors of the Tityran mode but here cut off from the surrounding winter.

Withdrawal to the background, 'home', by the goatherd-narrator signals the close, as we have seen, of the interlude that opened with the arrival of the goats of Meliboeus in the seventh piece. It began with 'play' (vii 17) and ends in 'toil' (x 1); it has sorted out the initiating-moving-energetic (Tityran) tendencies in Virgil's art from the retaining-contriving-calculating (Menalcan) which pass into the Arcadian form. While other tasks remain suspended in the background (the residue of expressed ambition), assiduously the poet plunders Tityran to produce Arcadian myth. By the end he has given the *epos* what he conceived in the fourth piece, a new version of its bucolic mode disguised as a return to origins. His version of the hero does not have to summon the inventor from Arcadia to Sicily to take back the pipe. Pan comes to Gallus on Pan's home ground. Arethusa is still at her source.

The pith of Arcadian pastoral is the idea, 'as before', without the other Tityran idea, 'bucolic growth'. Arcadia in the tenth eclogue is a world of goats and sheep, pigs, and a hint of men that consumed acorns before the moon was born (x 19-20). Bulls and cows are absent. Of the neatherd, 'Gallus' is a surrogate and trace. Here the ideal would be time without change. So 'Meliboeus' perceived and mistook Tityran bucolic—*quae semper* (i 53), 'as always', time conceived as ever one-the-same within the encircling spell of natural song inducing sleep (*saepes ... saepe*). Against this static vision, 'Tityrus' urged his journey and new god. 'Gallus' urges a new subject for Arcadian song (x 31-34). 'Arcadians' are imagined slow to comprehend his cause (x 21), able to articulate, not mitigate (22-30). In both the first and the tenth eclogues, longing of the *personae* in the dramatic fiction subserves a higher ambition: contact with heroic myth or distillation of new pastoral, pretext for a favor from the Arcadian nymph at home. Elegy may find fame, its erotic fable magnified in that of the bucolic hero. But the elegiac persona authenticates in turn the construct, vivifies through contrast, and becomes the real content of Arcadian myth. Love's soldier defeated, Virgil celebrates the triumph of Arcadian pastoral in the ruins of bucolic, first step in new epic design.

PART THREE: DESIGN

Chapter 7
THE POETICS OF DESIGN

All the antic lover's talk of 'tender feet' and 'tender trees' may have caused some readers to lose sight of the underlying design. Closing the tenth eclogue, the heavier shadows give their warning that both the day and the year are dead. Two converging temporal rhythms signal the accomplishment of a plan that started out with search of shade (E.i 52). Last comes the charge to goats: (x 77)

ite domum saturae, uenit Hesperus, ite capellae.

Go home, goats, with enough! Vesper's coming. Go!

'Home' does recall Meliboeus' ambivalent arrival in the foreground (*quid facerem? ...domi...*, vii 14-15); but now 'cold' has invaded the foreground and work is completed, hunger satisfied, while the background is imagined as pure shelter, for once making no demands of its own. These goats are greedy, snubnosed trimmers of tender shrubs (*tenera... uirgulta*, x 7). Virgil has to invoke the time and cut them off. Thus it is a vigilant, measuring craft that closes, reverses the imagined natural spontaneity of the goats' arrival (*ipse*, vii 7), and implies, perhaps, a certain insatiabilty behind that image of the pure attraction of the perfect place.

The goats of the fourth eclogue needed no direction in the spontaneous wending with full udders 'home' (*ipsae... domum*, iiii 21). But we remember that the goatherd-narrator's perfect retreat in the tenth echoes and in a certain sense supplants the original despairing cry with which Meliboeus, poignantly and expressly homeless (i 67-73), looked beyond Tityrus: (i 74)

ite meae, felix quondam pecus, ite capellae!
Go on, my goats, once prosperous herd, go on!

Something, as we inferred earlier, is supposed as changing for the better from beginning to end. Goats, in the last analysis, remind us of design and thematic development in the book.

As we look back, some implications of the design emerge more fully:

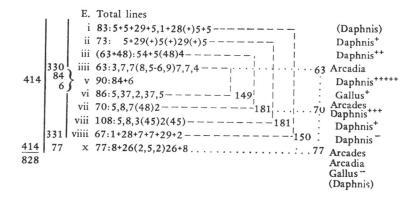

E. Total lines

		i	83:5+5+29+5,1+28(+)5+5 —————————	(Daphnis)
		ii	73: 5+29(+)5(+)29(+)5 ———————	Daphnis⁺
		iii	(63+48):54+5(48)4 ————————	Daphnis⁺⁺
	330	iiii	63:3,7,7(8,5-6,9)7,7,4 ———········63	Arcadia
414	84	v	90:84+6	Daphnis⁺⁺⁺⁺⁺
	6	vi	86:5,37,2,37,5———————149	Gallus⁺
		vii	70:5,8,7(48)2————————181···70	Arcades⁺⁺⁺ Daphnis⁺⁺⁺
		viii	108:5,8,3(45)2(45) —————————181	Daphnis⁺
	331	viiii	67:1+28+7+7+29+2 ——————————150	Daphnis⁻
414	77	x	77:8+26(2,5,2)26+8................77	Arcades
828				Arcadia
				Gallus⁻
				(Daphnis)

Beginning with the group of the first four pieces, we recall how the first places the epiphany of the god at the center, reaffirming commitment to bucolic material yet authorizing growth, while the second goes beyond this implicit claim to outdo Theocritus by suggesting direct succession from him, excluding bucolic mannerism. The third, then, claims at the center authorization from all georgic and bucolic nature in the spring season, after which the fourth finds its occasion like the first, but more emphatically, in the imagined moment of real events and ideological myth. Already in the first we saw a suggestion of *tripertita uarietas* in the distinction and disposition of bucolic, georgic, and civic-historical-heroic themes. This disposition recurs in a linear and parahistorical form in the fourth piece (where centering structure virtually disappears) in the paradigm of growth. Most fully we see it in the large middle portion: beginning miracles (8 lines: bucolic themes); middle, transition, mingled progress (5 lines: georgic) and persistence, even reaction (6 lines: 3 lines, georgic, civic, marine iron age; 3 lines, violent heroic); then end, full golden age (9 lines: georgic-bucolic miracles). The prominence of georgic then bucolic images at the climax of the scheme of growth anticipates the poetics of the fourth eclogue itself and finally of Arcadian myth. Parenthetically we may again note that the figure of the Theocritean bucolic hero remains in the background: implied in the figure of the absent cowherd (E.i 36-39), a cynosure of beauty (ii 26), a hunter deprived of his tools (iii 12-13).

Readers will have to recall for themselves the specific steps in growth through contrast (the *uariatio per alterna* that the Camenae love, iii 59), from *formosam* (i 5, taken for granted) to *formosum* (ii 1, not to be taken), or up from *fagi* (i 1) to *fagos* (ii 3), down from *deus* (i 6) to *domini* (ii 2), or the differences in outside observers, from Meliboeus (between realism and hyperbolic mythopoeia, E.i 46-50/51-58), to the disdainful narrator (E.ii 3-5), to the appreciative convalidating neighbor (E.iii 55-59, 108-111), to the eager Roman making short work of slight stuff (E.iiii 1-3); or other continuities and turns. The method appears to be one of now generalizing, now specifying in retrospect, varying the dosage at different thematic levels at different moments, for example the outrageous compression of the bucolic at the start of the fourth eclogue, followed by the ebullient expansion of georgic-Hesiodic themes and the strong mix of historical and heroic. Also notable in the fourth, of course, is the way that Pan is advanced from a vague figure of generic origins (E.ii 32-33), in parentheses behind the immediate predecessor indicated at the center of the eclogue (ii 35-39), to a potential object of competition, even in Arcadia itself. That, in our chart, is the righthand margin. In Virgil's design it is the high point of his first assault, a culmination which also spells the undoing of Tityran bucolic.

The method of revising in retrospect comes into its own in the fifth eclogue, which stands apart and responds to the group of four. The context particularly repays attention as a measure of return yet advance beyond the previous state of the bucolic mode in the aftermath of the fourth eclogue. We have seen that the song of Mopsus grows by reversing miracles of the fourth, while in reply the song of Menalcas (*maior*) draws positive themes from the first and fourth. The figure of Daphnis suddenly emerges as a hero-god, more than anything in Theocritus, resonant with the confident ideas and themes of the first four eclogues. We should remember that even as in the fourth piece Virgil drew on a form of *epos* beyond Theocritean bucolic proper (the Callimachean and Theocritean adaptations of the hymn) so here he turns to the post-Theocritean Greek bucolic for the form of the lament, which he integrates, as we suggested earlier, in this fashion into the genre as a formal sequel to the first idyll. Thus his version of Daphnis goes beyond the first idyll in form as well as theme.

In the chart, we divide the fifth eclogue and indicate the actual division between half-books in order to call attention to the moment in which the implied method of generalization in retrospect becomes most explicit in one of Virgil's most self-conscious and emphatic signals of

poetics. The device recalls that of the library; the technique
of labelling and cataloguing poems by first lines was that
of Callimachus' *Pinakes*, and the number of lines was
also occasionally recorded: Greek papyri have been found
with marks for every 10 or 20 lines and totals for every
100 or 200.[1] Virgil has adapted, refined and integrated
but not invented these particular techniques of measuring
and referring summarily to written work.

In this bibliothecal, retrospective modulation, Mopsus
gives up the Hesiodic and prophetic staff (token of his
role in Gallus, Euphorion, Hesiod competing with Calchas
in the 'Grove'?). Fresh from *alterna* against the prophetic
fourth piece, as we have noted, furnished with the ret-
rospective and generalizing 'hemlock', it is the figure of
Mopsus that provides the point of reference in the imagin-
ation for considering the second half book: prophetic old
Silenus, vatic Thyrsis, *mala carmina*, defeated Moeris, up
and down of the poet of the 'Grove'. After the generally
positive reply through Menalcas to the Tityran mode, the
particular critique, piece by piece, in a chiasmic progress,
takes up here.

Tityrus returns, promptly reduced from cattle to Hesiodic
shepherding: some expansiveness still allowed in pastoral,
but above all now the fine drawn, derivative song (E.vi
3-5). *Deductum carmen* evokes the generic idea of slight
style, but also signals the retrospective and reinterpret-
ative method of the second half book. Beginning with
the sixth eclogue, each piece repeats but reverses or
reduces in some way some functions, accentuating others,
of the piece to which it answers. Just as the first series
built up to the fourth, then took stock in the fifth, so
this series analyses that increment, gradually amplifying the

[1] Pfeiffer 1968.126-29; C. Wendel, *Die Griechisch-Römische Buchbeschreibung* (Halle 1949) 36.

design for Arcadian pastoral and diminishing the force of Tityran myth.

Virgil invents a succession of intricate dramatic fictions, the anecdotes effecting this design: the teasing and seduction of Silenus, chance session with Daphnis and whim of Meliboeus' buck, stupefaction of nature, exceeding eagerness for song, and need to do a little something for Gallus. Silenus in this light can be interpreted as the oblique and figural recollection of the poetic energy that went into making the Tityran mode from the first desire for *Libertas* to the full range of the fourth piece: an outburst that, when summarized in retrospect (for example, from the imagined viewpoint of this Mopsus) without the order of ideological myth, which justifies the paradigm of historical redemption, can well be reduced to grossly naturalistic and Dionysiac terms. The old fellow full of yesterday's revel. In the fourth eclogue, ideological commitment and poetic ambition reversed the Hesiodic-Lucretian model of decline. It returns in the sixth eclogue in the images of natural generation and human degeneration. A trace of centering structure returns. The first human voice, and echo, evoked is the lament for Hylas lost. The 'Grynean Grove' surfaces after having contributed Mopsus, if not more, to the preceding growth.

The contest was an affair of love in the third eclogue. In the seventh it is a matter of will. Damoetas and Menalcas were to tell contrasting songs, under the tutelage of Palaemon, and with the encouragement of all nature, because the Camenae love alternate songs (iii 55-59). That was represented as a direct drama. In the seventh, Meliboeus remembers a will to compete in remembering alternate verses. The differences are those between the expansive, Tityran series and the retrospective, anti-Tityran. We have seen that the dynamic tendencies of the Tityran mode fall to Thyrsis, the containing and Menalcan to Corydon. Reduction to musical shade and 'play' of memory sifts out the values that will find a home in Arcadian myth. Productive enterprise remains suspended in the background. The outside observer hails Corydon as the essential, apolitical, unheroic, self-contained thesis. In such a situation, to outdo, and Thyrsis does, is to lose.

In the progressive reinterpretation of the group of four, the eighth eclogue looks to the second. Its narrator was imagined in the background, disdainful perhaps, but fully attentive to the fore and middle grounds. That was where the action was, Corydon displaying his charms. Such a simple narrative structure served to integrate directly Corydon's amplifications in bucolic-georgic themes into the Tityran frame. Narrative in the second half-book, retrospective and reductive, becomes less simple. Tityrus, in the sixth eclogue we remember, aspired but was forced to settle for Apollo's dictates at more than second hand: through Pierians, Mnasyllus et al. from Silenus, through laurels (Daphne) thanks to Eurotas (the critic who gave the order to preserve) from Apollo because of love and beauty. Meliboeus *redux* heard the Arcadians remembering 'alternates' from the past, the Muse's or their own, but in any case originating at two removes from the narrative present. Like these two predecessors, the narrator of the eighth eclogue is imagined as ambivalent, caught between alternatives, only his case is more extreme. In the background, the promise of accomplishment by his original authority summons, but before him is a spell-binding clash of opposites within bucolic. Since the hero may be only coasting (*siue oram . . . legis*, viii 7), the action already under way prevails: *certantis* (viii 3) warns that we can expect replay and amplification of the *certamen* of the rivals (*E.vii* 16).

Damon's song, then, recalls the form and plot of

Thyrsis' song of Daphnis dying (Id.i), although the final leap to death echoes the paratragic threat of the goatherd (Id.3) as well. Thyrsis' refrain invoked the Muses to begin 'song of the cowherd (*boukolos*)', i.e. 'bucolic song', thus defining a new mode in *epos*.[2] Replying to this, and drawing now on the experience of the seventh eclogue, Damon's song is punctuated by the invitation to begin 'verse of Maenalus', a hint of the Arcadian myth that is to supplant the Tityran. But, in an important departure from Theocritus, here the refrain is imagined as sung by the subject of the song, hence it is the lover who is portrayed as calling for Arcadian form, evoking Maenalus and the myth of Pan's invention (viii 22-24). In poetics, this amounts to a trial of Arcadian myth by the needs of a passion for the unattainable that recalls the first Corydon (not the second, not the contained Arcadian). We have already discussed the result, its articulate despair with tragic parallels and perversion of golden age motifs: 'let Tityrus be Orpheus' (viii 55), bitter adynaton in the dramatic fiction, but in poetics a reminder of the associations of the Tityran mode with Orphic powers, by contrast with this Arcadian incapacity to do aught but deploy the proper literary precedents and highest skill, original myths to express the devastating force of love. In the second eclogue, Corydon's songs at least held and filled the foreground and suggested an orderly alternative in the middle ground.

We remember that Theocritus called the Pierians Love's only cure (Id.xi 1). With an echo, now, of Corydon's self-limitation (vii 23) and Tityrus' dependence (vi 13), the narrator makes his famous refusal to tell the song of Alphesiboeus. Here, as we have remarked, the Tityran mode makes a last show of strength, drawing on a Theocritean resource as yet untried, the second idyll, and thus showing, incidentally, that the arranger of Theocritus'

[2] VS 1976.32.

poems in the vulgate order was not alone in recognizing the formal affinity and thematic complementarity of the second idyll to the first.[3] By contrast with Corydon's *carmina* (E.ii 6) in that wide nature, rich land, delicious bower, these are nighttime, hermetic incantations, in the enclosure of the house, and of course imagined female passion drawing Daphnis back and down (again explicating Theocritus, where Delphis, Id.ii, was only an implicit surrogate, complement to Daphnis, Id.i).

The design of the eclogue suits both its ideas: the perfection of Arcadian form (*uersus*), yet the forced and intriguing, calculating and unrelenting passion (*carmina*). The inner dialectic of the eclogues reaches an extreme in this tormented web, desperate and exasperated *uariatio* in every sense. The reader may well wonder how the Medicean, Palatine, and, known through the Bernensian, Roman scribes all three came to feel authorized to intervene in this design, inserting the odd refrain (E.viii 76). Did they feel the attraction of the insistent theme of threes and mark off a group of three (viii 73-75)? The magical saw at that juncture might seem to justify it: *numero deus impare gaudet* (75), though the 'god' will not be expected to take equal delight in the even number of lines that follows (77-78), where the theme of three continues. Evidently the scribes, whatever the cause for their unanimity on this point, would not know that they were introducing an uneven number to the entire poem and the book (an even greater delight for this god?).[4]

Paradoxically, the last, perverse vestige of vatic and Orphic force in Tityran bucolic was directed to bringing a wayward Daphnis from the 'city' back to hearth and

---

[3] VS 1976.37, nn. 103, 104; and n. 6.71.b.

[4] Cf. n. 6.71. Servius' note shows that E.viii 75 did set off numerological speculation. He retails lore concerning both three and seven.

'home' in a passion-ridden, intensely grasping foreground.
In the thematic system of the book, as we noted earlier,
this effected a further reduction of the figure of the hero
of the Tityran mode from its association with ideological
myth and higher thematic registers. In terms, then, of the
same system, the plot of the ninth eclogue serves, as we
have seen, both locally to reverse the bucolic holding action
of Alphesiboeus' song and generally to criticize, in part
suspend, the formulation by the first eclogue of the found-
ing myth of Tityran bucolic. To this end, the narrative
framework, with its positive, still potentially productive
links to the background, is now itself reduced and criticized
in a new dramatic fiction. Instead of the narrator-observer
imagined as belonging to the middle ground or set there
(E.vi, vii, viii), the personae of the ninth eclogue are
portrayed traversing the middle from a foreground now
expropriated to a background that can not be put off. Their
memory of the powers of Menalcas generalizes in retrospect
about the mediating framework and positive relations be-
tween upper and lower registers originally worked out
in the first half-book. Ironically, one of the recollected
fragments of Menalcas' songs even evokes a Theocritean
pastoral moment, imaginatively prior to the situation of
the first eclogue, Tityrus pressed into service as a goatherd
while another goes to Amaryllis (23-25); while the other
Menalcan fragment (27-29) evokes the actual historical
plight of Mantua with a directness imaginatively prior
to the dialectical mediation and dissimulation of the
first eclogue and Tityran bucolic myth. Characteristically, it
is the young Lycidas who remembers the erotic pastoral
bit while Moeris remembers the verse of crisis; and
Lycidas replies by proposing song from Moeris, too:
an exchange. If the *mortalia* of Moeris seem to leave
intact the mind of Lycidas set on song, this must be yet
another ironical representation of the attitudes and ideas
gathering into Arcadian myth. Lycidas, we note, elicits

the narrative of trouble from Moeris only because of rustic surprise at movement to the city (1, cf. E.i 26, 36), a motive plausible at this point in the book only in a character imagined as not involved in the vicissitudes of Tityran-Menalcan bucolic (hence by contrast with Moeris an element on the "Arcadian" side). Consequently, when we find Lycidas refusing to associate himself with Moeris as a *uates* at the center of the eclogue (34), we recognize both the structural analogy with the first and second pieces, and the rejection, for Arcadian poetics, of the vatic development of Tityran myth. Finally, the two recollected fragments of Moeris also imagine situations prior to Tityran bucolic. Use of ecphrasis to tempt Galatea from the waters suggests the situation in Id.xi before it furnished a precedent for Corydon's plea (E.ii) and a detail for Tityrus' plenty (E.i 79-81); an elusive Galatea also recalls the pre-Roman slavery of Tityrus to love. [5] On the other hand, Moeris reproved Daphnis for observing the rise of old constellations when Caesar's new star makes the fields produce and assures continuity from generation to generation (46-50). This recalls the vignette of georgic arts on Menalcas' cups (iii 41-42) and imagines, as we noted before, the completest possible separation, even to indifference, between the elements that were synthesized in the Daphnis of the fifth piece. In retrospect, through the device of remembering old songs by an old 'poet-*uates*', we are reminded of the bucolic 'play' and the georgic and

---

[5] E.viiii 39-43, reinterprets Theocritus, Id.xi 42-49. It also recalls E.ii 45-55, vii 9 (*huc ades*); the flowers of iiii 18-20; grotto of E.i 75, v 6, vi 13; pliant vines, e.g. iii 38, vii 48; weaving in the natural context, vii 12, cf. *tegit*, vii 46; and it adds a refinement to the vocabulary of the bucolic locus in *umbracula*, 'shelters', from *umbra+culum*, a suffix for nouns "denoting instruments, places, etc." OLD. Flintoff 1976.17 argues that 'Galatea' is one person in the eclogues, against Mynors. 'She' is certainly one name and thematic fiction.

ideological (vatic and didactic) 'work' of the Tityran mode.
But this Daphnis is less and other than any bucolic figure.

After loss of the foreground, flight through the preter-
naturally silent middle ground, and effective collapse of
Tityran bucolic into the background whence it took force,
the status of the narrator has to be defined afresh. The first
line of the tenth eclogue sets narrative in the context of
the book itself (*extremum hunc*, x 1), a new step upward
in the progress of retrospective generalization. 'Arethusa',
then, at first seems to imply Theocritus (hence still Tityran
bucolic), while necessity to tell songs for Gallus, with an
eye to an urbane reader, bespeaks responsibility to Rome.
The bucolic and the urban, foreground and background,
after their forced union in the ninth, seem still to
have a narrator between them. But then the hint of
Arethusa's non-Theocritean state and the project of telling
Gallus' *Loves* come as an *interpretatio* that puts a different
construction on the initial signs. This narrator like the
others is in the middle, yet not between high and low but
between two versions of the low, Arcadian and elegiac.
Elegy as a genre has associations with both city and country
(cf. Theocritus, Meleager, in epigram; also Id.vii, Id.viii;
E.ii). Thus the narrator, securely located in the context
and matter of the book (x 1, 7-8), can place elegy in the
imagination where he will. The important point here is
that he conceives it as a genre in which the operative myth,
so to speak, is that of the poet-lover, whose writing, then,
is conceived as being a rhetoric designed to move, per-
suade, and teach or an expression of the soul's movement,
or solace and remedy for love. We have only to recall the
Aitia to remember that an elegist can also describe his
work by the operative myth of poet-initiate in Hesiodic
tradition; and we should recall that Mimnermus, remem-
bered by the image of poet-lover, also wrote on varied
subjects, including the origins of his town; and that
Hermesianax applied the myth of poet-lover to writers in

divers genres, such as Homer and Hesiod, Mimnermus and Philetas. [6] This is not to imply that Gallus in his elegies did not write of love, his own or others', but only to warn against supposing that a generalizing myth or fable of poetics reflects the specific content of all that a poet wrote. The principle applies equally to Theocritus, who come to be known as the Bucolic Poet because of the fame of those few poems; eventually it appears that all his works became known as *Bucolics*: the dominant operative myth concealed a variety of subjects and mixes of generic types. [7] Elegy, then, from the imagined viewpoint of the end of the eclogue book, is perceived, no doubt simplified and to a degree parodied and misread, through the operative myth of the poet-lover. The perception inevitably becomes colored by the forms that love has taken in the book, especially now in the sharpening distinction between Tityran bucolic and Arcadian myth. In this sense, Thyrsis was a precursor, and especially Damon's song, that set the plot of love, recalling the first idyll, in the context of Arcadian form. There, however, the figure of Daphnis was still encumbered with Tityran associations. Now it has been demythicized and reduced. *Irritus*, it can serve the need to give elegy bucolic form so as to shape the definitive contrast between Tityran and Arcadian in the book.

The meeting of opposites seems a bit awkward. The sheep stand about, perhaps stunned like nature in the eighth eclogue. Arcadians drop what they were doing. As if a bit at a loss themselves, they inquire what is going on. The narrator assures the elegist that sheep are nothing to be ashamed of. Adonis, too . . . In the dramatic fiction, Virgil deftly shows the nature and limits of literary mixing. Sheep also set Gallus apart and a little above the

---

[6] VS 1976-1977.329-330.
[7] VS 1976.32. Also the heterogeneous content of Bion's *Bucolica*.

narrator (goatherd) on the pastoral scale, a trace of Thyrsis and Tityrus (E.vii, E.vi 4) as opposed to Corydon and Meliboeus (E.vii), Menalcas (E.v). Cattle, as we have remarked, are absent. Moeris was the last cowherd. At least Lycidas so styled him (viiii 31). Insensitive prayer. He had nothing left but kids for the town (viiii 6).

The imagined wish of 'Gallus' that Arcadians tell his 'Loves' reflects the very form of the tenth eclogue, where Arcadian context surrounds the persona of the lover. In turn, the allusion to 'oat of Sicilian *pastor*' also reminds us that the figure of the lover has a Theocritean precedent and stands, in the design of the eclogues, as the climax in a progressive emulation. It began, we recall, by reversing the seventh idyll, which in poetics at least was Theocritus' last bucolic. Now the emulation closes with the first idyll, which Virgil has saved till last (having provided it with an ambitious sequel in the fifth eclogue). Finally Virgil bids to supplant Theocritus' Sicilian cowherd with the Roman elegist on Arcadian ground.

We have already studied the way that Virgil uses the elegiac persona to construct the perfected image of Arcadia in the center of the eclogue, drawing on the center of the second piece. The evidence of vestiges reconstituted suggests a final reflection on the layout of the book as a whole.

The trouble with those so-called static-concentric readings of the whole design was their assumption that "eclogue rings" had somehow to embrace the fifth piece even at the cost of leaving the tenth in the cold as the appendix, afterthought. A look at the ground plan of the tenth in relation to the second and first shows how captious that notion was, even apart from evidence for linear and dynamic development through the book: 'Daphnis' is not the fixed body, the kind of immaculate sun at the center, of Maury's vision but a changeable form that itself waxes and wanes in the progressive seasons of the design; Arcadia is not the universal and omnipresent idea but a construct only gradually brought to the fore toward the end. The structure of the tenth has a bold symmetry. In the ninth, the vestiges are slighter. The ninth sets out finally to eradicate Tityran bucolic. The tenth amplifies and demarcates the Tityran pattern of framing and centering as befits the positing of a new myth in and through the traces of the old. Together, then, the last two eclogues recall and reinterpret the first pair, as even their respective lengths might imply. The four pieces form a framework for the entire design, interwoven, introducing, then returning to exhaust, the variants of the leading motives, *Roma* and *Amor*: $(83+67=73+77)$

E.i   83: *ROMA deus*$^+$/ *barbarus miles*$^-$
            (*AMOR* Amaryllis$^+$/ Galatea$^-$)

E.ii   73:   (*ROMA*$^+$ implied order, narrator, *dominus*)
            AMOR Alexis$^-$/ Amaryllis, Menalcas, Amyntas$^+$

E.viiii 67: *ROMA* implied, *possessor*$^-$, *urbs*$^-$/ Caesar's star$^+$
            (*AMOR* Menalcas, Amaryllis$^+$/ Moeris, Galatea$^-$)

E.x   77:   (*ROMA* Gallus$^+$, Lycoris / *miles*$^-$)
            AMOR Lycoris$^-$ / Gallus$^+$ (x 1-8, 70-77)

Other details confirm the pattern. 'Beech', we recall, the tree (i 1), then woods (ii 3), but then old with broken tops (viiii 9); cool shade to be sought (i 52, ii 8), but then lost (viiii 20), being stripped (viiii 60-61), or menacing (x 75-76); goats, travail and remnant (i 11-18), once prosperous (i 74), attractive occupation (ii 30), again poor remnant (viiii 6), again prosperous (x 7, 77). Such signs, and there are others, justify and explain the image—generalizing in retrospect about the whole—of having sung, while seated to contrive a small containing form.

Epilogue: the Prospect and the Music of Order

Two final reflections suggest themselves, one retrospective, the other directed toward the further development of Virgil's work, both arising from the poetics of design.

The prospect of larger interests suspended haunts the second half of the eclogue book until the background presents a figure, Gallus, that can be reduced to bucolic guise. But the closing return home in its finality suggests that those larger aims, chores, horizons, and demands will now receive their turn. Their range became abundantly clear in the fourth eclogue. The assault on Arcadian origins has been carried off. The challenge remains open to Orpheus, Linus, Apollo, Calliope, and beyond it the aspiration to tell of *facta* that give body to Roman fate.

The *Georgics* turn to with method. The approach is familiar from the *Bucolics* although the contrasts and increments now progress through the larger units of books and then half-books. The first proem establishes a hierarchy of themes: earth, plants, animals (large, middle, small), rural divinities and heroes (benefactors, inventors of arts), then above them the historical and Roman hero to be a heavenly god. The ensuing growth through contrast will return to fill out and realize this design. Caesar holds the highest place at the beginning and shows the way. The project of an epic representation of Caesar's deeds (by Mincius' bank) looms in the middle. At the end, Caesar thundering in the East, affecting Olympian designs, marks the poetic horizon. Within, then, a familiar if vastly amplified framework of ideological myth and epic ambition, the *Georgics* take up their growth.

The first Georgic posits the whole frame, then deals with earth and sky, the extremes. The theme is toil, disorder. The second, then, rises by contrast to the things that grow from the earth, themes of plenty and order. The close signals this dialectical progression by echoing the close of the first. There the final image was a runaway chariot, driver not in control. Here the driver is expressly the poet, unharnassing after a long race.

In the third, the pace intensifies. Virgil amplifies the image of the driver out of all proportion—he will drive a hundred chariots—as he projects his ambition for heroic *epos*. He articulates the idea of centrality for Caesar—*in medio mihi Caesar erit*—but covertly in the exact center of his entire work he sets the image of the underworld: Envy with Ixion, Sisyphus—figures of frustrated and punished designs (G.iii 37-39). Horses, then, from figures of poetic passion become a subject of the half-book (with cattle, sc. large animals), the theme of driving passion for victory and in sex. Concluding with the etymology of *hippomanes* (cf. Id. ii), Virgil breaks the book precisely in half, redoubles again the theme of poetic passion, moves down the scale to the middle range of animals (pastoral: goats, sheep), then expands by the end of the book to a whole pastoral world afflicted by death. Thus far we have glossed over the specific literary precedents that he evokes, emulates, assimilates and overcomes. But Virgil's plague marks a major reinterpretation of Lucretius, assimilating and subordinating the end of that work, thus by implication its whole structure, to this larger design, after the earlier *recusatio* of non-mythological *epos,* of pure *rerum causas* (G.ii 475-86, *inglorius*): Virgil's etiological *epos* (*causas,* A.i 8, cf. E.i 26) has historico-heroic myth as its frame.

The paradoxes of growth through contrast intensify in the first half of the fourth book, where the slightest georgic matter is imagined as offering scope for the greatest themes, a rehearsal for *reges et proelia,* yet pure exercise of the imagination, without the express form of Roman fate: high moment subject to deflation by a handful of dust. Retrospectively the themes of the first and second halves of the third Georgic are negated by a return and synthesis of those of the first two books: here's passion, but for work only; here's immortality, continuity of the race, production, victory, without sex.

The bees, then, are the figure of the fullest possible georgic order in its fullest possible implications. In poetics they signal accomplishment of a middle *epos* beyond Hesiod and Lucretius: *in tenui labor, at tenuis non gloria* (G.iiii 6). The poetic toil is in slight (sc. Hesiodic) style. The reward heroic (countering G.ii 486). Yet even this still falls short of the highest register in the hierarchy of themes established at the start; the heroic and divine inventors of georgic arts, beyond which also stands the ultimate heroic and Roman authority. In other words, in poetics, Virgil has exhausted a level indicated by the *Works and Days*, but has not moved to the level of the so-called epyllion and erroneously labelled "little *epos*", short mythological subjects (cf. G.iii 2-8), which was implied in the thematic hierarchy as the last stage before full heroic (sc. Homeric) and Roman *epos,* the ultimate aim.

For this final move upward, the method is familiar: generalization in retrospect about the accomplishment thus far. The way is doubly prepared, since the theme of inventing georgic arts lends itself to reflection on the art of the *Georgics* and since the figures of the inventors, minor deities or heroes, promise suitable subjects for epyllion. The actual advance, then, as repeatedly in the *Bucolics*, comes in "an anecdote invented for its pith," here an epyllion: in short, one of those dramatic fictions that reflect because they draw on the work itself, producing a new moment by recasting what came before. For instance, we saw 'Menalcas' emerge as the figure of continuity in retrospect by contrast with 'Mopsus', the figure of ambition, at the close of the fifth eclogue; then 'Menalcas' return in the configuration of Arcadia, which summarized continuity and containment in the entire book, by contrast with 'Gallus', the figure recapitulating the poetics of ambition, striving and defeat.

Similarly, in the fourth Georgic, at the center, a passage

that modulates, posits the loss of bees—figurative negation of the entire georgic order accomplished thus far in the work—and their recovery by an Arcadian's invention. The story of this invention, its *aition,* is the "anecdote" that reflects on the ideas of poetry implicit in the creating of the *Georgics* themselves: passions are the causes and the causal chain articulates contrasting types of passion as the motives in the work (cf. G.iii). The strong and immediate passion of Arcadian Aristaeus is for his lost bees and disrupted productivity on the farm. Desperate, he flees (*fugiens,* 317). But it turns out, of course, that he himself was the ultimate cause of his own troubles. He set the causal chain in motion by trying to rape Eurydice, Orpheus' wife. Fleeing, she died (*fugeret,* 457). Orpheus was on the verge of recovering her, as we know, through the power of song, when sudden passion overcame him and he violated the restraining rule. She fled away (*fugit diuersa,* 500). He fixed attention on her memory until Thracian mothers, passionate and ignored, tore him limb from limb. His soul fled (*anima fugiente,* 526), body returned to the land. His anger deprived Aristaeus of all his georgic property. But killing cattle can produce new bees. Egypt preserves the technique in refined form.

In the figure of Aristaeus, concerned above all about property, not an impassioned though an occasional lover, we may recognize some traces of Menalcan character, transformed and amplified in the generalization about georgic order that places bees at the top, their loss a cause for abandoning all the rest: not realistic but a real reflection of the imaginative hierarchy of materials established through the poem as a whole. In Orpheus, then, we may recognize the pattern of Tityran passion, though amplified through recollection of the themes of the third Georgic. But Aristaeus is an Arcadian who tries a rape, then forgets all about it. Not quite Phyllis and Amyntas in the shade. Casual sexual violence initiates the etiological anecdote that reflects on the character of the art of the *Georgics*. Self-irony in Virgilian poetics acquires a new edge. This cause is more sinister than the elaborately casual straying of a goat by which Virgil first brought Arcadians to the narrative present (E.vii 7). The effect is a chain of exiles more desperate and final than the first arrival of a figure of comprehensive order lost (*nos patriam fugimus*, E.i 4), if less portentous than the founding flight (A.i 2, *fato profugus*). By comparison, the boast of poetic victory in the fourth eclogue seems a purely theoretical militance (E.iiii 53-59). Here the idea of violence becomes subject to moral evaluation. The anecdote, "doctrinal in design," shows attempted violation at the root of specific, irreparable loss though ultimate generic gain: a conflict of values and interests that cannot be reconciled, an ambiguity in the character of the ordering (civilizing and poetic) act. [8]

Inventing the "anecdote" of the Arcadian inventor, Virgil not only fills out the immediate scheme for middle *epos* that he implied from the start but he points beyond it to his ultimate literary ambition. The literary precedents for Aristaeus, calling on his goddess Mother in his distress and binding the *uates* Proteus to learn its true origin and solution, are well known: the *Odyssey* (Menelaus, Proteus) and the *Iliad* (Achilles). Again a myth of Arcadian origins serves to give Virgil access to a literary past in order to

---

[8] On the idea of violence in order, D. Halperin, "Man's Fate in the *Aeneid*," *Virginia Quarterly Review* 53 (1977) 58-72. For elements of a dialectical interpretation of G.iiii, see C. P. Segal, "Orpheus and the Fourth Georgic: Vergil and the Nature of Civilization," *AJP* 87 (1966) 307-325, a study not understood by L. P. Wilkinson, *The Georgics of Virgil* (Cambridge 1969) 120, who simply fails to account for the relations of Aristaeus and Orpheus to the entire work. On the dialectic of the *Aeneid* growing out of the *Bucolics* and the *Georgics*, see Johnson 1977.20-21. Modern editors are not so attentive to number as some ancients (n. 7.1): Mynors (Oxford 1969) omits G.iiii 338 although it is required by the symmetry of G.iii and G.iiii, not to mention the trace of centering structure in the whole.

complete a present design. In the tenth eclogue, Arcadian myth took the shape and appropriated the hero of Theocritus' first idyll. Here Homer is the object, barely broached. But in the allusion to Achilles, the heroic type that was superseded in the fourth eclogue by the idea of the bucolic-georgic heroism of the child, returns to the threshold as Virgil reaches the limits of bucolic-georgic order and prepares for the Homeric mode.

In the "anecdote," both Aristaeus and Orpheus in their fashions seek the same object that eludes. *Eurydice*, like *hippomanes*, that Arcadian plant which shepherds indicate by a name that reveals its nature (*uero nomine*, G.iii 280-81), is a name that has the truth of its bearer's nature in its Greek roots. But unlike *hippomanes, Eurydice* yields its etymological pith not at the level of theme, subject matter or anecdote, not in the narrative fiction, but as an idea in poetics. The Greek roots mean 'wide-ranging order, general writ' (cf. Latin *dicio*). They suit a figure represented as the object of desire for both tendencies in the art of the *Georgics*. Here the role of the figure in poetics can be said to determine the choice of the name, since tradition offered both *Eurydice* (*Epitaph. Bion.* 124) and *Argiope* (Hermesianax 7.14 Powell) as names for Orpheus' wife; and the new detail, that Orpheus failed to bring her back, also reflects the poetics of this work (and the continuity with defeated 'Gallus'). *Eurydice*, the figure of the comprehensive language that eludes, lost, indeed destroyed by the attempts, becomes at least the occasion for an idea of completeness and self-renewal in the lower, non-human, non-heroic georgic order. The attempted rape leads to the "discovery of a technique" (sc. the reflection on development through contrast in the poem) that the death of bulls can always produce a new order of bees (as the third book gave rise through dialectical progression to the fourth): crude bucolic matter, passion and mortality, becomes, in the design of the *Georgics*, the prelude to slight, perfected and immortal form.

On the other hand, Orpheus, after a violent end, returns to the land where the work began. Both the order and the passion remain within the circle of the containing frame.

At the end, Virgil imagines himself at last in the middle, like those narrators in the eclogue book, hearing epic thunder on the horizon, remembering bold youthful play beneath the beech. His perspective is that of the narrator and poetic protagonist ('Meliboeus—goatherd') looking down (and now back) at 'Tityrus'. The suggestion of *tripertita uarietas* and the specific gesture to the *Bucolics* are more than justified (although inevitably such explicit generalizations must simplify and reduce) by the employment of the method of the eclogue book written larger, the transmutation of bucolic matter into georgic form, and the final invention of another Arcadian myth in dynamic contrast with passionate power as another return to the origin of another epic mode.

The final mode of *epos* remains for the "anecdote" of the *Aeneid*. The work begins by establishing its own programmatic hierarchy of 'arms' and 'hero', travel and war, Troy, Italy and Rome: in poetics aiming to assimilate and surpass the *Odyssey*, the *Iliad*, in short the Greek origins, but also the epic of Rome. The background and the horizon of the previous works have become the narrative present.

Such a design, of course, is not merely of the poet's chosing. It imposes itself with the authority of tradition, history, ideology as an impersonal order of which the particular implications are by no means clear at the start. They remain to be elaborated through work. These qualities of the design, its import in poetics, are summed up in the "anecdote" by a word that appropriately for an idea of poetics means determining utterance—*fatum*, 'fate': what the Parcae establish, Varro says, by uttering (*fando*) at the time of a child's first significant speaking (*fatur*), hence called *fatum et res fatales*, 'fate and fated things' (*De ling. lat.* 6.52; cf. E.iiii 46-47).

The *Aeneid* is Virgil's poetic fate. Its personae are his

final reflective instruments, enlarged vestiges of Orpheus and Aristaeus. The figure of Aeneas the Trojan, heir to Hector in a sequel to the *Iliad,* progresses through an Odyssean plot. The typology of the *Iliad* remains, the greater challenge: *maius opus,* as the poet reminds us in a characteristic modulation, assuming for the first time the name of *uates* as he approaches his 'end of toil' (A.vii 37-45). 'Achilles' was the type of violent heroism superseded in the vision of the fourth eclogue; but now the task presents itself of absorbing his traces in 'Aeneas'. In Virgil's literary victory, the Trojan figure will supplant Homer's first hero, much as 'Gallus' in the tenth eclogue in Arcadia supplanted the Sicilian Daphnis. The Virgilian conquest of the entire tradition of *epos* will be complete. As before, Virgil carries it off with a trace of Arcadian invention.

In the last scene of the poem, which recovers the pattern of Achilles killing Hector, Aeneas is imagined killing Turnus (the native hero who fought for passion) not merely on his own initiative but provoked to vengence, indeed acting as the surrogate of the young Arcadian Turnus killed: 'Pallas sacrifices you, Pallas exacts the penalty' (A.xii 948-49). Even here, perhaps we should say "above all here," the invented anecdote reflects the character of Virgilian poetics as articulated in the recurrent transformations of contrasts between figures of order (Arcadian) and of overreaching passion: Arcadians/Gallus, Aristaeus/Orpheus, Aeneas (Pallas)/Turnus. In each case the Arcadian element figures in a literary triumph, some conquest of tradition, as the fourth eclogue seemed to imply (E.iiii 53-59). But the "pith" of the invented anecdotes becomes progressively more bitter in reflecting on more ambitious ordering acts.

The last lines of the *Aeneid,* like the close of Virgil's previous works, reinterpret traces from the beginning of the *Bucolics:* (A.xii 951-52)

...ast illi soluuntur frigore membra
uitaque cum gemitu fugit indignata sub umbras.

...but his limbs grow slack with chill
and with a groan his life flees outraged to the shades.

This chill is that of death. This final victim of Roman
order flees to an exile in shadows that seem to allow no
return, no reintegration of Meliboeus to observe play, no
reincorporation of Orpheus in the basic matter. This
separation sounds brutally final, as befits this moment in
the order of the works. The design for *epos* stands complete
and with it ideological myth. The *fatum* of the com-
prehensive literary-historical design has been realized. Hence
there can be no desire for further contrast (in letters), no
room for it (in ideology). Just as the kindling of Turnus'
passion made a story where there was none (A.vii), now
the story requires a definitive end, one that leaves no fur-
ther cause for growth and change. If we require any further
measure of the distance between that first moment in Vir-
gil's imagination and this, we may reflect that here the
imagined cause of flight is not a *miles* but a demi-god,
perhaps *barbarus* but not by any stretch of the imagination
impius. His action is presented metaphorically as a sacrifice
(*immolat*, A.xii 949, cf. A.ii 223-24), in which a hero, not
a lamb, is the victim. Yet perhaps even this grim finality
must be read, like Virgil's others, in relation to the end of
the first half of the work, which does present its vision of
return of souls to the struggle. 'Turnus', then, may sug-
gest not only Rome's achieved domination of her neighbors
but also the inevitability of new reaction against order,
hence new ordering struggles in history and ironies of am-
bitious designs.

Our final reflection, now, on the poetics of design
takes us back not to Meliboeus' flight but to the orderly
music of Tityrus. The images of music in the eclogue book
are so familiar that they seem part of the generic scene,
like cows and goats and shepherds, milkmaids, beech and
Pan. Hence, like these persons and materials, music must

have import for poetics, though likely to be even richer because of the varied practice and elaborated theory of the art. Song is its most characteristic bucolic form: the regular work that broadcasts echoes of requited love (i 2, 5), play as expression of whim (i 10), song as accompaniment of pastoral ease (i 75-78); singing as rhetoric, suasion against unrequited love, the instrument as valuable property (E.ii); song as skill in its own right, validated by the recollection of the erotic uses already touched (E.iii); song as prophetic enunciation, as moving and instructing rhetoric to the 'boy' (cf. E.ii), as capable of utterance like the very 'fates' of the Parcae (E.iiii); song as consolation and praise, lament and hymn, the instrument as formal control, teaching the singer (E.v); song as generating and consoling, even transforming power, inexhaustible story (E.vi); but verse, not song, as recollection of contrasts (E.vii); verse, then, as narrative recollection of despair in love, song as repairing material force (E.viii); song as failure to repair, memory of lost powers (E.viiii); song as imperative of poetic love, as immortalizing and consoling form, as rhetoric of love, as alternative and drug, failed remedy. Each of these ideas has a separate history which leads back into poetic tradition, philosophy, and musical theory. [9] The whole subject invites another book, no doubt, written from the viewpoint of Virgil's design. But taken for the moment in the context of the design itself, the musical ideas and the others in their variety, development, returns and transformations, bring to mind a moving pattern in music: [10] contrast (calm/motion), gradual build up to oracular 'Graze cattle as before, breed bulls!', return and development of calm, but fuller restatement of exile overwhelming, yet calm of close (E.i); then

[9] On the Muses as *pharmakon*, for instance, see n. 6.88 and the suggestive study of Id.xi by Spofford 1969.

[10] Benevelli 1973.263 suggests that critical thought adopt "la metafora del diagramma musicale." Cf. n. 1.57.

calm but tension, energetic rise, sharp fall, minor tones, closing middle tone (E.ii); staccato, sudden discord, strident crescendo, new harmony in fuller tone, sudden high note (Jove, iii 60), then lower pitched, intense concerto, replaying loves but playing itself out in edginess for work, envy, before the comprehending close (E.iii); sheer musicality of returning, swelling pattern, Jove's scion, Arcadia, Pan (E.iiii); modulation, soft-pedalling, 'shade' yet 'shade to dell', bold recapitulation, first minor, but then still more exuberant major, but the close breaks on-going rhythm, punctuates by literal restatement, thus necessitates new gathering of forces (E.v); again start, Tityrus, a new divine utterance 'Graze sheep fat, draw out song!', no cows, let alone bulls, the tickling of Silenus' fancy, vast upswelling, furtive continuos, monstrous inversion (lust for new breeding by a bull), intermezzi, love sublimated into woods, dissonances, unwilling gods, night (E.vi); but after the cosmic storm, a casualness, circumstantial, only intense anamnesis, Arcadians, only a trace of larger order past in the network of designed, exhaustive variations, then sudden, final shift to intense commitment, poetic love (E.vii); the intense note grows, a clash of opposites, symmetry forced to extremes (E.viii); more strained replay and reversal of old motifs (E.viiii); but then finale, restatement, modulating and interweaving, the dominant and contrasting tones, coda (E.x).

Some such memory of the eclogues' order might well approximate to an idea of music as internally articulated, varying and coherent structure, perhaps also with a sense of the rhetoric of the structure, the way that its *uarietates* and *colores*, modes heard successively, might grip and please, perhaps dispose. But the underlying plan of the eclogues also invites comparison with the idea of music as a rational system formed on the order of the cosmos. This, too, would merit much further study in the light of what we have seen of Virgil's order; but we must close with two instances.

Quintilian refers to the cosmos as composed according to system, which then was imitated by the lyre: *ipsum mundum ratione compositum, quam postea sit lyra imitata.* More fully, Varro Atacinus in the *Chorographia* spoke of Apollo's music as echoing the music of the seven planetary spheres: (p. 97 Morel)

Vidit et aetherio mundum torquerier axe
et septem aeternis sonitum dare uocibus orbes
nitentes aliis alios, quae maxima diuis
laetitia est. at tunc longe gratissima Phoebi
dextera consimiles meditatur reddere uoces.

He saw the cosmos turn on its etherial pole
and seven spheres with timeless voices give out sound
supported by each other: that is greatest joy
for gods. But then, by far most pleasing, Phoebus' hand
begins to work to give back voices like to like.

Varro's terms for echo resemble those of Lucretius, sighting echoes: *loca uidi reddere uoces* (iiii 577). That context in Lucretius also gave Virgil the echoic poetics of the 'woodland muse', as we have seen, (E.i 2, 5)

siluestrem tenui musam meditaris auena,
formosam resonare doces Amaryllida siluas,

where the verb, 'you work to make', is that which Varro uses for Apollo's music with the lyre. The number of the spheres itself is of course a commonplace and fixed, like the number of the strings (cf. the image of Orpheus' lyre, A.vi 646). But Virgil chose to introduce it into the poetic aition at the center of the second eclogue (E.ii 35-39), where he established himself as Theocritus' successor, by contrast with the 'nine-voiced' pipe in his source (Id. viii 18). Thus 'seven' as much as the expansive command of the 'god' (E.i 45) became a sign of Virgil's difference from Theocritus and an element in the poetics of the eclogue book, a formal condition that shapes, links, and 'instructs' (cf. *docuit* of the *cicuta*, E.v 87). [11] Joy of the gods at music was a motif of the *Theogony*, as we noted in discussing the sixth eclogue (their displeasure when Silenus ceased, E.vi 86, constrained to silence by Vesper, who also ordered the 'sheep' to be numbered, after Apollo authorized 'fat sheep' at the opening of the piece). Joy, then, a cosmic tremor of anticipation for the 'child' (E.iiii 52), and natural celebration of Daphnis (E.v 62-63), is a motif at the high points in the eclogues. But beyond these thematic links, we recall the first cause of song in the sixth eclogue was Apollo, working it up (in unrequited love), *Phoebo meditante* (vi 82). A song of order in nature, disorder in human love, decline in civilization, if Apollo sings it, can please the gods as much as the echo of the music of the spheres.

Poetry that claims start from an oracular *responsum* (E.i 44-45), posits a *principium* in Jove (E.iii 60), and could presume to put words in the mouths of the Parcae, or at least approximate their 'fates' ('*talia saecla...currite*', "such as those" just described in this piece, Virgil makes them say, or the editors mispunctuate, E.iiii 46-47), poetry that could pretend in an exemplary anecdote that it caught Phoebus' eye (and he, its ear) and that it could report even

[11] Seven was assigned meanings both popular and learned (see n. 7.4). On the lyre (A.vi 646) see Desport 1952.162 and A. D. Nock, "Varro and Orpheus," *CR* 61 (1927) 17. Callimachus, fr. 202 Pf., is a poem for the seventh day festival of a little girl; it tells of a song Apollo sang for Demeter's daughter on her seventh day, the finest gift of any god. Callimachus, H.iiii 249-253, says that swans circled Delos seven times at Apollo's birth, hence the lyre has seven strings. Varro, *Hebdomades* (Aul. Gel. 3.10), gives other speculations with sevens: 28 is four hebdomads, comprises the first seven numbers, equals the period of the moon; the development of the fetus proceeds by hebdomads, the seventh seven being the time of full formation as a human being (cf. E.iiii 49). Varro closed by saying that he had entered his twelfth hebdomad of years (39 B.C.) and had completed seven hebdomads of books up to that time.

snatches of the song that he worked up that pleased the gods, such poetry ought to aspire to the condition of music as a rational, constructed and instructing, moving discipline, informed by number and fitted to the rational order of the heavens, moved by love. Hence such poetry ought to make at least something like the allusion to numerical order that we find in the eclogue book. Something like this must be the largest reason for the design. Here again we come to a beginning as much as an end of study; and as readers we are again challenged to venture beyond our tested range— whether the play of what is now called intertextuality or the work of theme and variation, or merely such more diffused realities as drama, landscape, 'thanks to the Emperor', and the rest.

APPENDIX

One valuable study, long promised by its publisher, arrived too late to be taken into account: I. M. LeM. DuQuesnay, "Vergil's Fourth *Eclogue,*" *Papers of the Liverpool Latin Seminar 1976, ARCA 2* (Liverpool 1977) 25-99. Its formidable array of historical and literary traces will clearly have to be reckoned with. It offers welcome reinforcement for what we have said about the prophetic or vatic character of the fourth eclogue, but without going on to consider the role of the vatic in the design of the book as a whole.

Indeed, a similar reflection passed through my mind repeatedly while reading, since so many of the particular observations took on a different cast when viewed in the light of my general arguments: that the fourth eclogue plays an integral part in the design of the eclogue book, and that the whole design makes a new program in the tradition of Greco-Roman *epos*. For instance, *siluae* (E.iiii 3) was rightly glossed by Greek *hyle*, 'wood; material to be worked up' (cf. *materies, agger,* 'timber'), but without recognizing *siluae* also as a retrospective reflection on the matter of the preceding pieces, one of the class of natural objects that figure bucolic art (e.g. also *liber,* 'inner bark; book'). Or again, Virgil's relation to Catullus (*C.* 64) was discussed, but without attention to the programmatic typologies of *epos;* and the background of *epos* would have helped, too, in giving its due to Virgil's transmutation of Lucretian *isonomia* from an idea of the redistribution of matter between systems to an idea of the reforming of a single system, changing its old matter into new (e.g. ... *ferrea primum / desinet ac... surget gens aurea,* E.iiii 8-9; and *uestigia... / irrita... soluent...*).

Bibliography

Alpers, P. J., 1972. "The Eclogue Tradition and the Nature of Pastoral," *College English* 34: 352-371.

Badius in *Vergilius Maro, Publius, Opera*, Venice 1544, repr. as The Renaissance and the Gods, n. 7 (New York 1976).

Barsby, J. A., 1974. "The Composition and Publication of the First Three Books of Propertius," *G and R* 21: 128-137.

Bayet, J., 1967. *Mélanges de littérature latine* (Rome).

Becker, C., 1955. "Vergils Eklogenbuch," *Hermes* 83: 314-349.

Benevelli, E., 1973. "Strutturalismo e/o Scritturalismo (A proposito di *S/Z* di Roland Barthes)," *Strumenti Critici* 21-22: 257-268.

Berg, W., 1965. "Daphnis and Prometheus," *TAPA* 96: 11-23.

———, 1974. *Early Virgil* (London).

Berkowitz, L., 1972. "Pollio and the Date of the Fourth Eclogue," *CSCA* 5: 21-38.

Beyers, E. E., 1962. "Vergil: Eclogue 7—A Theory of Poetry," *AClass* 5: 38-47.

Bowersock, G. W., 1971. "A Date in the Eighth Eclogue," *HSCP* 75: 73-80.

Büchner, K., 1955. "P. Vergilius Maro," *RE* 2.15.

Cartault, A., 1897. *Étude sur les Bucoliques de Virgile* (Paris).

Clausen, W., 1964. "Callimachus and Latin Poetry," *GRBS* 5: 181-196.

———, 1972. "On the Date of the First Eclogue," *HSCP* 76: 201-206.

———, 1976. "CYNTHIVS," *AJP* 97: 245-47.

Coleman, R., 1977. *Vergil Eclogues* (Cambridge).

Damon, P., 1961. "Modes of Analogy in Ancient and Medieval Verse," *UCPCP* 15: 261-334.

Desport, M., 1952. *L'incantation virgilienne: Virgile et Orphée* (Bordeaux).

Di Benedetto, V., 1956. "Omerismi e struttura metrica negli idilli dorici di Teocrito," *ASNP* 25: 48-60.

Dick, B. F., 1970. "Vergil's Pastoral Poetic. A Reading of the First Eclogue," *AJP* 91: 277-293.

Duckworth, G. E., 1969. *Vergil and Classical Hexameter Poetry. A Study in Metrical Variety* (Ann Arbor).

Elder, J. P., 1961. "NON INIUSSA CANO: Virgil's Sixth Eclogue," *HSCP* 65: 107-125.

Fabiano, G., 1971. "Fluctuation in Theocritus' Style," *GRBS* 12: 517-537.

Fedeli, P., 1972. "Sulla prima bucolica di Virgilio," *GIF* 3 (24): 273-300.

Flintoff, T. E. S., 1976. "Characterization in Virgil's Eclogues," *PVS* 15: 16-26.

Fredricksmeyer, E. A., 1966. "Octavian and the Unity of Virgil's First Eclogue," *Hermes* 94: 208-18.

Frischer, B. D. 1975. *AT TU AUREUS ESTO. Eine Interpretation von Vergil's 7. Ekloge* (Bonn).

Galinsky, G. K., 1965 (1968). "Vergil's Second Eclogue, Its Theme and Relation to the Eclogue Book," *C et M* 26: 161-191.

Geymonat, M., 1973. *P. Vergili Maronis Opera* (Torino).

Gow, A. S. F., 1952². *Theocritus* (Cambridge).

Grube, G. M. A., 1965. *The Greek and Roman Critics* (Toronto).

Hahn, E. A., 1944. "The Characters in Vergil's *Eclogues*," *TAPA* 75: 196-241.

Hanslik, R., 1955. "Nachlese zu Vergil's Eclogen 1 und 9," *WS* 68: 5-19.

Hardie, C., 1966². *Vitae Vergilianae Antiquae* (Oxford).

——, 1970². "Virgil," *Oxford Classical Dictionary* (Oxford).

——, 1971. "The *Georgics*: A Transitional Poem," The Third Jackson Knight Memorial Lecture (Berkshire).

Johnson, W. R., 1977. *Darkness Visible. A Study of Virgil's* Aeneid (Berkeley).

Kidd, D. A., 1964. "Imitation in the Tenth Eclogue," *BICS* 11: 54-64.

Klingner, F., 1967. *Virgil* (Zurich).

Koster, S., 1970. *Antike Epostheorien* (Wiesbaden).

Leach, E. W., 1971. "*Eclogue* 4: Symbolism and Sources," *Arethusa* 4: 167-184.

——, 1973. "Corydon Revisited: An Interpretation of the Political Eclogues of Calpurnius Siculus," *Ramus* 2: 53-97.

——, 1975. *Vergil's Eclogues: Landscapes of Experience* (Ithaca).

Maury, P., 1944. "Le secret de Virgile et l'architecture des Bucoliques," *Lettres d'Humanité* 3: 71-147.

Otis, B., 1964. *Virgil, A Study in Civilized Poetry* (Oxford).

———, 1971. "The Eclogues: A Reconsideration in the Light of Klingner's Book," *Vergiliana*, edd. H. Bardon and R. Verdière (Leiden): 246-259.

Perret, J., 1970². *Les Bucoliques* (Paris).

Perutelli, A., 1973. "T. S. Eliot e il concetto di 'Tradition' nella critica anglo sassone su Virgilio," *Maia* 25: 118-136.

———, 1976. "Natura selvatica e genere bucolico," *ASNP* III, 6, 3: 763-798.

Pfeiffer, R., 1943. "A Fragment of Parthenius' *Arete*," *CQ* 37: 23-32.

———, 1951. *Callimachus* II (Oxford).

———, 1965. *Callimachus* I (Oxford).

———, 1968. *History of Classical Scholarship* (Oxford).

Pöschl, V., 1964. *Die Hirtendichtung Virgils* (Heidelberg).

Posch, S., 1969. *Beobachtungen zur Theokrits Nachwirkung bei Vergil* (Innsbruck): rev. E. A. Schmidt, *Gnomon* 44 (1972) 771-76.

Pucci, P., 1977. *Hesiod and the Language of Poetry* (Baltimore).

Putnam, M. C. J., 1969. *Virgil's Pastoral Art* (Princeton).

Robinson, D. M., and E. J. Fluck, 1937. *A Study of Greek Love Names* (Baltimore).

Rossi, L. E., 1971. "I generi letterari e le loro leggi scritte e non scritte nelle letterature classiche," *BICS* 18: 69-94.

Schmidt, E. A. 1972. *Poetische Reflexion. Vergils Bukolik* (München).

———, 1974. *Zur Chronologie der Eklogen Vergils* (Heidelberg).

Segal, C. P., 1965. "*Tamen Cantabitis, Arcades*: Exile and Arcadia in Eclogues One and Nine," *Arion* 4: 237-266.

———, 1976. "Vergil's *caelatum opus*: An Interpretation of the Third Eclogue," *AJP* 88: 279-308.

Serrao, G. 1971. *Problemi di Poesia Alessandrina. I. Studi su Teocrito* (Rome).

Skutsch, O., 1956. "Zu Vergils Eklogen," *RhM* 99: 193-201.

———, 1969. "Symmetry and Sense in the Eclogues," *HSCP* 73: 153-169.

———, 1970. "The Original Form of the Second Eclogue," *HSCP* 74: 95-99.

———, 1971. "The Singing Matches in Virgil and Theocritus and the Design of Virgil's Book of Eclogues," *BICS* 18: 26-28.

Soubiran, J., 1972. "Une lecture des 'Bucoliques' de Virgile," *Pallas* 19: 41-75.

Spofford, E. W., 1969. "Theocritus and Polyphemus," *AJP* 90: 22-35.

Syme, R., 1939. *The Roman Revolution* (Oxford).

VS: Van Sickle, J., 1966. "The Unnamed Child: A Reading of Virgil's Messianic Eclogue," *HSCP* 71: 349-52.

———, 1967. "The Unity of the Eclogues: Arcadian Forest, Theocritean Trees," *TAPA* 98: 491-508.

———, 1968. "About Form and Feeling in Catullus 65," *TAPA* 99: 487-508.

———, 1969a. "Is Theocritus a Version of Pastoral?," *MLN* 84: 942-46.

———, 1969b. "The Fourth Pastoral Poems of Virgil and Theocritus," *Atti dell'Arcadia* 3, V, 1 (Rome): 129-48.

———, 1970a. "Poetica Teocritea," *QUCC* 9: 82-97.

———, 1970b. "Studies of Dialectical Methodology in Virgil," *MLN* 85: 884-928.

———, 1972. Rev. T. Rosenmeyer, *The Green Cabinet: Theocritus and the European Pastoral Lyric* (Berkeley 1969), *AJP* 93: 348-354.

———, 1973/1974. "The Structure of (Theocr.) *Id*.8," *Museum Criticum* 8/9: 198-199.

———, 1974. "Propertius (*uates*): Augustan Ideology, Topography, and Poetics in *Eleg*. IV, 1," *Dial. di Arch.* 8: 116-145.

———, 1975. "Epic and Bucolic (Theocritus, *Id*.VII / Virgil, *Ecl*.I)," *QUCC* 19: 45-72.

———, 1976. "Theocritus and the Development of the Conception of Bucolic Genre," *Ramus* 5: 18-44.

———, 1976-1977. "*ET GALLVS CANTAVIT*: A Review Article," *CJ* 72: 327-333.

———, 1977a. "Virgil's Sixth Eclogue and the Poetics of Middle Style," *Liverpool Classical Monthly* 2: 107-08.

———, 1977b. Rev. *Ancient Pastoral*, ed. A. J. Boyle (Melbourne 1976), *RFIC* 105 (1977) 194-201.

———, 1978. "Revising the Eclogue Tradition," *Studi in Memoria di Marino Barchiesi* (Roma).

Wendel, C., 1900. *De nominibus bucolicis* (Leipzig).

———, 1920. *Überlieferung und Entstehung der Theokrit Scholien* (Berlin).

West, M., 1966. *Hesiod Theogony* (Oxford).

Williams, G., 1968. *Tradition and Originality in Roman Poetry* (Oxford).

Williams, R. D., 1967. *Virgil* (Oxford).

Wormell, D. E. W., 1969. "The Originality of the Eclogues," *Vergil*, ed. D. R. Dudley: 1-26.

Wülfing-Von Martitz, P., 1970. "Zum Wettgesang der Hirten in der siebenten Ekloge Vergils," *Hermes* 98: 380-82.

INDEX

Aeneid: 230-32; anticipated by E.iii, 130, by E.iiii, 70; Arcadian poetics in, 231; continues dialectic (q.v.) of *B.* and *G.*, 228 n.; 'seven' important in, 22; vatic poetics (q.v.), 174 n. 58, 231.

allegory: autobiographical, 18, 82, 95 n. 29; of ideology (q.v.), 52, 92, 97, 101-02, 145; of poetics (q.v.), 91-92, 96-97; cf. dramatic fiction, Servius (*latenter ostendit*).

Alpers, P.: his belief in demise of eclogue (q.v.) tradition premature, 101 n.

alterna (sc. *carmina*, q.v.): term of principle of bucolic composition, 130-31 (cf. *amoebaea*, contrast, *uariatio*); implies growth-through-contrast of Tityran mode (q.v.), 211 (cf. 'Camenae', 'love', dialectic); as variant and reduction of E.iiii, 140 n. 85 (cf. 'Mopsus'); *alternos* (sc. *uersus*, q.v.) as retrospective generalization (q.v.) and reduction (q.v.) of contrast, 175 (cf. 'Arcadia', performance); in reduction (q.v.) of Tityran mode (q.v.), 213-14 (cf. *deductum dicere, irrita*).

'Amaryllis' ('sparkling', 120): 48-49, 218; available female, 56; enchantress in E.viii?, 179 n.

amoebaea: 20, 23; technical term in bucolic (q.v.), 130 n. 68; 48-line convention, 24, 129 n.; cf. *alterna.*

amplificatio: 29, 130, 215; cf. 'growth'.

anaphora: 82, 117, (196); cf. repetition.

'Apollo': 64, 133, 146, 155; *meditans* (q.v.), 158, 215, 235-36.

Apollonius of Rhodes: added to canon of *epos* (q.v.), 106, 112; in E.vi 155-56.

Aratus: added to canon of *epos* (q.v.), 106, 112; type for middle register, 130-31.

'Arcadia': growth (q.v.) of image, 22, 24, 71-72, 160 n. (b), 163-64, 168, 187, 193-94, 214, 222; import for poetics (q.v.), 80 n. 2, 93-94, 138, 182, 192-93, 204, 227-230 (in *G.*), 231 (in *A.*); as origin of bucolic (q.v.), 80 n. 2, of *epos* (q.v.), 137-38, 145, 190, 205; Snell's view wrong, 72 n. 46, 168 n. 43, 190 n. 82; as subtext in E.vi, 156, 158 (Eurotas' source).

'Arethusa': "at home," 188-190, 203-04, 220; cf. 'Arcadia'.

Asclepiades of Myrleia: 11; brings Theocritus (q.v.) to Rome, 101; influence in *B.*, 129 n. 65b, 131 n. 70.

ideology: 32, 68-70, 74, 89, 92, 101; definition, 35; devising positive moment, 31, 35-37, 61 (cf. 'Muse', 'woodland'); dissembling negative moment, 31, 47, 66, 185 (cf. deferral, dissimulation); proto-Augustan (themes of Tityran mode, q.v., 'as before' / 'growth', q.v.), 30-41, 35, 43-48, 52-55, 59, 64, 66, 69, 95, 138 (cf. 'Arcadia'), 145 (cf. 'Daphnis'); reactionary (theme of Arcadian poetics, 'as before'), 41-43, 45, 48; resolved conflict, 48, 54; frame for *G.*, 68, 224, for *A.*, 68, 230; cf. myth; performance; Vergilius, celebrity of.

interpretatio: 117, 167, 169, 193, 201, 220; cf. 'growth'.

irrita ('unratified, reversed', 66): idea of social change (q.v.), 66; implied process of change in poetics (q.v.), 164, 168, 199, 221; cf. *deductum dicere*; reduction; Tityran mode, gradual deconstruction.

'Juppiter': 44, 67; figure of mythic order, 61, 67-68; theme in upper register (q.v.), 63, 136, 176; cf. myth.

labor: cf. 'work'.

lament: typology for Mopsus' (q.v.) song in E.v, 18, 140, 212; cf. bucolic, post-Theocritean.

'*Liber*': cf. Dionysiac.

libertas (cf. '*Liber*'): 45-46, 57, 177, 214; cf. Tityran mode.

'love': 34-35, 56, 61; and Rome, 223; constructive cause, 34, 61, 125-27, 131, 183, 204, 214, 225; disintegrating cause, 30, 34, 59, 182, 216; heterosexual, 56, 60, 131; homosexual 57, 125-27, 131; medicine for, 128 n. 62, 202, 216, 233; permutations, 129, 130-31; visual stimulus, 120 ('Amaryllis'), 147 ('Aegle'); cf. causality.

Lucilius: type of lower register for Varro, Horace, 111, 114.

Lucretius: country idyll, 122, 127 n. 63, 150 n. 10 (cf. 'Muse', 'country'); critique of bucolic myth (q.v.), 89, 122, 150 n. 10, 235, (echo; cf. 'Muse', 'woodland'); Epicurus as 'god', 50, 122 n. 49 (cf. Octavian); language in E.vi, 155; emulated in *G.*, 225; *isonomia* reinterpreted as transformation of old system into new, 65, 239 (cf. change); idea of irreversible decline countered by E.iiii, 133, 214, returns in E.vi, 157.

ludus: cf. 'play'.

'Lycidas' ('of wolf', 183): Id.vii, 109, 121, 124; persona in Arcadian mode, 186-87, 218.

Lysias: type of low or plain style, 102.

'Maenalus' (*mainomai*, 'to rage', 179 n.): 158 n., 182, (191), 200, 216.

Mariotti, S.: Gallus' fragment transformed by Ovid, 197 n. 87.

meditari, 'to devise, rehearse, work up or over': 87-88, 124 n. 59, 158, 162 n. 30, 235; cf. 'work'.

204, 211, 215; suspended, 218; new status, 220; representational form, 20, 37, 131.
numerical order: 28, 70-71; cosmic imitated by music (q.v.), 235, hence by poetry, 235-36; in eclogue book, 20-24, 217; in E.i-iiii, 22-23, 70, 120 n., 126 n., 129 n., 132 n.; in E.viii, 180 n.; in Theocritus (q.v.), 132 n., 180 n.; by 'sevens', 217 n. 4, 236 n. 11, as sign of *oppositio in imitando* (q.v.), 235.

Octavian: 35, 42-48, 52, 96, 97; focus for centering structure (q.v.) in E.i, 27-29; basis for ideology (q.v.), myth (q.v.), 180, upper register in *epos* (q.v.), 224-25; cf. Tityran mode, *aition* (Roman).
omnia, 'all': 60, 68, 135 n. 77, 176, 185 n., 186, 202; cf. Tityran mode, growth and gradual deconstruction.
oppositio in imitando: defined, 90; cf. change, emulation, tradition, *urbanitas*.
'Orpheus': 232; founder of *epos* (q.v.), 129, 136, 224; mythic analogue for Tityran mode (q.v.), 140 n. 86, 154 n. 20, 171, 173, 216; recurrent dialectic (q.v.), Arcadian/Orphic, 93 n. 16, 172, 194, 204, 227, 231; cf. Dionysiac.

Pacuvius: used for Caesarian propaganda, 52; type of upper register, 111, 114; cf. Sophocles.
'Palaemon' *uicinus* ('wrestler'?, sea-god's name, 129 n.): *oppositio in imitando* (q.v.) Id.v, 130; thematic character, 60, 203; validating lower-middle registers (q.v.), 128, 131, 211.
'Pan' ('all' implied, E.iiii 52, 58-59): inventor of bucolic (q.v.), in Id.i, 127 n. 63, 137, 212, 216; in E.ii, 127 n. 63; in E.iiii, 137; in E.viii, 145 n. 2; cf. 'Arcadia'.
pastoral: concept of genre, 12, 41, 101, 118 n. 42; replaces bucolic (q.v.), 205.
performance: technique in Arcadian poetics (*cantare*, distinct from *canere*, cf. 'singing'), 169 n. 44; of *B.*, 9-10, 91 n. 14, 102, 114; cf. Vergilius, celebrity of.
persona fictional: 18, 20, 91; as vehicle for themes, 47-48, 87, 123, 171 n., 193; limited consciousness imagined in, 47, 142, 166 n., 175; significance of names, 118 n. 43 (cf. etymology); unifying function in book (q.v.), 74, 83, 126 n. 61a, 170; cf. dramatic fiction.
Philetas of Cos: 106; authority for Theocritus, 109; shown as poet-lover, 221.
placement, significant in book (q.v.): 19 (*sic insigniter*), 23, 31, 35, 37, 79 n., 88, 90, 94, 113, 141, 152-53, 222-23; cf. *uariatio*.
Plato: 202; *Phaedrus*—three registers of discourse, 102-03, —love as visual, 120, —high and low discourse, 155 n. 21.
'play': 44, 95, 113, 149, 151 n. 10, 163, 166, 204, 215, 219, 230, 233; ideal in poetics (Alexandrian, neoteric) 124 n. 49; *seria/ludo*, 180 n. 73, 203.

siluae (*hyle*, 'wood; matter', 239): 49, 56, 60, 63, 132, 149, 151 n. 10, 160, 201, (223): cf. bucolic, symbols of; 'Muse', 'woodland' (*siluestris musa*).

'singing': 62, 73-74, 120 n. 43 (a, c), 126 n. 62, 169; older, higher mode (distinct from 'writing', q.v.), 124, 138, 233; in Theocritus (q.v.), 109; magical charm (*carmina*, q.v.), 182, 217, 233; cf. vatic poetics; *uersus* (distinct from); performance (*canere* to generate, *cantare* to repeat.)

Snell, B.: his conception of 'Arcadia' wrong, 72 n. 46, 168 n. 43, 190 n. 82.

Sophocles: 103; type of upper register, 181 (cf. style, tragedy and comedy; Pacuvius).

Spenser, E.: 24 n. 26; cf. seasonal imagery, time, numerical order.

Stesichorus: 103.

Stevens, W.: "The Comedian as the Letter C," cited 91, 92, 228, 230; poet as symbolist, 94 (cf. poetics).

spontaneity, natural as bucolic theme: 67, 75 n. 49, 83 n. 7, 135 n. 77, 163, 167, 172, 209.

structure: CONCENTRIC, 27-29, 32, 33, 41, 53, in separate eclogues E.i, 120 (cf. Tityran mode, *aition*-Roman), —E.ii, 126 (cf. Tityran mode, *aition*-bucolic), —E.iii, 129, —E.vi, 214, E.viiii, 184 n., —E.x, 189 n., 196-97, 219, 222; not in book (q.v.), 79; in G., as whole, 225;
LINEAR, 29-30, 33, 68-71, 79, 94, in separate eclogues—E.i, 120, —E.ii, 126, —E.iii, 129, —E.iiii, 132, —E.viiii, 184 n.; in G. as whole, 224;
CHIASTIC, 213-14 (cf. chiasmus, retrospective generalization); NUMERICAL (q.v.), in E.iiii, 22, 131, in E.viii, 180 n.; woven in book, 203, 222-23; cf. placement.

style: 'slight' or 'thin', 63 n. 33, 87, 105, 118, 151 n. 10 (Hesiod, q.v., type of for Alexandrians; Theocritus, q.v., type of for Virgil), 226 (cf. 'play', 'work'); 'grand', 152 (cf. Homer); middle—not in Alexandrian poetics, 103-111,—Hesiod becomes type for Virgil, 152-54 (cf. 'sheep'); tragedy and comedy as 'grand'/ 'slight' 114, 180; cf. registers, tripartite ordering, *epos*.

'sweet': 'music' (q.v.) in Id.i, 119 n.; 'plowlands' in E.i, 49, 101; cf. 'Meliboeus', *oppositio in imitando*.

Theocritus of Syracuse: Arcadian origin of bucolic (Pan, Id.i), 190; generic mixing, 106, 221, in *epos* (q.v.), 109-10, 116, with epigram, 109, 220; Idd.i-vii a unique group, 106-08; Idd.i, ii perceived as complementary by Virgil, 179 n., 217; challenged by E.i, 12, 119-123 (cf. Tityran mode, *aition*-Roman); claimed as predecessor in tradition (q.v.) by E.ii, 126-27, 221 (cf. Tityran mode, *aition*-bucolic); surpassed by return to source of tradition, 146 n. 7, 202 (cf. 'Arcadia', 'Arethusa'); in E.iiii, 122 n. 72 (cf. 'Muses', *Sicelides*); in E.vi, 156; in E.x, 189 n. (b), 222; cf. bucolic, emulation, *epos*, Hesiod.

61), 34, 186; sprawled 'beneath crag' (E.x 14), 192; seated in (now threatening) shade (E.x 70-77), 203, 223.

Varro, Atacinus: 124; music of spheres imitated by Apollo (q.v.), 235.
———, Reatinus: *fata* (q.v.), 230; '*Hebdomads*', 236 n. 11; names of Muses (q.v.), 132 n.; *tripertita uarietas* first applied to poets, 111-12.
vatic poetics: 174 (Thyrsis, q.v.; Horace, q.v., Epd. 16); 176; 182 (reduction, q.v., in concept of *uates*); 186-87; 200 n.; 213; 217; 219 ; 228 (Proteus); cf. Hesiod, 'Mopsus', prophecy, 'singing', *carmina*, Tityran mode (*responsum*, 'oracle').
Vergilius Maro, P.: ambitious artist, 122, 137-38, 145, 224; celebrity caused by *B.*, 9-10, 52, 92, 102 (cf. performance, myth, rhetoric); works emulated, 10, 24; relations with scholarship, 10-11, 101, cf. Asclepiades of Myrleia.
uersus: 147, 149, (159), (163); distinct from *carmina* (q.v.), 178, 197-98, 214, 216, 217 (Arcadian form); cf. 'singing'.
urbanitas, poetica, 'nicety in craft': 12; cf. emulation, *oppositio in imitando*, tradition.

'work': 95, 203, 204, 220, 233; Alexandrian-neoteric ideal poetics (q.v.), 124 n. 59, 150, 189 n.; cf. *meditari*, 'play'.
'writing': theme in Tityran mode (q.v.), 124 n. 59, 140-42, 147 n.; cf. 'bark', 'beech'; hypothetical models of Virgil's, 25-26.